HISTORIC HALIFAX

IN

TALES TOLD UNDER THE
OLD TOWN CLOCK

HISTORIC HALIFAX

IN

TALES TOLD UNDER THE
OLD TOWN CLOCK

By WILLIAM COATES BORRETT

A series of Broadcast Talks designed to make us familiar with our City and Province and to revive memories of days and events which have made Nova Scotia Canada's most storied Province.

THE RYERSON PRESS

TORONTO   HALIFAX   VANCOUVER

PREFACE

DURING the past seven years, a number of "Tales Told Under The Old Town Clock" have been selected for broadcast, as a weekly radio feature, dealing with a variety of historic days and events in Halifax.

While many tales dealt with the individual persons, who by their activities, have made history, many other tales dealt with buildings and other structures, and their locations, as Halifax has grown from its founding, and progressed through many exciting times, including two world wars, which have definitely left their mark on the historic old City of Halifax.

With the Celebration of its 200th Birthday in 1949, Haligonians will be called upon to entertain many thousands of visitors from all over North America, including many former citizens, who will return to their native City, for this special occasion.

Among the subjects that will receive much attention, in the conversations of old friends meeting under such circumstances, will be the historic buildings and places of interest in the vicinity and the changing scene from years ago.

It is with the idea of bringing these very things to the attention of Haligonians and their guests, that a number of the radio talks broadcast or published separately have been put together in one book, in the hope that they will serve a useful purpose on this auspicious occasion.

WM. COATES BORRETT.

Halifax, N.S., 1948.

CONTENTS

CONTENTS

HISTORIC HALIFAX

IN

TALES TOLD UNDER THE
OLD TOWN CLOCK

I

HISTORIC HALIFAX

The Warden of the Honour of the North

Two hundred years ago, in what is now Halifax Harbour,
around a table aboard the transport *Beaufort,* The Honourable Edward Cornwallis and his advisers gathered to decide
the exact location to establish His Majesty's township of
Halifax beside the waters of Chebucto.

From that day onward, Halifax has become the scene
of increasing activity, especially in times of war and has

1

been host to thousands of soldiers and sailors, in the Service of the Empire, down through the years.

History has repeated itself over and over again, and never was Halifax more busy than during the conflict of 1939 to 1945. During this, the Second Great War, thousands of Canadians, and nationals of other allied nations, were temporary visitors to Halifax. The fact that within two years the population was doubled, made it impossible for these temporary visitors, mostly in the Services, to get a true picture of Halifax, and Haligonians. Far too often, they walked Barrington Street, and perhaps Water Street and back to barracks or aboard ship and formed their opinions, based on such scant acquaintance with the venerable "Warden of the Honour of the North"—Halifax. How sad it seems that no organized effort was made to give the Service personnel at least, the background of history played down through the years by the famous British regiments, since its founding in 1749, as an outpost of Empire, a role it has played exceedingly well on every occasion the Empire has had trouble on its hands.

Nova Scotia has become known as Canada's Most Storied Province and Halifax has been the centre of the many historic events which have taken place since the memorable day in June, 1749, when Colonel the Hon. Edward Cornwallis entered its magnificent harbour to firmly plant the Union Jack upon the Citadel. Within ten years of its establishment as the capital city of Nova Scotia and chief guardian of British prestige in North America, both Louisburg and Quebec had fallen and the first real start was made in the development of this great Canada, of which we are all so proud.

Each year on June 21st, as a rule, Haligonians celebrate the City's natal day. Halifax came into being, unlike the majority of large places, in that it did not grow from a small fishing village into a world port, but was created by man, in one day so to speak, and started life with a population of

2,576 people, which must be admitted, is a fair sized town to start with.

Halifax, the metropolis of Nova Scotia, and the chief city of the Acadian or Lower Provinces, was founded in the year 1749, at the expense of Government, under the direction of the Lords of Trade and Plantations, and was named in compliment to George Montague, Earl of Halifax, then at the head of the Board under whose immediate auspices the settlement was undertaken.

From the Treaty of Utrecht, in 1713, when Acadia was ceded to the Crown of Great Britain, to the year 1749, no progress had been made by the British in colonizing the country.

The necessity of a large permanent British settlement and Military Station on the Atlantic Coast of the Peninsula, had long been considered the only effectual means of preserving British authority, as well as for the protection of the coast fishing, which at this time was deemed of paramount importance to British interests. The continual breaches of neutrality on the part of the French, together with the loss of Louisburg, under the treaty of Aix-la-Chapelle, in October, 1748, rendered such an establishment indispensably necessary to the support of the British Crown in Nova Scotia and for the protection of the sea route between New England and Great Britain.

A plan for carrying into effect this long-cherished design was brought to maturity by the Board of Trade and Plantations, in the year 1748, and submitted to the Government in the fall of that year. It was warmly supported by Lord Halifax, the President of the Board and an advertisement soon appeared under sanction of His Majesty's authority, "holding out proper encouragement to officers and private men lately discharged from the Army and Navy, to settle in Nova Scotia." Among other inducements was the offer to convey the settlers to their destination, maintain them with food and drink for twelve months at the public expense, and to supply them with arms and ammunition for defence, and with materials and articles for clearing the land. The British authorities also promised to carry out the erection of dwellings and to prosecute the fishery. The advertisement in the London *Gazette* was as follows:

Whitehall, March 7, 1748-9.

A proposal having been presented unto His Majesty, for establishing a civil government in the Province of Nova Scotia, in North America, as also for the better peopling and settling the said Province, and extending and improving the fishery thereof, by granting lands within the same, and giving other encouragement to such of the officers and private men lately dismissed His Majesty's land and sea service, as shall be willing to settle in the said Province; and His Majesty having signified his Royal approbation of the purport of the said proposals, the Right Hon. the Lords Commissioners for Trade and Plantations, by His Majesty's command, give notice, that proper encouragement will be given to such of the officers and private men lately dismissed His Majesty's land and sea service, and to artificers necessary in building or husbandry, as are willing to accept of grants of land, and to settle with or without families in the Province of Nova Scotia.

To the settlers qualified as above:

1. Will be granted passage, and subsistence during their passage, as also for the space of twelve months after their arrival.

2. Arms and ammunition, as far as will be judged necessary, for their defence, with proper utensils for husbandry, fishery, erecting habitations, and other necessary purposes.

A civil government to be established, with all the privileges of His Majesty's other colonies or governments in America, and proper measures will be taken for their security and protection.

The lands granted shall be in fee simple, free

from the payment of any quit rents or taxes, for the term of ten years; at the expiration whereof, no person to pay more than one shilling sterling per annum for every fifty acres so granted. The lands are to be granted with the following qualifications and proportions:

50 acres to every private soldier, or seaman, and 10 acres over and above to every person (including women and children) of which his family shall consist, and further grants to be made to them as their families shall increase.

80 acres to every officer under the rank of an Ensign in the land service, and that of a Lieutenant in the sea service; and 15 acres to every person belonging to the family.

200 acres to every Ensign, 300 to a Lieutenant, 400 to a Captain, 600 to every officer above the rank of a Captain, in the land service. In the sea service, 400 acres to a Lieutenant, 600 acres to a Captain; 30 acres to every person belonging to such families. Reputed surgeons, whether they have been in His Majesty's service or not, shall be in the capacity of Ensigns.

All persons desirous to engage, are to enter their names in the month of April, 1749, at the Trade and Plantations office, or with the Commissioners of the Navy residing at Portsmouth and Plymouth.

The encouragements appeared so inviting, that in a short time 1,176 settlers, with their families, were found to volunteer, and the sum of £40,000 being appropriated by Parliament for the service, the expedition was placed under the command of Col. the Hon. Edward Cornwallis, M.P., as Captain General and Governor of Nova Scotia, and set sail for Chebucto Bay, the place of destination, in May, 1749. The fleet consisted of 13 transports and a sloop of war, the *Sphinx*. Altogether 2,576 men, women and children came to Chebucto, the total number of males, exclusive of children, was 1,546; of this number above 500 were man-of-war sailors.

On the 21st of June, 1749, the Sloop of War, *Sphinx*, arrived in the Harbour of Chebucto, having on board the Honourable Edward Cornwallis, Captain General and Governor-in-Chief of the Province of Nova Scotia, and his suite. They had a long and boisterous passage across the Atlantic Ocean, being at sea roughly six weeks.

Governor Cornwallis' first dispatch to England after arriving at Chebucto, was sent via Boston, and bears date 22nd June, the day after his arrival. In this letter he says: "The coasts are as rich as ever they have been represented; we caught fish every day since we came within 50 leagues of the coast. The harbour itself is full of fish of all kinds. All the officers agree the harbour is the finest they have ever seen."

On Friday, the 14th of July, the civil government was organized, and Colonel Paul Mascarene, Captain Edward How, Captain John Gorham, Benjamin Green, John Salsbury and Hugh Davidson were sworn in Councillors on board the *Beaufort* Transport, and the Commission and Royal Instructions were then read. The table around which this Council assembled, is now in the Council Chamber in the Province Building. "The formation of the Board was announced to the people by a general salute from the ships in the harbour and the day was devoted to festivity and amusement." The first three gentlemen named in the Council were officers from Annapolis; Mr. Green was from Massachusetts, and had been with General Hopson at Louisburg, and the latter were of His Excellency's suite; Mr. Davidson acted as secretary.

Early in the month of July, a spot for the settlement was decided upon near Point Pleasant, then called Sandwich Point, and people were employed in cutting down the trees; but the wants of sufficient depth of water in front, its great exposure to south-east gales and other inconveniences being discovered, it was abandoned for a more eligible situation to the northward, commanding a prospect of the whole harbour and on an easy ascent, with bold anchorage close to the shore. Here Mr. Bruce the engineer, and Captain Morris the surveyor were ordered to lay out the town.

Buckingham Street was the north and Salter Street the south limit. It was surrounded by a strong palisade of pickets with block houses or log forts at spaced intervals. Foreman's new division was afterwards added as far as the present Jacob Street. The north and south suburbs were surveyed about the same time.

Great difficulty was at first experienced in the erection of dwellings; the British settlers being totally unacquainted with the method of constructing wooden buildings. Frames and other materials for building, were however, soon brought from Massachusetts and before the cold weather set in, a number of comfortable dwellings were erected. Provisions and other necessary supplies were regularly served out in the camp, and every exertion on the part of the Governor was made to render the settlers comfortable before the approach of winter. Several transports were detained and housed over to accommodate those settlers whose houses were not complete.

Mills were also erected at the expense of the Government for sawing lumber, and a mill master appointed, and every facility held out to enable those settlers, who had not yet been accommodated, to complete their dwellings on the approach of spring.

The plan of the town having been completed and the building lots marked out, in order to prevent dispute and discontent among the settlers, it was deemed best that they should draw for the lots. Accordingly, at a Council meeting held on the 1st of August, it was resolved that on Tuesday following, the 8th August, all heads of families who were settlers, should assemble at seven o'clock with the overseers, and single men should form themselves into families, four to each family and each family choose one to draw for them. Mr. Bruce the engineer, being present on the occasion, distributed the lots according to arrangement, and the locations and owners of each lot were entered in a book of registry which was to be kept for the purpose to constitute evidence of title and possession.

The next object of importance was the erection of proper defences for the protection of the Settlement. The harbour being broad and easy of access, the selection of proper positions for fortifications, which would command the entrance, was given first consideration.

It was accordingly decided that Sandwich Point and the high lands opposite (now called York Redoubt), and George's Island were the most suitable positions for the erection of the necessary defences. On the latter position Cornwallis immediately placed a guard, landed his stores and planned and proposed to build thereon his magazines for powder.

After the evacuation of Louisburg the population received a considerable increase when a number of the English inhabitants came with Governor Hobson and became settlers, and many from New England were daily arriving, and upwards of 1,000 more from the old provinces had expressed themselves desirous of joining the Settlement before winter. The Governor therefore gave orders to all vessels in the Government service to give them a free passage. It was not long before the New England people soon formed the basis of the resident population, and they are the ancestors of many of the present inhabitants. It is recorded by historians that many traders came here for the purpose of making money; these people infested the Settlement in great numbers, and gave Governor Cornwallis and his successors much trouble and annoyance in demoralizing the people by the illicit sale of bad liquors, and in other ways retarding the progress of the country.

On the 30th of August, a sloop from Liverpool, Great Britain, with 116 more settlers, arrived after a passage of nine weeks. Two streets were then added to the town and lots assigned to these people. This area was known as Foreman's new division.

Information having reached the Government that the Indians of Acadia designed to molest the new settlement at Halifax on the approach of winter, it was deemed advisable to erect outworks for its defence; accordingly the troops and inhabitants were immediately employed to construct a line of palisades around the town in connection with square log forts which were to be placed at conveniently spaced distances. A space of thirty feet was cleared outside the palisades and the trees thrown up by way of a barricade, which constituted a complete defence against any attempt on the part of the Indians. Those settlers who had built their houses without the town had arms given them, and their dwellings being built of logs were musketproof.

An order was sent to Boston for a supply of lamps to light the streets during the winter nights. Col. Gorham was sent to the head of Bedford Basin with his company of Rangers for the winter, with an armed sloop to assist him, and every preparation possible was made for the protection of the people during the ensuing winter.

This was the first outpost of defence and owing to the frequent alarms of invasion from the Indians and French stragglers during the winter, it was resolved in Council to organize a militia force for the protection of the settlement, and on the Sunday following, the 6th day of December, after divine service, all the male settlers, between the age of sixteen and sixty, were assembled on the parade, and drawn up in the following order: "Those of Mr. Ewer's and Mr. Collier's divisions to face the harbour, those of the quarters of Mr. Galland and Mr. Foreman to face the Citadel and those of Mr. Callendar's division at one end of the parade." The proclamation bears date the 7th day of December, 1749. This was the start of the Militia from which the Princess Louise Fusiliers and the Halifax Rifles of today trace their ancestry. It is proper to observe that in founding the City, the spiritual wants of the settlers were not lost sight of by the British Government. On laying out the town, a spot was assigned by the Government for the church. The site was first selected at the north end of the Grand Parade, where the City Hall now stands, but it was changed immediately after for the present site of St. Paul's Church.

Governor Cornwallis in 1749, also assigned the lot at the south-west corner of Prince and Hollis Streets for a Protestant Dissenting Meeting House. The old building known as Mather's, or as it was afterwards called St. Matthew's Church was soon after erected on this site. This old church was destroyed by fire, which consumed a large portion of the buildings in Hollis Street, in 1859. The lot of ground on which it stood is now the location of the Eastern Trust Building.

And so in 1749, a complete British community, to be known as Halifax came into being, under the able direction of Governor Cornwallis, whose statue you will find on the square before the Nova Scotian Hotel, which faces toward the entrance to the harbour, into which he led his 2,500 settlers and Council two hundred years ago. With grateful thanks, we Haligonians, honour his memory and celebrate the birthday of our City, which is known far and wide as the "Warden of the Honour of the North."

As we think about war and the part the Port of Halifax has so recently played, our thoughts go back over the years, before there were any of the modern weapons of destruction, and when it took weeks to find out what was going on over the other side of the ocean. It is interesting to review the defences of this port at the time when Halifax was first founded and in later years as it was growing up to become a city.

Many visitors walk through Point Pleasant Park in the south end of the city, and look at the Martello Tower, or perhaps come across Chain Rock on the shores of the North West Arm, and wonder why those big ring bolts were put in the large solid rock, or perhaps they hear about a boom of logs and chains which were anchored to these ring bolts.

Such military objects of bygone days make one wonder how they defended the city when it was first founded and probably start a visitor off on an inspection tour of what fortification—or ruins—are still left standing, as they imagine themselves living in those days, wondering all the time how they would have stood up to the trials and tribulations of the early settlers, and the more they found out, the greater their admiration would be for those hardy pioneers.

From the year 1749 to 1754 or 1755, the defences of the town consisted of palisades or pickets placed upright, with blockhouses built of logs at convenient distances. This fence extended from where St. Mary's Cathedral now stands to the beach at the south end, and on the north along the line of Jacob Street to the harbour.

A large portion of the front of the present Citadel Hill was originally private property; a small redoubt stood near the summit with a flag staff and guard house, but no traces of any regular or permanent fortification appear until the commencement of the American Revolution. There were several blockhouses south of the town—at Point Pleasant, Fort Massey and other places. A line of blockhouses was built at a very early period of the settlement, extending from the head of the North West Arm to the Basin, as a defence against the Indians. These blockhouses were built of square timber, with loop holes for musketry—they were of great thickness, and had parapets around the top and a platform at the base, with a well for the use of the guard.

In 1755, four batteries were erected along the beach— the centre one, called the middle or Governor's Battery, stood where the King's Wharf now is—another where the Ordnance Yard was afterwards built, called the Five or Nine Gun Battery; the third was situated further north, and the fourth called the South or Grand Battery, where the Nova Scotian Hotel now stands and which property was for years known as the Lumber Yard. These fortifications were removed about the year 1783, and the ground appropriated to their present purposes. The Ordnance Yard, then a swamp around the battery, and the King's Wharf, were both filled up and levelled by stone and rubbish removed from the five-acre lots of the peninsula which were beginning to be cleared about this time.

There were blockhouses along the beach, near the Dock Yard wall, built by Colonel Spry about 1775. The drawings of the town, published about the year 1774 or 1776 show a strong fortification on George's Island. About the year 1778, the Citadel Hill appears to have been for the first time, regularly fortified; the summit was then about twenty-two feet higher than at present; the works consisted of an octagonal tower of wood of the blockhouse kind, having a parapet and small tower on top with port holes for cannon—the whole encompassed by a ditch and ramparts of earth and wood, with pickets placed close together slanting outwards. Below this there were several outworks of the same description extending down the sides of the hill a considerable distance.

The Lumber Yard, Ordnance Yard and King's Wharf were all commenced about 1784. The buildings which were until recently at the head of Sackville Street, known as the South Barracks, were erected under the direction of the Duke of Kent, as also were the North Barracks destroyed by fire some years ago.

A building called the Military Office stood at the south corner of the market wharf. It was used as a military office until 1800 or perhaps later. At this time a guard was kept at the Prince's old playhouse, where the old Acadian School building now stands, and is now used as a printer's shop on Argyle Street. Jacob Street was a barrack site as early as 1769. It was the site of one of the old blockhouse forts erected at the first settlement. It continued to bear the name of the Grenadier Fort until removed.

The old wooden fortifications were removed from Citadel Hill about the time Prince Edward was Commander-in-Chief.

The remains of this work were removed at the commencement of the present fortifications. Much of the old work was performed by the militia drafts from the country, embodied at Halifax at the close of the 18th century, particularly in 1793, during Sir John Wentworth's administration, and at subsequent periods.

Martello Towers on George's Island, Point Pleasant, The East Battery, Meagher's Beach and York Redoubt were built at the commencement of the 19th century. The Prince established signal stations between Halifax and Annapolis, the first post being on the hill behind his residence on Bedford Basin. He levelled the ground called the Grand Parade, in front of the City Hall. The Chain Battery at Point Pleasant was first constructed, it is said, by Lord Colville, in or about 1761. The present ring bolts were put down during the War of 1812-15. The old blockhouse at Fort Needham and one on the south-east corner of the intersection of the present North and Windsor Streets, which was then the road leading to the Basin called the Blue Bell Road, were built during the American Revolution, and reconstructed during the Prince's time. Windsor Street was evidently an extension of what we now call Bell Road; apparently its proper name is Blue Bell Road.

As early as 1761, there was a good road to Point Pleasant; it was a continuation of Water Street and was said to have passed through or near the site of the Lumber Yard grounds, where the Nova Scotian Hotel now stands, following the shore of the harbour.

What stories these old forts and other objects of historical value could tell of how they were constructed during the different periods of wartime activity which have come in regular cycles of time.

Since 1749, the date of its founding, the City of Halifax has become the Crossroads of Empire on every occasion of war, and throughout its history has experienced a housing and feeding problem, every time that military activity has been stepped up, and never has it been more active and had greater problems than during the Second Great War, beginning immediately at the outbreak in 1939, and growing more complex with every month.

It must not be assumed, that our problems today are any more complicated or difficult than those experienced by our forefathers.

Just try to imagine the problems of the Honourable Edward Cornwallis when he arrived here in 1749 with twenty-five hundred people. Trees were cut down, and mills erected to make boards, and great difficulty was at first experienced in the erection of dwellings. Frames and other materials for building, were however, soon brought from Massachusetts and before the cold weather set in, a number of comfortable dwellings were erected. Provisions and other necessary supplies were regularly served out.

Not ten years had gone by, from the date of its founding, before Halifax was faced with the problem of a sudden increase in population to feed and house. Generals Amherst and Wolfe arrived in 1758 before the siege of Louisburg with 159 ships and some twelve thousand men. General Wolfe had some tart remarks to make in reference to the feeding problem in particular. The situation was no doubt relieved when they sailed to attack Louisburg, but a similar problem came up next year before the fleet and troops left to attack and conquer Quebec.

Things went along fairly evenly for the next twenty years and then the American Revolution broke out. Many Nova Scotians were favourable to the Americans, they having come up here at the invitation of the Government to occupy the lands vacated by the Acadians, and were not ready to fight against their former friends and relatives.

In the American colonies, however, there were thousands who could not agree to fight against the old flag. In March, 1776, General Howe evacuated Boston, and arrived in Halifax with 3,000 troops and 2,000 women and children, along with 1,500 settlers and their families, and some ten thousand Loyalists arrived in Halifax up to 1782-1783. Governor Parr at Halifax had his hands full, feeding and housing this group.

Saint Paul's and Saint Matthew's Churches were used as dormitories, and a city of tents sprung up on the Citadel and Common. Crime increased, and Halifax spent a most uncomfortable year, until this new population was gradually settled throughout the Province.

Another period of thirty years passed, when war again overtook this great Canadian East Coast Port—The War of 1812. During this conflict, while the Mother Country, Great Britain was in open conflict with the United States, the Provinces of Nova Scotia and New Brunswick on the one side and the New England States on the other, carried on trade as usual—a most strange procedure—and both issued proclamations warning their citizens not to molest the other. For instance, according to Murdock's history, the people of Eastport, Maine and Moose Island desired to keep amicable terms and the Lieutenant-Governor and the Admiral acquiesced on that plan, therefore on July 3, 1812, His Excellency issued a proclamation, forbidding any persons under his command from offering molestation to the American people living on the frontier of New Brunswick or interfering with their goods or their coasting vessels. The war was equally unpopular in the Eastern States, and when President James Madison of the United States declared war on Britain, all the vessels in Boston Harbour flew their flags half mast, except three, and the populace compelled them to follow suit.

Halifax became the great East Coast port of call for the British Navy, and carried on the war at sea, yet business as usual was carried on on land.

The following passage from Murdock's history affords a lively picture of the condition and aspect of Halifax at this period:

The effects of the war upon the people of Halifax were very marked. Our harbour had become the temporary home of the ships of war, and the place where their prizes were brought and disposed of. Our youths were eager to participate in the path that seemed to lead by a few steps to honour, glory and fortune: and, indeed when it is borne in mind that several Halifax lads rose to be admirals, we can hardly wonder at the school-boy's desire to wear the white stripe on his collar and the ivory-handled dirk that indicated his authority to command men. The little capital, then occupying a restricted space, became crowded. Trade was active, prices rose. The fleet increasing provisions were in great demand, and this acted as a large bounty in favour of the agriculturist and the fisherman. Rents of houses and buildings in the town were doubled and trebled. A constant bustle existed in our chief streets, cannon were forever noisy; it was a salute of a man-of-war entering or leaving, practising with guns or celebrating something or somebody. There is another side to this picture which must not be omitted. The moral condition of the town had become dreadful in the extreme. Eight or ten thousand soldiers, sailors, and prisoners of war let loose in a little town of less than 10,000 inhabitants can well be imagined.

Commenting further on the condition of Halifax in 1813, Doctor Akins, the historian observed:

The upper streets were full of brothels; grog shops and dancing houses were to be seen in almost every part of the town. A portion of Grafton Street was known under the appellation of Hogg Street from a house of ill-fame kept by a person of that name. The upper street along the base of Citadel Hill between the north and south barracks was known as "Knock Him Down" Street in consequence of the number of affrays and even murders committed there. No person of any character ventured to reside there.

After the war of 1812, Halifax settled down to another drab existence, this time for a period of nearly fifty years, until the American Civil War broke out. Immediately it sprung into prominence again, as the principal port of call and supply for the Southern blockade runners during the years 1863 and 1865. The Harbour was ever active and fortunes were made in supplying the Belligerents.

The South African war, again saw Halifax being used

as the port of embarkation for troops and supplies to help the Mother Country, around the turn of the century.

The first Great War, 1914 to 1918, saw Halifax spring to life as the great East Coast Port of Canada, and shipping sailed in and out of the port in greater quantities than ever before in its history. Retail and wholesale trade reached figures never heard of before. The Halifax Explosion of 1917, when the munitions ship *Mont Blanc* loaded with four thousand tons of T.N.T. blew up, killing some twelve hundred citizens, and wounding and making homeless some twenty to thirty thousand, presented the greatest housing and feeding problem the city had ever faced.

On December 6, 1917, the city of Halifax went through the worst explosion the world had ever known, in a seaport town of its size.

In the main hallway of Broadcasting House in Halifax there are three large pictures taken a few days after the Halifax explosion. These pictures are looked at with great interest by the many young men in the three services who visit the station. Many of these young fellows were yet to be born when this terrible disaster overtook us.

The older people of Halifax don't need to be told what war is, they know only too well. They have many sad memories of their relatives and friends, who were numbered among the twelve hundred odd killed and the twenty thousand wounded. Many of the older men you meet on the streets of Halifax were heroes on December 6, 1917, even though they wear no ribbons to bring their bravery to our attention. Many of them were among the thirty thousand homeless people of that day, when the total damage ran up to around $30,000,000. It has been said on more than one occasion during the war that Halifax is the most war-minded city in Canada. Is it any wonder after their experiences in the last war, when half the city was wiped out in faster time than it takes to tell it?

As one stands by the Old Town Clock on Citadel Hill, of Halifax, it is easy to transport oneself in spirit back to the days of "wooden ships and iron men." It is not hard to look back over the years and be reminded of tales of adventure and romance that have been enacted in real life down through the years, and the famous men that have trod the streets of Halifax, "The Warden of the Honour of the North," since its early days.

Cornwallis, the founder—Prince William—Edward, Duke of Kent—Wolfe, the conquerer of Louisburg and Quebec—Amherst—Monckton and other generals such as Sir John Moore of Peninsula War Fame, and Sir John Inglis—Joseph Howe—Samuel Cunard—Enos Collins and many more come to mind. Every inch of old Halifax and every old stone building has a tale it can tell.

Halifax played important roles in the Seven Years' war with France, the War of American Independence, the War of 1812, the United States Civil War, as a centre of intrigue for emissaries of both factions and a port of supply for Southern blockade-runners. In the Great War, 1914-18 its well-guarded harbour was the headquarters of transport convoys, and for examination and internment of suspected cargoes. Again Halifax carried on with its job in the Second Great War and as in the First Great War received war wounds which have left their mark.

If love of country, pride in past achievements or the knowledge of where British history began in North America means anything to you, Halifax ever beckons, inviting you to delve into its storied past.

May I suggest that you visit at your leisure, the following historic spots of Halifax and get an appreciation of our venerable past:

Saint Paul's Church, built in 1750.

The Public Gardens, first started in 1753.

The Memorial Tower across the Arm, which commemorates the establishment of Representative Government in 1758.

Chain Rock in Point Pleasant Park, used for a boom in 1762.

Prince's Lodge on Bedford Road, where H.R.H. the Duke of Kent lived in 1794.

The Martello Tower in Point Pleasant Park, erected in 1796.

The Old Town Clock built in 1803, on instructions of H.R.H. The Duke of Kent.

The Shannon Tablet and graveyard by Admiralty House, which commemorates the famous Shannon-Chesapeake Battle of 1814.

Dalhousie University, established from funds collected during the British occupation of Castine, Maine, from 1812 to 1814.

The Province House, built in 1818 with its historic contents, especially the table from the transport *Beaufort*.

Government House, the residence of the Lieutenant-Governor.

Eastern Passage, where the Tallahassee made her famous escape in 1864.

Mount Olivet Cemetery, where you will find a special series of rows of graves of the Titanic victims.

The Nova Scotia Provincial Musuem in the Nova Scotia Technical College Building.

The Nova Scotia Archives Building at Dalhousie where you can find out more about Halifax, Nova Scotia, and the early history of Canada, than any place I know.

Go down to the square in front of the Nova Scotian Hotel, and look at the statue of the founder of this historic city, The Hon. Edward Cornwallis. Visit His Majesty's Canadian Dockyard where ships of Britain have made their headquarters every time the Empire has had trouble on its hands, during the past two hundred years. Do this and the words of Rudyard Kipling in respect to Halifax will come to mind:

> Into the mists, my guardian prows put forth,
> Behind the mists my virgin ramparts lie,
> The Warden of the Honour of the North,
> Sleepless and veiled am I.

II

THE HALIFAX SCENE

Today and Yesterday

WHEN one becomes familiar with the history of Nova Scotia, as recorded in Archives, and when you read the publicity compiled by the Provincial Bureau of Information and the City of Halifax, you will learn that Halifax, the great East Coast Canadian Port, is the centre of an unspoiled region of parkland and forest, hills, lakes and rivers. Capital of Nova Scotia, a peninsula province of Canada, stretching so far towards Europe that "Atlantic Time," an hour in advance of the rest of the Continent, is the standard. A point from which the whole of Canada's Atlantic Playground can be explored conveniently and at leisure, and that there are few other cities in America which can equal Halifax in romantic charm, history and beauty of setting, coupled with such wealth of sport so near at hand by land and sea.

The city occupies a unique situation—on a peninsula which is almost an island, with the Citadel in the centre, beneath which, at foot of the glacis, the tight packed streets of the old town nestle. Back of the Citadel, the handsome avenues of the newer city extend for miles, bounded at one side by the spacious harbour and on the other by the romantic and beautiful North West Arm, with its aquatic clubs and lovely homes dominated by the grey Memorial Tower, commemorating the advent of representative government in Nova Scotia in 1758.

Every corner of Old Halifax teems with interest and Haligonians who seldom go themselves, will insist on the visitor climbing up the road to the Citadel, where from the fine road encircling the top, one can enjoy a magnificent view on all four sides of the city and harbour.

Just below, on the harbour or eastern side is the Old Town Clock, erected under orders of the Duke of Kent in 1803; Old Saint Paul's, a Royal foundation and the oldest Protestant Church in Canada, erected in 1750 with tattered battle flags and memorial tablets, and in its vaults, the tombs of great men of an earlier age; and the Province House, one of Canada's finest examples of Georgian architecture.

To the north, the King's Dockyard, off which His Majesty's Ships can be seen lying at anchor, Admiralty House and Wellington Barracks, or Stadacona as it is now called, since having been taken over by the Royal Canadian Navy, with their memories of Military and Naval pomp and circumstance.

In the harbour, Georges and McNab Islands with their fortifications and not far off to the north, the scene of the Halifax explosion of 1917 and still further north on the other side of the harbour, in Bedford Basin, the scene of the explosion of 1945.

To the south, can be seen the entrance to the magnificent harbour, while to the west lies the wide Halifax Common, one of the finest civic lungs on the continent, where children, citizens and soldiers relax in games today, even under electric lights at night, where formerly the Imperial troops of early days spent long hours in ceremonial drills for the benefit of the Commanding General, and to the delight of the populace on every public holiday.

Within its boundaries, Halifax today has 288 acres of public gardens and parks—the Spring Gardens, considered to be the finest on the continent containing eighteen acres of loveliness.

Point Pleasant Park, two hundred acres of natural beauty on the tip of the Peninsula, threaded by ten miles of shaded walks, seashore drives, bridle paths, three old forts and an interesting old Martello tower erected in 1796—overlooking the beautiful North West Arm, on the other side of which is the Sir Sandford Fleming Park with its birch groves and public picnic grounds and the old Military prison at Melville Cove.

There is much to see in Halifax today, both old and new. Those of you who only know Halifax as the great Eastern Canadian Seaport, have little idea of the tremendous changes that have taken place in the peninsula of Halifax over the period of the last century.

The second Great War made tremendous changes in Halifax. During the first three years, the civil population grew from around 70,000 to around 130,000. Prefabricated houses, as well as permanent structures have taken up practically all the vacant places, and thousands of war workers from Upper Canada came to live amongst us, who otherwise would never have set foot in the Maritime Provinces.

The first Great War had a similar effect, but not nearly to the extent of this last war. The Halifax explosion which took place in 1917 and wiped out half the city, started an era of change in location for business, railway terminals, docks and homes, such as the city had never known before.

In fact, Halifax, which was founded by a military and naval expedition to establish British prestige in North America in 1749, has ever since been a centre of naval and military activity, with a swollen population every time the Empire has had a war on its hands, and has rested, so to speak, in its progress between wars. Every emergency in which it has jumped ahead, has left its mark, and never has it slipped back as far as it has gone ahead and a comparison with the Halifax of a little over one hundred years ago, will prove this in no uncertain tone. The foregoing remarks must not be interpreted to mean that Haligonians have gone to sleep between wars. Far from it. What it does mean, is that it is only when a war is on that many people realize the importance of this wonderful seaport with the third largest harbour in the world.

A classic example of this is the "official" inquiry made during their Majesties' Canadian Tour, as to whether the S.S. *Empress of Britain* could turn around in Halifax Harbour, when it was suggested by local authorities that the ship sail up the harbour from the South End terminals and then turn around and sail out, so that all the citizens and visitors would get a good look at her before she left our shores with their Majesties and their naval escort.

However, in war-time, the naval authorities, who know, have not hesitated to send in and out the world's largest ships, both naval and transport.

During the war years an article was published in the New York *Herald Tribune*, and distributed all over Canada, which stated in no uncertain terms with its headlines, that Halifax was "The World's Busiest Port." When a New York paper will admit that much, you can be sure it's a fact, as our cousins to the south very seldom admit that anyone else has the world's busiest or largest "anything."

But now, let's go back a little over one hundred years

and make your own comparisons as you learn a few things about Halifax in the so-called "Good Old Days." Those people who continually are preaching that the younger generation of today is going to the dogs, and that the people generally are not observing Sunday as they might, will perhaps be somewhat surprised when they are made aware of conditions in Halifax, in the so-called good old days—around the early 1800 period.

In those days, Halifax was a very small place. The town was bounded on the north by Grenadier Fort on Jacob Street, and on the south by Salter Street at the foot of which was a tavern with the name "The Sign of the Split Crow." All beyond was called the suburbs, the North End was styled Dutchtown, and the South, Irishtown. The army numbered about 4,000 men and the civilian population about 8,000 people. The Leading Inn of early Halifax was "The Great Pontack," a three-story building erected by the Hon John Butler in 1754 at the north-west corner of Duke and Water Streets. "The Great Pontack" was patronized by the leaders of Halifax society for many years.

According to the Provincial Bureau of Information in its publications on historic Halifax, life was gay in Halifax for the upper class, or well-to-do, at the beginning of the nineteenth century. The Duke of Kent had established all manner of festivity during his stay, and the social set largely composed of well-to-do army officers, were resolved that their pleasures should continue. The Coffee-Houses were used as banqueting halls, and nomadic minstrels, rhymers and silhouette artists helped entertain. Sundays were gay days. The taverns conducted a thriving trade and society paraded in all its finery. Ladies with high ostrich plumes, fans and rustling silks, and gentlemen in knee breeches, coloured waistcoats, stocks and frills, wearing wigs and queues, indulged in extravagant ceremony. In addition to The Great Pontack other famous inns of early Halifax were The Golden Ball, The Split Crow, The Blue Bell Inn, and The Crown, The British and the Jerusalem Coffee Houses.

The streets were colourful with traders from West Indian ports, many wearing large gold rings in their ear, and bright red sashes about the waist. The Indians had curb markets where squaws sat during the day with bows and arrows, axe handles, baskets and even canoes, to sell. There were apple and cake stalls for fishermen and dock labourers, and these also sold hard-boiled gulls' eggs and lobsters. Red woollen caps were worn by market fishermen as a distinguishing mark.

Many homes had wells in their yards, but others depended on the town pump, which was an evening rendez-vous for boys and girls getting water for tea. Rum was plentiful. Labourers and charwomen were allowed two glasses per day by their employers. Pails of rum, and dipper, were in each shop for the needs of customers. Boarding houses kept an ever-ready supply for the sideboard. Licensed chimney sweeps made their rounds, and the law demanded that their services be employed. Smoking on the streets was prohibited. Sedan chairs were used as taxis and the regular fee was one shilling. Auctions of church pews were held each year. A town crier called out all important sales and trans-actions, and at New Year's made his rounds, ringing his bell and reciting poetry at each house. He was busily employed during spring months when fur buyers were active, crying different prices each day.

Dancing and singing classes had large attendance, as it gave the young folk an excuse for meeting. Day schools were private and expensive, with classes early in the morn-ing, and in the evening as well. Girls received instructions in "knitting, sewing-plain, ornamental and flourishing-purse work, bead work, shell work, wax work, and drawing." Curi-ous advertisements were displayed at the taverns. "At the Sign of the Hand and Pen, spelling, reading and writing taught. Arithmetic in all its parts." "Reading school of children kept." "Gold and silver lace cleaned. Mourning stiffened."

It was thirty years after the founding of Halifax before

all stumps were removed from its streets. Settlers were reluctant to occupy lots over an old Indian burial ground near the centre of the city. 'Casks were filled with sand and gravel and placed about the Governor's house, and cannon mounted on them. Wildcats were often shot near the buildings and the last one killed in the city was mounted, and is now on display in the Provincial Museum. The town firemen were assisted by soldiers, who were more proficient with the buckets than the regular fire brigade. Amateur plays provided entertainment, and two announcements were always made: "Will the ladies please dress their heads down as low as possible"—"No children in laps will be admitted."

Just one hundred years ago, in the the first paper to be published in the wake of the arrival of the year eighteen forty-eight, reference is naturally made to the Levee held at Government House. The report was not extended for things were tersely reported in those earlier papers—that is with exception of letters bearing on some philosophical or political dispute. Then the contributions were very apt to run into many columns and be continued issue after issue.

However, here's what the *Novascotian* had to say about the Levee on New Year's day a century ago. "Friday being New Year's Day, His Excellency the Lieutenant-Governor, held a Levee at Government House, which was numerously and respectably attended. Lady Harvey also held a Drawing Room at the same time. Gentlemen who attended the former being severally introduced to Her Ladyship by the Aide-de-Camp in waiting." Certainly the scribe of a hundred years ago did not waste much ink in writing descriptive or colour matter when His Excellency received the Sovereign's loyal subjects at the turn of the year. Also missing in those days was the means of recording in picture form the prominent personages at the Levees as they shook hands —the news photographer and the eye-starting bulbs of his camera flash gun, were things yet to become known, and the art of engraving in the modern manner, which sees pictures taken, developed, printed and an engraving made all within the hour, had not been dreamed of.

Speaking of photographic pictures, there's interesting passing reference in the same issue of the paper which bore the report of the Levee. It is in a column devoted to the readers of the fair sex and bearing the interesting title "Making Mouths." Here's what it has to say: "It is rather important to ladies to know how to place their lips when they desire to look amiable, dignified, etcetera. This column of the paper published 100 years ago suggests that when a lady would compose her mouth to a bland and serene character, she should just before entering the room say, "Besom" and keep the expression into which the mouth subsides, until the desired effect upon the company is evident. If, on the other hand, she wishes to assume a distinguished and somewhat noble bearing, not suggestive of sweetness, she should say "Brush," the result of which is infallible. If she would make her mouth small and pretty, she must say "Flip," but if the mouth already be too small, and need enlarging, she must say "Cabbage." "Perhaps due attention to these rules might be useful to all persons intending to submit to the modern process of Daguerreotype portraiture," the piece concludes. Well, it may be a hint even today when you face the modern camera, which is such a vast stride over the type of equipment used to produce the now outdated daguerreotype. I can hardly imagine many modern young girls, with the manner in which they generally without concern breeze into a room, standing outside the door before entering a social gathering —standing there and whispering words over to get just the right position of the lips, before making an effective entry to join the other guests.

Much interesting material can be found in some of these old papers of a century ago—and which picture life as it was being lived by the people of Halifax of those times.

For instance, some of the means of entertainment provided for the people of Halifax during the winter season of the year just a hundred years ago. It is recorded that a

highly successful concert was presented by the choristers
of the Universalist Church. The writer of that time, says
that the neat church was nicely decorated for the occasion—
and that the audience was large and respectable—and that
the performance of the various pieces was worthy of com-
mendation. The concert was presented under the direction
of Mister James Croskill and one of the highlights was a duet
sung by two children, who had been well trained by Mister
J. S. Cunnabell.

One hundred years ago writers of the press did not go
into much detail. In dealing with the performance at the
Royal Theatre, it was said the pieces presented were satisfactory to the visitants—but no mention is made as to the
titles, although the reviewer does record that the scenery as
usual was magnificent. Of an extravaganza sung during the
evening, notation is made that the acting of a Mr. Ibbertson
alone made it tolerable—certainly this is not the kind of
praise likely to create a longing on the part of the theatre-
going public to attend any subsequent performance.

Today our newspapers, when tragedy strikes, go to great
lengths to provide us with copious details of what has
occurred (too much at times in my humble opinion). The
newspaper of a hundred years ago contents itself with printing in a line and a half that "A shocking fratricide was committed on Saturday, last, at Kingston, Kings County, New
Brunswick—and leaves the reader not even one word more
information.

The *Novascotian* reports that in 1848 the weather in our
city was remarkable for a New Year's Day—a heavy rain
commenced early in the morning and continued till evening. It is further printed that the numerous young gentlemen who paid their annual visits to the ladies, got their boots
soiled and the evening parties were somewhat dampened.

Today news events which happen in all parts of the world
are made known through the medium of press wires, and the
radio broadcasts in sometimes a matter of minutes, after they
happen, or—in some instances, with on the ground or as we

call them "Remote Broadcasts" taking place—just as they are happening. Things were not considered so hurried in Halifax a century ago. The Editor of the *Novascotian* on his first publication day of the new year wrote that his American and Colonial exchange papers which had been received the day before, contained a variety of interesting intelligence, which, to use his words, he promised to "dress up" for his readers in future numbers of his newspaper.

Travel, too, in those times, was not anywhere approaching the speedy means provided today. For example an advertisement appears in the issue of the newspaper which we are scanning and which tells of a new arrangement for the Eastern Stage Coach. It was said that under a new arrangement it would leave Halifax every Wednesday and Saturday morning at half past six o'clock. The stage was also scheduled to leave Pictou every Monday morning at four o'clock and travellers aboard the horse-drawn vehicles were given assurance that they would arrive in Halifax the same day. The notice said also that to provide accommodation to all, the stage would leave Pictou every Thursday at two o'clock in the afternoon, or immediately after the arrival of the Antigonish mail. The stage and its travellers were given a chance to rest up in Truro over night and at nine o'clock the following morning, would proceed on to Halifax.

Further evidence of the great difference between transportation means then and now is provided by another notice in this first of the year newspaper of 1848. Tenders are called for, in the matter of conveying the mails between Truro and Amherst. It is stipulated that a person tendering, would have to be prepared to make two trips a week over the route. He would have to furnish a suitable wagon to be drawn by no less than two horses. It is also set down in the notice that a tenderer must pledge that the rate of speed would not be less than eight miles an hour, except in the more severe months of the year, and even then he must not let his horses move at a pace that would be less than six miles an hour.

But let's turn to another issue in this bound volume of

newspapers issued in Halifax a century ago. Times were different in those days in respect to law and order, so it appears. It was lamented by the editor that there was not a sufficient police force provided to put down rows, and it was said that between two hundred and four hundred rowdies had been traversing the streets with no one daring to halt them in their so-called fun of disturbing citizens. One of these bands of young men and boys had adopted the name of "Christmas Boys" and had been roaming the streets at that season molesting citizens. Some of the gang had annoyed a local watchman to the point where he had unsheathed an old sword, and so severely wounded one of the boys that he had died a few days later. Another of the gang had also been seriously stabbed. At the inquest which was held it was found by the jury in its verdict to be "mere manslaughter."

Earlier I made mention of the difference in conditions for transmission of news. An article printed early in January a hundred years ago, records that the Saint John (New Brunswick) *Courier* had just printed intelligence on a proposed telegraph between Halifax and Montreal, and the scheme was said to have originated with the Montreal Board of Trade.

It was reported the Trade Board had addressed a memorial to the Governor-General, relative to the establishment of such an electric telegraph, to run through New Brunswick by the present post route. It was urged that the project be undertaken without delay and without waiting for the running of a railway line, which was then being proposed. The Montreal Board contended that a single wire could then be established at a cost of twenty-five pounds per mile, and that a double wire could be provided at a cost of thirty-seven pounds a mile. It was urged that the Governor-General communicate with the Lieutenant-Governors of the Provinces of Nova Scotia and New Brunswick in an effort to have these two Provinces co-operate in making the project possible.

The editor of those days said:

It would not at all astonish us, surprising as it may seem, if within two years, the first information of the Mail steamer being off Halifax should be made known almost simultaneously in Halifax, Saint John, Fredericton, Quebec and Montreal. Yet, the Editor continued, such would be the case and any news arriving on the mail ship, could be received within fifteen minutes of docking and dispatched and made known in all the other cities linked up by the telegraph.

Winter also brought seasonal problems in Halifax a hundred years ago, for the press reported that within two days the editor had noticed two accidents caused by skaters who sped down the hilly streets. One of the youthful skaters ran into a young woman, knocking her to the ground, and in another the skater himself was the victim. In speeding across a city street intersection, the youth was knocked down by a vehicle. "Is there no law to prevent skating on public thoroughfares?" the editor wanted to know. A hundred years later, we are still trying to cope with the problem of providing skating places for present residents of the city.

Early in the new year of a hundred years ago, Halifax social life was granted an event which had been lacking for several years—a fancy ball. The paper recorded the fact that picnics and dinners without number had helped entertain the people—but a fancy ball had not been attempted for some time. A correspondent in the press of that time, in fact, had written "that we were in danger of becoming a gloomy and savage people"—but the fancy ball was attempted as a remedy, and proved a marked success. The report of the scene says that "Old Mason's Hall looked like a great Ark, dedicated to the preservation of fine specimens of the whole human race, gathered from every region beneath the sun." In describing the variety of costumes to be seen, and commenting on some of them, the writer of that day said in part: "Little Red Riding Hood, beware of the wolves in red clothing." . . . So we see that the use of the word wolves with its modern meaning, can be found to have much the same attached to it a century ago. It was reported that overlooking the gay groups below were a bevy of dowagers, who, "redolent of smiles, and living over, in the forms of their daughters, they contemplated with so much pride, the triumphs of their youth." I like the use of the word "redolent" in this newspaper report.

In one of the papers I noticed another word we seldom see or hear these days. It is the word "Soiree," and is used in announcing that "a soiree will be given on Thursday evening at the Harmonic Hall by the members of the Episcopal Methodist Church, in aid of their building fund.

Not bearing on Halifax, but of interest in these days when we have seen the results of aerial bombings in modern warfare, is a little paragraph in the press of 100 years ago, which reads: "We see by our English papers that three thousand pounds had been awarded by the British Government to Captain Warner in order to test his experiments of destroying cities, etc., with long range shots. The experiment was attempted by sending two balloons to the height of about a mile and dropping therefrom the shot, which neither fell in the right place or exploded. The editor then writes: "We imagine that this scheme, which has occasioned much discussion in the old country, is now for ever put at rest." How wrong he was.

Certainly that Halifax editor a century ago did not dream of the wholesale destruction that could be launched from the skies just a hundred years after he published his reaction to the idea in the Nova Scotia paper.

Yes, it's interesting to look back at life and ideas of a century or more ago.

Before concluding our picture of the Halifax Scene, let us take a glimpse at old Halifax of just over half a century ago, the memory of which will no doubt be recounted during the Bicentennial celebrations by many of our older citizens, as they entertain visitors old and young, on this auspicious occasion, in the life of Historic Halifax.

The great extent of the changes that have been wrought within the lifetime of many of us was forcefully brought home to me in a few hours in which I spent in interested study of the Carnival number of *The Evening Mail* which was issued in 1889, just a bit more than half a century ago. To publish such a pretentious volume at that time was indeed an ambitious undertaking, and one which undoubtedly won for the publishers of the newspaper, the warm congratulations from readers of that day. Of course Haligonians know the newspaper now as *The Halifax Mail*, but in those days it was *The Evening Mail*, and continued as such until fairly recent years. Then, as now, it was a thoroughly progressive publication, and full evidence of this was given by the Carnival Number, which was in the form of a large magazine-like supplement. On the cover, which was replete with art work, there is a picture of the city in those earlier days as captured by the skill of the artist. It shows a much smaller group of buildings about the base of the Citadel Hill than we see today, and church spires stood out in striking isolation. Today they have to vie with such other structures against the skyline as the towering Federal Building, Eatons, the *Herald and Mail* building with its great Neon sign atop it, with the advertising sign etched against the sky.

In the Carnival Issue, pictured along the waterfront are the towering spars of the windships which used to frequent this port, in that colourful time when the wooden ships went from Nova Scotia's shores to all parts of the globe. There is prominently shown in the stream a proud steamer, but it is brought home to us by this picture that in that area of ocean travel, the engines were not considered entirely sufficient, and this craft, too, has tall masts, four of them, with the yards stretched for sails which could augment the other means of propulsion.

In glancing over this Carnival Number of *The Halifax Mail* of 1889, which I chanced upon during a visit to the Nova Scotia Archives where it is preserved, one of the things of major interest to me was to read the pages which carried the advertisements. They brought to memory a variety of business establishments which have gone with the passing of the years. Of course, many of the advertisers of that last part of the nineteenth century still are operating in the city today, some of them on greatly expanded scale but a number of them have passed into history, and except to older Haligonians, are now forgotten.

Take the back cover of the Carnival Issue, for instance. It is given over to a highly coloured drawing of The Halifax Hotel, and the name of the operators of that popular hostelry at the time is given as H. Hesslein and Sons. Those living here in the days of the fateful Queen Hotel fire will recall that among the buildings also to fall prey to the flames was one known as the Hesslein Building, which housed stores, offices and living apartments. It was in the same block as the Halifax Hotel, but separated from it by the Queen Hotel building. Once Halifax's best known hotel, the "Halifax" seemingly has outlived its usefulness. After ceasing operation as a hotel, a few years ago it was taken over as a barracks for the expanded forces of the Royal Canadian Mounted Police, which had so many additional men here to meet the requirements of safeguarding the port. Now it is apparently doomed to fall under the hammers of the wreckers to make way for an additional federal building.

What memories the Halifax Hotel holds for many of us who enjoyed the old world type of service which was linked with it, even up to the time when it suspended operations of catering to the public.

For instance there was the dining room, which while not as luxurious as the rivals which came to challenge its position as a leading hotel, it still boasted a charm and individuality which was its own. There no single dinner plate heaped with vegetables was placed before the diner. Attentive waiters, or waitresses came with silver dishes from which the diner could select portions to meet the individual taste. Then there was the Saint Julian room, a marvel of its time. Certainly it could be slipped into a section of the Lord

Nelson's Georgian Room, or the ornate banquet room of the Nova Scotian Hotel, but what memories it holds—of those gatherings of the North British Society or the Charitable Irish Society—truly it was a hotel that had a definite part in the history of Halifax.

But we mustn't tarry too long considering the picture of The Halifax Hotel, for between the covers of the *Mail's* Carnival Number of 1889 are many other things to gain our attention, and be worthy of consideration, as we familiarize ourselves more fully with our city as it appeared over half a century ago. So let's turn to some of those other interesting pages.

When I referred to the picture of the port on the cover, I mentioned an ocean vessel which had masts both for sail as well as a smokestack to carry off the clouds of smoke from her engine. It is not the only such picture of this type of ocean transport. One of the advertisements on an inside page shows just such another. It is pictured in the advertisement of the Canada Atlantic Steamship Line, which made claim to being the shortest and most direct route and linked Nova Scotia and Boston. It is heralded that, to travel by this line meant spending only one night at sea—and that would be amid all the luxury afforded by the then new steel Clyde built steamship *Halifax*. Superlatives are employed by the compiler of this advertisement and in use of adjectives he would have no cause to take a backseat to any of the writers of modern advertising copy. Of the steamship-*Halifax*, it was said in the advertisement, that the ship was "the finest, fastest and most palatial steamship on the Atlantic coast, and that it boasted magnificent accommodations and was electric lighted throughout. The liner *Halifax* was said to have a grand promenade deck 240 feet in length, and in that day and age such a boast would be considered something worthwhile. But place that deck in comparison with the great liner *Queen Mary*, now so familiar a caller on the Halifax Waterfront—and what a contrast you would have. It was stated in the schedule of sailings, that the liner *Halifax* would sail from Nobel's wharf here every Wednesday at ten o'clock in the morning, and would leave Boston for the return trip to Halifax on each Saturday morning at noon. Chipman Brothers served as the Halifax agents for the line.

A picture in an advertisement holds added interest, for it shows a horse-drawn omnibus proceeding along Water Street, in front of an establishment. Another means of transportation shown was a horsecar, drawn by two horses, and speeding over a single line of rails on Hollis Street passing in front of the hotel.

Speaking of sea transportation, I was intrigued by study of an advertisement inserted by Pickford and Black, still as then among leading ship brokers and steamship agents here. Among the number of lines which they then served as agents was the Furness line, and in this connection mention was made of the ships *Ulunda* and *Damara.* For these two ships it was claimed in the announcement that they offered splendid passenger accommodations, "carrying a Stewardess and no cattle." Among other ocean runs advertised in the publication by the same firm was that of the Halifax and Prince Edward Island Steamship Company which operated the steamship *Princess Beatrice,* commanded by A. H. Kelly, and which sailed each week for Charlottetown from Halifax. She had a number of ports of call *en route,* including Sheet Harbour, St. Mary's, Canso, Arichat, Port Mulgrave, Port Hawkesbury, Port Hastings, Bayfield, Port Hood, Souris and Murray Harbour. Those were the days before railway travel, and motor busses, which so deeply cut into coastwise transportation. Nowadays it is possible to go by plane almost in the matter of minutes, shall we say, from Halifax to the Island capital, where once it embraced a considerable sea voyage. The same advertisement spoke of the steamer *Harlan,* commanded by J. A. Farquhar, a name which was later to loom large in Nova Scotia sea history, and which then travelled every two weeks to Newfoundland. A number of other lines are mentioned such as the Donaldson between

Halifax and Glasgow and the Bossière Line between Halifax and Havre, but no individual ships are mentioned.

In those days the papers quite freely carried the advertisements of establishments dealing in the manufacture of alcoholic drinks. For instance, in the advertisement of S. Oland Sons and Company, it was said of their English Table Beer, their Schenck Beer and Hop Beer, that as the three did not contain "sufficient alcohol to bring them under the provisions of any existing Act for the regulation of the sale of intoxicating liquors, they could then be sold without licence. The Oland works were then at Turtle Cove in Dartmouth and the office and vaults located at 243 Hollis Street.

I wonder how many will remember the Saint James Billiard Hall, which at that time operated the establishment at 117 Hollis Street, and of which Richard Shepeard was the popular proprietor. The advertisement offered a strange variety of services to the patrons of the Saint James Hall, for it read, "English and American Billiard and Pool Tables. American Bowling Alleys and Shooting Gallery. English Ales and Porter on draught. Choicest wines, Finest Havana Cigars. Fresh Milk and Buttermilk."

There is one distinctive advertisement in the issue which I am sure will strike a responsive chord in the hearts of many of our older citizens—for it is that of an establishment which had a wide clientele. It is that of the Pictou House, which was at 34 Salter Street. It was just around the corner from the Old Academy of Music, which had its entrance where the present canopy of the modern Capitol Theatre now spreads over the sidewalk of Barrington Street. The Academy of Music later became the Majestic Theatre. But, coming back to the Pictou House, it was on Salter Street, just about where the stage entrance of the Capitol Theatre is to be found. C. Woolnough was the proprietor of this well known place of refreshment. What a scene it presented in the days when the gentlemen of Halifax dressed in festive raiment for attendance at the Academy performances—and when they found the Pictou House, with its well-stocked cellars, an ideal

place to drop around the corner for a between-the-acts visit—
and a quick pick me up before the curtain was scheduled to
rise again on a succeeding act. Yes, the Pictou House was
certainly an institution in the social life of Halifax of earlier
days. The advertisement, too, was striking. It merely bore
the simple name, "Pictou House Restaurant," the name of the
proprietor and the address. The entire central part was given
over to an etching showing a regal turkey standing, feet
apart, on the back of a turtle, while from a branch coming
down from the frame, were suspended a pair of smaller
game birds—evidently the piece of art being intended to
convey to the reader some of the things for which the old
Pictou House was justly famous—along with its succulent
oyster dishes.

At the time the Carnival Number was issued many inno-
vations were the subject of proud boast, which today we
accept as a customary service without giving them second
thought. Take the advertisement of the Intercolonial Railway, which proudly claimed its express trains ran between
Halifax and Montreal in thirty hours and particularly noteworthy, that through express train cars were brilliantly
lighted by electricity and heated by steam from the loco-
motive. Such a luxury in travel was a novelty then—and
today we accept air conditioning without batting an eye.

Today, we can walk into any number of our comfortable
theatres and enjoy the marvels of talking pictures—we accept
this form of entertainment as an everyday occurrence—it's
just there and we think little about the development of the
entertainment on the screen in recent years. But half a century ago in Halifax an announcement to be seen in the press
blazoned the wonders of the new Edison Kinetoscope. The
public was invited to visit Pauley's Amusement Hall to view
this miraculous new form of entertainment. Pauley's Hall
was located at the corner of Barrington and Duke Streets.
The announcement said in part: "Be sure and view this wonderful machine, the life producing marvel, giving an exact
reproduction of nature itself—figures and scenes in actual

motion." Perhaps some of our older citizens of today can recall visits to Pauley's and what they saw there and what they thought of Edison's Kinetoscope. It would be interesting to hear their comments.

Today, the motor car has to large measure ousted the horse, and even in the war era of gas and tire rationing, there were comparatively few who depended on the horse for transportation. But times were different a half century ago. I noted where somebody had broken the large plate glass window of A. Hutt, Dartmouth carriage builder. As a sequel to the breaking of glass in the Portland Street establishment about twenty dollars worth of whips were stolen. Today, even if he found such a quantity of whips easy to steal, this would hardly form a paying type of loot, for where could the thief find customers to whom he could offer such merchandise.

There are no doubt many of our citizens who will recall happy hours spent skimming over the ice surface at the old Exhibition Rink. Half a century ago it cost fifteen cents as price of admission to the rink to attend an ordinary session without a band, but when there was a band in attendance in the old Exhibition Rink an additional five cents was exacted, while for carnivals admission to the rink cost a quarter.

Today, our mouths water—and our hearts almost break— as we read the announcement by Hartlen's Market at 116 Barrington Street. Hartlen's reported they had just received from Montreal a carload of 200 quarters of choice beef. Then they gave their schedule of prices per pound. Think of it. Sirloin steak was offered at twelve cents a pound and Porterhouse was just the same. Pork steaks were offered to Halifax housewives for only a dime a pound. Today Halifax housewives can hardly imagine their grandmothers getting a sirloin roast at twelve cents a pound and a pork roast at only ten cents a pound.

Yes, there is some truth in the words of the old timers of Halifax, when they speak of "The Good Old Days."

E MARI MERCES

III

THE FIRST MAYOR

A Pompous Gentleman

THIS is the tale of Stephen Binney, first Mayor of Halifax, elected to that high office in 1841, an office which he apparently thought was superior to head of the Provincial Government.

Once again I must thank Dr. D. C. Harvey, Provincial Archivist, for material to make up the continuity of this tale, which I feel will be of special interest, in view of the fact that Halifax is approaching the two hundredth anniversary of its founding.

After nearly one hundred years of struggle for efficient and responsible government between the reformers and the local authorities, on April 19, 1841, the town of Halifax was incorporated as a City by an Act of the Provincial Legislature. Though the struggle became acute after the trial of Howe in 1835, the movement for incorporation had begun with the grant of representative government to Nova Scotia in 1758. During the first session of our legislature, a bill was introduced, but was vetoed by the council of twelve as "Contrary to His Majesty's Instructions."

In these early days in our history, the Imperial Government was very much concerned about the democratic organization and the tendencies of the Townships in New England, and insisted that the Governor and Council of Nova Scotia should guard against the appearance of "Democracy" in the Province and maintain control through the careful selection of all officials. It was under such a system that Halifax was governed for almost the first hundred years, although not without much protest from time to time, until finally in 1841, it was incorporated as a City to have its own elected municipal Government.

It is interesting to note that a combined celebration of the founding and incorporating of Halifax was held by the Nova Scotia Philanthropic Society on June 8, 1841, only four days after the organization meeting of the first City Council.

The Nova Scotia Philanthropic Society had been formed in 1834 as a tangible expression of that growing national consciousness which spurred Nova Scotians on to the achievement of responsible government for the whole province and of a charter of incorporation for the capital. Unable to find a Nova Scotian saint or national hero to honour, it inaugurated the custom of holding an annual picnic to commemorate the founding of Halifax. At that time, and for many years afterwards, Haligonians regarded June 8th as their natal day. It was not until 1860 that the late Dr. Akins discovered, on having some dispatches of Governor Cornwallis copied in London, that the true date of the founding was June 21st.

In 1841 it decided to show its appreciation of the new
honour that had been conferred upon Halifax by including
divine service and a procession in its programme of festivities,
with the City Council as guests of honour.

Altogether it was to be a very colourful procession, and
after following its route of march to the steps of Saint Paul's,
and then to the ferry at Market Wharf, was to recognize both
the founding and the incorporation by three hearty cheers
for the future prosperity of the "Infant City" over the spot
supposed to have received the first footsteps of its founders.
They then on the ferry crossed to Turtle Grove, Dartmouth.
There, athletic games occupied the time until four o'clock,
when the Society and their guests, three hundred in all, sat
down to dinner. "Numerous flags and banners helped to
enclose the dining area, and had a very imposing effect
amid the sylvan pillars.

The Hon. J. Leander Starr, President of the Society, presided and proposed several toasts. Those to the Mayor,
Aldermen, Common Council men and Recorder of the city
were received with great enthusiasm.

At the approach of dusk, the company marshalled and,
preceded by the band, marched on board the attending
steamer. The deck was occupied by parties engaged in
quadrilles, contra dances and waltzes, while the boat pro-
ceded down the harbour, round George's Island, and into the
wharf. The company again formed, the band struck up and
an escort of some thousand persons waited on the mayor to
his residence. Three hearty cheers were followed by the
thanks of His Worship, Mayor Stephen Binney, the first
Mayor of Halifax. Similar honour and acknowledgment
were given at the residence of the President of the Society
and the National Anthem by the band closed the proceedings
of the day.

Observers of the general struggle for responsible government in Nova Scotia have noted that the most bitter
opponents of that principle were among the first to offer
themselves as confidantes, and thereby get control of the

new civic government, and so look after their own interests, and maintain their old policy of social and political exclusiveness.

One of the chief offenders in this respect was Stephen Binney, the first Mayor of Halifax, who had been prominent in the official, business and financial clique in Halifax in those days. In exalting his office and himself, he clashed first with the Lieutenant-Governor Lord Falkland over an alleged slight to the Mayor's high office during the entertainment of the Prince de Joinville, and later with the Duke of Cornwall. The first incident led to a prolonged discussion in the newspapers of the day, and the later led first to a public meeting of protest in Halifax and by various stages paved the way for the election of a new mayor.

When the news reached Mayor Binney that the Prince de Joinville, son of Louis Philippe, would visit Halifax during the week of September 6th, he went ahead with arrangements to welcome him as if the visit were to Halifax, rather than Nova Scotia, and to him, the Mayor, rather than to the Governor of the Province, the official representative of Her Majesty in Nova Scotia. At that time there were three imperial regiments in garrison besides detachments of imperial artillery and engineers, and several British warships in the harbour. It was obvious, therefore, that the Mayor's part in the official reception must be secondary to that of both the imperial and the provincial representatives; much to the Mayor's chagrin, that was how the ceremony of welcome was arranged.

On Monday, September 6, 1841, the Prince landed at Queen's Wharf at noon, and was received by the Commander of the Imperial Forces, the Governor's aides and several military gentlemen, and was accompanied to His Excellency's carriages to the cheers of the citizens. After his visit to Government House he returned to the wharf, visited the Captain of the *Winchester*, and received a salute.

On Tuesday evening the Prince and his suite attended a dinner at Government House, and another on Thursday evening, after which he was expected to visit the Regatta Ball in which the Mayor was especially interested.

It was over this second dinner and the Regatta Ball that the Mayor took offence. On that date Captain Grey, Lord Falkland's aide, invited the Mayor and Mrs. Binney to call at Government House on their way to the Ball to be presented to the Prince; but the Mayor declined the honour, refusing to be introduced to the Prince by the Lieutenant-Governor in this way, and reminded the Governor's secretary that he was the Mayor of the Capital of the Government of Nova Scotia. He also reminded the secretary, that as Mayor of Halifax, he considered himself next in power and authority in this good city, to Lord Falkland himself and that the Governor might at least have invited him to his second dinner to the Prince, and not merely sent for him and his wife to come and look at the Prince for five minutes.

On receipt of the Mayor's note of refusal, Lord Falkland dismissed the Mayor from his staff, and that was the final insult in the Mayor's opinion. Though the Mayor and a delegation from the City Council presented an address to the Prince on Saturday and he was invited to the Garrison Ball on the following Tuesday, he never forgave the social affront of ranking him below the members of the Provincial Government, and for weeks after the Prince departed, the Tory newspapers kept up an attack on Lord Falkland, and the *Novascotian*, which defended him against the Mayor's friends. In the course of the controversy, the *Novascotian* devoted several pages to the instruction of Mr. Binney in the etiquette of international courtesy.

The news of the birth of a son to Queen Victoria, on November 9, 1841, reached Halifax in the first week of December, and was received with great enthusiasm by all classes in the community. The Governor promptly celebrated the event by a brilliant ball, which was attended by the officers of the garrison, the members of the government and a select body of citizens, but the citizens in general wanted some vent to their patriotic feelings and looked to City Council to lead the way. The Mayor first proposed to give a subscription ball in Province House at two pounds a head, but on finding this proposal unpopular, and utterly inadequate, called a public meeting to discuss the matter.

At the meeting considerable opposition was shown towards the exclusive nature of the first proposal, and the Council was urged to devise some means of expressing the loyalty and happiness of the poor as well as the rich. The Council then fixed the date of the celebration for December 23rd, decided that the various societies should march in procession, that a feast should be spread for the poor and subscriptions taken to release some of the debtors, that a ball be given for the more wealthy, and that an address from the Mayor and Council be laid at the foot of the throne by the Mayor himself, who planned to go to England soon on private business.

On the face of it, the latter looked harmless enough, but those who knew the inside story were convinced that the proposal to send the address by the Mayor instead of through the Lieutenant-Governor was merely a means of revenge for the Prince de Joinville affair. Consequently, the members of Lord Falkland's Government and other leading citizens of Halifax favourable to him, called a public meeting of protest. At this meeting a lively discussion took place, and the Mayor left the chair when sentiment turned against him. Finally, a resolution was passed to the effect that the address from the city should be presented to the Queen through Lord Falkland.

At a later meeting of the City Council, it was decided to save face for the Mayor by allowing him to carry the address to England, but that another address should be sent to Lord Falkland explaining the reason. Thus the Mayor finally had his way, but not without further heartburnings.

On the day of the celebration his conduct brought him still further criticism because, in an excess of zeal for the poor, he attempted to exercise the royal prerogative, and release not only the debtors whose claims had been settled, but the whole lot as well as all the criminals in the gaol, including one who had been convicted by the Supreme Court, and was awaiting sentence. Fortunately for him the sheriff, knowing that he was exceeding his authority, waited until his back was turned and quietly turned his key on the prisoners.

In commenting on this bravado, the editor of the *Novascotian* wrote: "O'Connell has won from his countrymen the title of the great Liberator. There is this difference, however, that Dan did what he attempted, and the Mayor attempted what he could not do."

On January 3, 1842, Mayor Binney embarked for England with the address from the City of Halifax in his pocket. At the City Hall, Alderman Kenny acted as Mayor until the middle of March, when Binney's leave of absence having expired, his seat was declared vacant and Kenny was sworn in, as Mayor to complete the first Mayor's term; and Mayor Stephen Binney passed out of the picture. If ever there was a pompous man with exalted ideas of the importance of his office, it was Stephen Binney, first Mayor of Halifax.

In the following October, the next elections for civic honours were held and Alderman Williamson was chosen Mayor. His election indicated that the forces sympathetic to the new form of city Government had triumphed, and that henceforth more democratic policies would be followed in the City Council. He had led the petitioners for a charter of incorporation in 1823 and now, as the first citizen of Halifax, he was expected to represent their interests as a whole rather than exploit his position in the interest of the old clique: for the election contest had made it clear to all that Mr. Binney's whole career had been essentially anti-democratic, that his term of office had been characterized by extravagant display, well calculated to bring the new government into disrepute and that the citizens of Halifax wanted no one in office who would attempt to "nullify" the City Charter.

IV

CITADEL HILL

Our Military Diadem

ON Citadel Hill in Halifax the best known object on its easterly slope is the old Town Clock. One day I had occasion to call on the family physician and when I arrived at his office, the waiting room had some ten or twelve people there. Having nothing else to do but settle down and wait until my turn came, I naturally did what everyone else does; looked over the old magazines and then at the other people waiting to see the doctor, wondering what was the matter with this one, or what was the matter with that one and getting quite a bit of amusement out of the shy look of each

47

new arrival, as everyone tried to keep quite still and look unembarrassed.

There was one old gentleman who particularly took my eye; light spring coat, spats and a light coloured hat. He was joined by another old gentleman, small man with a round cheery face, who shook hands and the first thing I knew they were talking about Halifax. When the cheery one said, "I can remember Halifax fifty years ago, just as well as I can remember coming here today," I sat up and took notice. Then the thought struck me that if the many changes taking place in Halifax as compared to the old days were such a topic of interest in that room and made everybody feel so interested and at home, that there must be thousands more in Halifax who would like to have memories of by-gone days revived, and thousands of newcomers who would like to know more about the city in which they are living.

Among the places the old gentlemen talked about was the Old Garrison Clock on Citadel Hill and how they used to sit on the Hill in the shadow of the clock and talk things over, in the summer evenings or Sunday afternoons. It struck me as a mighty good idea.

If more of us would slow up once in a while and go find an old friend and relax for an hour or so by the Old Town Clock, we would be better able to carry on afterwards.

On one occasion I received from Mr. Barnes of Rolph Clark Stone, a beautiful calendar, which is now hanging up in my office. This calendar has a lovely illustration of the Old Town Clock with the following description under it:

The Halifax Town Clock took up its position two years and a day before the battle of Trafalgar. Plans were prepared on instructions from H.R.H. the Duke of Kent, while commanding His Majesty's Forces in Nova Scotia—the same Duke of Kent who was later to become the father of Queen Victoria. They were finally approved in 1801. The clock itself arrived from England on June 10, 1803, in H.M.S. *Dart* and was placed in position on October 20th of that year.

Those were trying days for England. The Garrison Clock,

as it was called then, ticked off the tragic hours of the Napoleonic War and the War of 1812. While still strange to its new surroundings, it recorded the time spent by Bonaparte in his fruitless preparations to invade England. It continued to serve the good people of Halifax during the dark days prior to Waterloo and the victorious days which followed. It told the time for all to see, during the depressing campaign in the Crimea. It said "Good-bye" and "Welcome Home" to those Canadians who fought in South Africa. It struck the departure hours for countless thousands, sailing from Halifax to do their part in the World War of 1914-1918, and struck as confidently during the retreat from Mons as during the last glorious hundred days.

And now, mellowed by the years, it looks on once more while the Empire fights its greatest fight—mildly amused, perhaps, by the same doubts and fears so often expressed during other wars it has watched. When the time comes to record the end of this war, the job will be done, and the faithful old clock, its roots in the past, its face to the future, will go on as before, keeping a kindly eye cocked towards the little island whence it came.

The Old Town Clock on Citadel Hill is a familiar sight to all of us, some more than others. For a number of Haligonians its North face is a guide as to whether they are on time for work, as they walk briskly over the diagonal path across the Citadel Hill, from North Park Street to Brunswick Street by Glacis Barracks, to reach the downtown section of the city.

Few Haligonians have ever been inside the Garrison Clock structure, which boasts such an unusual shape. This statement can be taken as fact from a man who lived there for thirty-three years. That man was the late Sergeant W. J. White, formerly of the Halifax Police Department. It is said that familiarity breeds contempt, and while it is not contempt in this case, few of us pause to wonder about the mechanism that has "ticked" faithfully on for nearly a century and a half, giving the time to Halifax people. According to Sergeant White a number of tourist visitors called from time to time at the Old Town Clock and asked to see the interior of the structure, but few regular residents of the town asked to see the faithful timepiece at close quarters.

However, let us pay our visit to the town clock. Let's pause to examine the too inconspicuous cornerstone in the wall, at the base of the hill—removed by a few feet from busy Brunswick Street itself. The stone seems to have been selected hardly with an idea to make it stand out with any prominence. Brown in colour, and with no relieving hues for the letters, it is necessary to bend forward to read the inscription.

This tells us of the erection of the clock in the days of the Duke of Kent, when that Gentleman whose name loomed rather large in the city's earlier days, made this city his home, while on duty on this side of the Atlantic and after whom the street in the rear of Broadcasting House was named—Kent Street.

The inscription on the stone tells us that the Town Clock was erected in 1803, and further that this particular stone was laid by H.R.H. the Prince of Wales, whom today you know as the Duke of Windsor. The ceremony took place in 1919 on his visit to the city, and was supposed to be the inauguration of the new foundation for the historic clock. True, a short retaining wall was erected, but today the immediate vicinity of the walls presents a sorry sight. There is litter about and plenty of mud, caused by water from the springs that abound on the Eastern slope of the Citadel Hill. Really it seems time that Halifax paid a little more attention to keeping the immediate vicinity of the clock in more presentable shape.

But let us get along with our tour of inspection. A long line of wooden steps leads us to the clock structure. Count them as you mount and excluding the upper platform, there are fifty-two steps. Rather fitting, don't you think, for the introduction to a place devoted to the telling of time—a step for each week of the year. It is rather a disappointment that the other set of steps, leading to the doorway lack a couple of an even dozen. If that was remedied, we would have one for each month, and then things would be complete in their significance.

Well—up we go, more and more steep stairways, with loose rope handrails, past one landing, then to the one directly behind the four faces of the clock. There, housed in a wooden and glass door box, are the works. The things that make the hands go around. In four directions the metal tubes and bars extend, through the faces of the clock, and to these the hands are attached.

A metal plate bears the name of the maker "Vuilliamy—London—No. 371"—but no date.

Every Saturday the keeper of the clock winds the clock—that is he turns the spindle to which is attached the thin steel cable to which a heavy weight is suspended, and which drops through a well that goes down through the whole tower, right through the living quarters and into a deep pit in the cellar. The weight once up—the clock is ready to keep on ticking for another week or even a day or so more. A pendulum with a massive circular weight, also extends downward for several feet, keeping the works moving at their regular, measured pace.

An interesting feature of the old clock and showing somewhat the trend of population in earlier days, is the fact that the face on the West side, where the Citadel towers above, and that facing South to Sackville Street are smaller than the others. It was not necessary for them to be designed to be seen from such distances as the faces on the East and North sides.

Let's hope that Halifax will not fail to realize the honours due such a venerable structure and that everything possible will be done to preserve this clock linked with the city's storied past. The surroundings are worthy of every attention.

Of course, in these days when watches are not so scarce as personal possessions, and clocks for the home can be secured at low prices and correct time is given by Radio, the need may not be so extensive for the friendly guidance of the old clock. But it *is* an old friend and as such, it deserves our affectionate care.

While the Old Town Clock on the Eastern slope of the Citadel Hill is an interesting old place, it's only one of the many features of interest about this section of Halifax, which catches the eye, bordering Brunswick Street. As we look up George Street from the Grand Parade, we see the clock, but higher still, as the eye travels upward there is the summit of the hill, which has upon it the granite walls and the Citadel itself.

I suppose that most of the newcomers to Halifax have already enjoyed a stroll around Point Pleasant Park and have been at the Point itself. It may surprise them to know that the expedition which arrived in the harbour on June 21, 1749, originally selected Point Pleasant as a place of settlement. It is recalled that this was then called Sandwich Point, at the mouth of the Sandwich River, now known as the North West Arm.

But lack of water, and the exposure to south-east winds and fog caused the clearing, already started, to be discontinued.

With good anchorage provided close to the shores, a bit further north, the settlement was then laid out. The first boundaries of the town were from Buckingham Street and Salter Street, as north and south boundaries, and this was later extended north to the distance of the present Jacob Street.

By the middle of October of the year of the city's founding a number of comfortable dwellings had been erected.

The central fort of the original fortifications, provided for protection from attack during the early building operations, was called the Citadel. A series of blockhouses at convenient points along picket stockades, extended along Jacob Street, thence to Citadel Hill and to the harbour again by way of Salter Street. The site of the modern Capitol Theatre of today was where Horseman's fort stood. It is interesting to know that even today the importance of this site is shown by the lines of Barrington Street. Perhaps you have wondered why Barrington Street broadens out south from Salter, in front of the Capitol building. Well, there was once the gate to the city there, and traffic moving outside of the gate, caused the route to fan out a bit—and so we still have Barrington Street following this line today.

As we mount to Citadel Hill and look out over the harbour we see small George's Island, jutting out from the water, not far removed from the great docks and seawall of the National Harbour Board property. George's Island loomed large in early defence plans of the city, for it was felt that an ever-present threat was attack from the sea. So George's Island was early fortified, and strong forts were also constructed close to the water at the foot of Jacob and Salter Streets, and an additional stronghold built between them close to the shore.

The Citadel Hill stands high above surrounding Halifax at the present, but according to early accounts and drawings, the summit was quite a bit higher than it is today. It was cut down some feet to a lower level in the process of carrying out the extensive fortification plans that came later. Despite the ever-present fear of attack, either by French or Indians, none such was ever experienced by Halifax itself, although Indians delivered a deadly attack on Dartmouth across the Harbour, and conducted a scalping foray under cover of darkness.

Historians recall that after cession of Canada to the British by the Treaty of Paris in 1763, the danger of attack from the Indians gradually diminished, but prior to that, egged on by the French, they made it dangerous for unwary settlers to venture too far north along the shores of the Basin and many a straggler failed to return.

The beginning of the first permanent fortifications on Citadel Hill was in the year 1761 by Bastide, and the work started by him was carried on for a number of years. Work was frequently interrupted and it is often quite difficult to arrive at any conclusion that certain works referred to were new works, or merely the repair or extension of works already begun. We read that in 1774 the subject of fortifying the town again came up for discussion, but owing to its not having been brought up early enough it was thought to be out of the question, the season being too late, the scarcity of workmen being every great and there being no troops for its defence.

Constant fear of invasion was still felt, and on September 11, 1775, it was proposed to throw up some temporary works in addition to the old works on Citadel Hill and to entrench about the Naval Yard, but again it had been left until too late in the season to do earth work.

The work started by Bastide on Citadel Hill carried on down to somewhere near the year 1779. At this time there was an octangular tower of wood of the blockhouse type, having a parapet and a small tower on top and the whole encompassed by a ditch and ramparts of earth and wood pickets. Five or six guns were mounted at each angle and there were numerous covered ways or passages leading into the fort. Below this were several smaller outworks, extending considerably down the sides of the hill.

Several other forts, such as the Grand Battery at the Lumber Yard (about where the Nova Scotian Hotel now stands) and Fort Massey and Fort Needham were erected, about the same period.

It is recorded that in 1793 when Prince Edward was Commander-in-chief, some five hundred and fifty men of the town militia assisted the Garrison in the works and remounting of the guns. There is a Maroon Bastion at the Citadel today, and its name was given in honour of the five hundred Maroon Negroes, from Jamaica, who were on board a ship which called here *en route* to Canada and were detained by the Prince to carry out work on the great Citadel. Sir John Wentworth, during his years as Governor, did much to strengthen defences, but it is said that by 1812 the works on the Citadel had again fallen into disrepair, and further work was then undertaken by Royal Engineers.

The Citadel we see today, the fourth one, whose proper name is Fort George, took nearly thirty years to build and was completed in 1856. It is of the Bauban trace system and called one of the finest examples of that type on the Continent. It is in the form of four bastions, or separate forts connected by a straight curtain or walls of masonry, and surrounded by a deep moat. This moat was of the dry type, and never intended to be filled with water, as were moats of the castles we recall reading about in days of youth when questing for sensational literature and accompanying thrills.

The Citadel cost sums that seemed terrific in those days, but would be dwarfed into insignificance by modern defence needs. It was said to have taken so long to construct that it was outmoded before completion—but unquestionably it is one of our great national monuments. It is a wonderful tourist attraction, although closed to casual visitors at the present time. It is a strange thing that very few Haligonians have taken the trouble to explore its interior in peace times to be shown around by one of the Canadian Corps of Commissionaires, who acted as guides. Most people were content to enjoy the beauties to be seen in a trip around the scenic drive that now encircles the summit, there to view the activities going on all around. Many people choose the Citadel from which to view the sports and other functions that take place on the part now known as the garrison ground.

After the Halifax Explosion these grounds were used for temporary housing facilities.

Later when we were to have the honour of a visit from their Majesties the King and Queen, a special pageant was put on there, and some 26,000 school children covered Citadel Hill. All, of course, remember the arrival of the Victory Loan Torch and the great crowd assembled there and also the most interesting ceremony of "Beating the

Retreat" by the massed bands of the Third Canadian Division Active Army.

The ceremony of "Beating Retreat," by the massed band and pipers of the Third Canadian Division, was one of the most colourful seen on the old Citadel Hill. No doubt the sound of their pipes was also the most welcome music to the people of Normandy.

To the school children, the visit of their King and Queen will remain the outstanding scene of their lives on Citadel Hill.

To the average citizen, the Citadel remains the symbol of military pomp and circumstance down through the years and is to Halifax its crown of authority as the Warden of the Honour of the North.

As previously stated, one of the Citadel's bastions is known as the Maroon Bastion.

The Maroons were the descendants of a number of African slaves, who when Jamaica was conquered from the Spaniards, took refuge on the island. They continued in a state of insubordination, but occasionally made treaties with the English. In 1796, they were in open hostility with the authorities, but had been overpowered, and it was arranged that a number of them should be sent to Canada as settlers. They were placed aboard ship and in due course, put into Halifax Harbour.

Their stay here and escapades during a three-year period, 1797 to 1800, left its mark, and it is another event which has contributed towards making Nova Scotia one of Canada's most storied Provinces.

Many tales could be told of their activities and the attempt to settle them in a group in Nova Scotia, and the heartfelt gratitude of the Governor, when Sierra Leone took them finally, off his hands.

There are few memorials of this fierce race extant, but while Ochterloney Street and Quarrel (now Queen Street) in Dartmouth, the remains of Maroon Hall at Preston and the Maroon Bastion survive, their memory cannot pass away entirely. If one remembers them in connection with the fortifications on Citadel Hill, they will always remain alive in the history of Halifax, for the Maroons played a very important part in making Citadel Hill the well nigh impregnable fortress it has remained since their time, although it never has actually been attacked.

Imagine a glorious day of warmth and sunshine, in July, 1796. It is the 21st of the month, the very height of midsummer in Nova Scotia. Three large transports in full sail are to be seen making their way up toward the centre of Halifax. The richly wooded shores, clad in every imaginable shade of green, the deep blue-green of the shimmering placid water, overarched by a sky as flawless as a sapphire in the diadem of a king, form a perfect setting for the dramatic arrival of a strange people to these shores. The transports prove to be the *Dover*, *Mary* and *Anne*. As soon as the water ripples and closes over the anchors, His Royal Highness, Prince Edward, the Duke of Kent, steps on board the foremost ship, to see for himself the people of whom he has heard weird tales.

The canvas flaps musically in the breeze to the accompaniment of the military band, as the Prince gives the Maroons the "once over."

They are drawn up the entire length of the ship, clad in neat military uniforms, and his Highness ever a connoisseur of soldiers conceives the idea that they can be of use and worth to the garrison at Halifax.

When the royal visitor makes his farewells and is about to be rowed to shore, he is lustily cheered by these African slaves and fighters, who are highly delighted at their reception by "Massa Prince."

The Maroons came from the Island of Jamaica. When this island was taken from the Spaniards in the seventeenth century, a large majority of their African slaves left the plantations, taking up their abode in the mountain fastness which were almost inaccessible to the white man. Here they lived a wild, free, uncivilized life and were called the

Maroons, probably more from the simple reason that they had gone off on their own hook, than for anything else. In their mountain fastnesses they carried on a vindictive guerilla warfare against the British. Battles were numerous, with all honours to the Maroons. These people despite their savagery, and hatred of the British, displayed courage, endurance, activity and loyalty to each other. By nature, however, they were wild and truculent, a race skilled in mountain warfare, and having a well equipped military force. They flourished in the hot climate of Jamaica, nourished on fruits and vegetables of the tropics. Their mountain quarters, abounded in cock-pits, precipices, impenetrable jungle growth of thorns, twisted roots, and ropy creepers. Expedition after expedition sent against them proved unsuccessful, until affairs reached a crisis—the Maroons took to stealing from the British, and this the British could not, and would not stand.

A larger expedition than usual was organized against them, and two British colonels and seventy-six men were slain. There was nothing for it but to let loose the bloodhounds. These animals could have been easily defied by the Maroons but for the superstitious fear and dread they had of them. The mental picture they conjured up of these beasts proved too much for them and to the delight of the British, they sent out a white flag. Six hundred of the most warlike were transported thus breaking their power in Jamaica effectually.

William Dawes Quarrel and Alexander Ochterloney, for whom two streets in Dartmouth were named, were the agents of the Jamaica Assembly and came to Halifax in control of the Maroons. They were appointed by Lord Balcarras, as principal and deputy commissaries, with a credit of twenty-five thousand pounds Jamaica currency, to do as they pleased with.

As soon as the Maroons disembarked, they were quartered two miles out of Halifax, also in Preston within five miles of Dartmouth, three thousand acres being laid aside for their settlement. Today, overlooking the blue waters of Cole Harbour, a few moss covered rocks and the pit of what was once a huge cellar, mark the place where for more than three years these people lodged in barracks under a certain amount of military discipline.

In all that followed the landing of the Maroons in Halifax, Sir John Wentworth, who was the Lieutenant-Governor at the time, was practically to blame more than anybody else. The Jamaica Commission desired to separate these people, spreading them out over the Province, so they could settle and form homes of their own, but Sir John, who had a will of his own, was not, always wise, and he determined to settle them collectively in one great body in one place on an estate he had in mind, five miles from Halifax. He foolishly flattered them, creating colonels, majors, captains and lieutenants among them, who strutted around lording it over their inferiors. They were dressed in scarlet, gold lace and cocked hats. Among the names that are recorded as officers of the Maroons are Colonels Montague and Johnson, and Majors Jarrett, Bailey and Mayers. There are others, of course, who had their vanity satisfied with lesser rank.

Sir John then asked for two hundred and fifty pounds a year for a chaplain to give them religious instruction. At this the Maroons laughed in derision, following their own customs, which it must be admitted were heathenish to say the least. The Governor raised their hopes to the highest pitch and then not being able to fulfil his promise, plunged himself with them into a painful and humiliating situation.

The Duke of Kent took a more practical and saner view of them, and employed them immediately overseeing at the Citadel. They worked well and faithfully for him, work that was arduous and to them unknown. The greater portion of the fortifications at that period were the labours of their hands, and to this day the Maroons bastion commemorates a portion of their toil. Working so well and cheerfully, it is not hard to see why the Governor and his Council wished to settle them here. The Assembly at Jamaica were pleased at the way affairs had gone and now washed their hands of them, leaving them on Sir John Wentworth's shoulders. They proved a white elephant later to the Province.

At the end of the second year of their sojourn, complaints began to come in more frequently. The Maroons became discontented, the novelty of their surroundings and position wearing off. They desired greater privileges, some wished to own estates, some servants to do their work, many of them turned up their noses at the mention of farming, but above everything else, they, one and all disliked and dreaded the bitter winter weather. They did not care to live in a state of peace, they were men of war, fighting was the breath of life to them, also hunting. One of the chief offenders confided to Wentworth, that yams, bananas and cocoa would not grow on his farm in Preston, there were no wild hogs to hunt either. They wanted to be sent to India. "Give us arms, and ammunition, put us ashore, and we will take care of ourselves," they begged. By this time Sir John was disgusted with them and deeply regretted his clemency.

Halifax had her hands full with her huge barracks of mountaineer banditti to support. They were for many weeks comparatively idle, work was not to be had all the time and the poor little struggling colony of Nova Scotia, to say nothing of the British Government, was put to the expenditure of fifty thousand dollars a year to support them. They had been kept in the event of the French fleet, under Admiral Richery, attacking Halifax, when they could have performed military duty, but that idea had faded, the French fleet minding its own business as far as Halifax was concerned; instead of guarding Halifax, Halifax had to guard them, a large body of troops being in encampment continually near Maroon Hall in case of trouble.

The chaplain employed by Wentworth reported no spiritual progress among his charges. "They worshipped false gods," he said. "On Sundays they have horse races among themselves, cock fights (a favourite sport) and gambling. They range the woods, hunting and fishing, and

Dartmouth is in a continual state of terror from them." The chaplain found to his surprise and disgust that they believed in more than one wife. That they buried their dead under a cairn of stones (traces of some of these cairns can be discovered today) and near them secreted a bottle of rum, pipe and tobacco, also two days' food rations for the ghost's journey to the undiscovered country beyond.

Winter alone conquered them and averted serious trouble. They hated the severity of the northern winters. It broke their proud spirits and they besought Sir John as piteously as children to let them die, any change would be a relief, they had stood as much cold as they could. "Send us anywhere else," they cried. Fortunately help was forthcoming for themselves as well as for the harassed governor. Sierra Leone had room for them, wanted them to help quell a rebellion that had arisen amongst a tribe similar to themselves. The foolish attempt to settle them collectively in Nova Scotia had cost five hundred thousand dollars.

Sir John declared that the happiest day in his life was when he watched the *Asia* sail down the harbour bearing the troublesome Maroons to Africa, thus relieving his Province, and incidentally himself, of a terrible financial weight and strain.

Two years after their arrival in Sierra Leone, Nova Scotia heard of their peaceful settling down in their far distant home, where they were respected for their courage, fighting qualities and independence. There beneath the fiery tropical sun they lived, free to dance their Coromantee war dance, practice polygamy, in short, live and hunt as they pleased.

All that is left of them are mutilated heaps of stones, that cover their dead in the vicinity in which they lived, the foundation of Maroon Hall, the Maroon Bastion on the Citadel and the Dartmouth streets named in honour of the men under whose care they came to these shores for a brief unhappy sojourn, nearly one hundred and fifty years ago.

As we glance at the Maroon Bastion on Citadel Hill, just above the Old Town Clock and also gaze across the Harbour at Dartmouth, the adventures of the Maroons came to mind. They certainly were not suited to become settlers in a northern climate, nevertheless we must give them their due, they must go down in history as builders and fighting men.

Along with Citadel Hill, the first place to be fortified after the founding of Halifax was George's Island, which can be seen so clearly to the south east, from the Citadel. George's Island, the small mound of land which emerges from the waters of Halifax Harbour, just off the Nova Scotian Hotel and the great seawall of National Harbours Commission. It once was an important fortification, actually bristling with guns.

Today it is almost deserted, and in fact, has no military significance in these days when great distances may so easily separate battling forces. Earlier in its history it had important batteries, but in the second world war, a lone gun was mounted on the island. That was an anti-aircraft weapon which occupied a vantage point on the island's peak. In the first great war, when the submarine net stretched from the island shores as a protection against undersea raiders from Germany, there were three guns placed on the southern side of the island. Then there were three, four point seven quick firing guns.

Interesting old blueprints and maps at the headquarters of the Royal Canadian Engineers show the extent of the scheme of fortifications once established on George's. Today these fortifications are crumbling away, for they are entirely outmoded. These plans show provision for at least eight great gun emplacements on the southern side of the island, where the muzzles would point towards the harbour mouth, a distinct menace to any enemy that might seek to approach from the sea. Still earlier other batteries were placed at other sections of the island.

In the office of the officer commanding the Royal Canadian Engineers here, there is an interesting picture. It shows Halifax as seen from George's Island in 1777, and is a far cry from the modern city of today.

The original picture was among the collection of the father-in-law of the Engineer officer and is in colour, and is considered of high value. The owner had a photostatic copy made for his son-in-law, and the picture is entirely fitting in the R.C.E. office.

One of the interesting points about the old blueprints of the fortifications—known as Fort Charlotte—on the harbour island, is the drainage system and the source of water, which is from a well dug deep in the island earth.

There is a legend in Halifax which frequently crops up, that there was constructed in the long ago, a big tunnel which linked the fortifications of Fort George atop Citadel Hill with Fort Charlotte, and which was said to have actually passed under the waters of the harbour. However, it is just one of those stories that grow up about a place of historical significance—for there is absolutely nothing in the plans to back up existence of any such passage way, or to suggest that such a project was even intended. There is a large sewer of about four or five feet in diameter, which runs from the Citadel down towards the old Gun Wharf Property, which no doubt is the basis of these tales of a connecting tunnel.

The establishment on the island in the years when it had real strategic importance, were very extensive, but today buildings have fallen into disuse and the once strong battlements would have little value in modern warfare.

The only "going" establishment on the island today is the lighthouse on the western shore, which was first established there as an aid to shipping in 1876 and improved on different occasions since. The only resident of the island, which once had large numbers of inhabitants, is Keeper Bedgood, who is at present in charge of the light.

There's a fact about George's Island that is forgotten by most, even if they have ever heard of it—namely that the body of d'Anville, head of the ill-fated expedition which loomed so large in our earlier history was once buried there. His remains did not join the bones of so many of his men along the shores of Bedford Basin, but after his demise, the body was interred on George's Island, according to legend. Later the body was taken to Louisburg, and there reinterred under the altar of the chapel.

Dr. D. C. Harvey, the Nova Scotia Archivist, says that when certain works were being carried on at the site of the Louisburg Chapel a body was found which was supposed to be that of d'Anville. The bones were carefully taken out and placed in a suitable receptacle and sealed. Then put back to remain in the place where they had rested for so long.

In those times when the French expedition came to such a sorrowful fate, the Island we know as George's was referred to as Isle Racket, or the Snowshoe Island. It was in the year 1746, a few years before the English came to found the settlement of Halifax.

It is an established fact that the little island received its permanent name shortly after Cornwallis brought his settlers to found Halifax, and as is quite evident, the name was bestowed in compliment to the then reigning sovereign. Halifax was founded on June 21st, 1749, and early in July some of the pioneers were landed on the island, to settle on the ground which presumably was previously utilized by the French at some periods. The occupations of the island ground was not intended as a permanent fixture, but only as a temporary expediency, until more ground could be cleared on the mainland. Then they quit the island for the settlement of Halifax proper.

There is evidence in correspondence between Cornwallis and officials in the homeland, that the founder of Halifax immediately saw the possibilities the island held in his scheme for fortifications. He informed the Secretary of State that the island made an ideal site for a battery which could play a part in defending both the harbour and the town.

Within a month of his writing, Cornwallis had a guard on duty on the island and he had under contemplation the construction of a suitable magazine for the storage of gunpowder. Also early in the English occupancy, it served as a place of landing for those who came on the transports Cornwallis had sent to Louisburg for means to carry out the evacuation of that stronghold.

The spring of 1750 saw men working under Cornwallis' direction to clear away much of the forest growth on the island, and before winter settled in, a part of the island had been fortified. One of the first tasks was erection of a palisade around the island, and seven thirty-two pounders were in position to defend the harbour against any possible attackers.

During the succeeding summer, that is in the year 1751, the undertakings on the island provided employment for a considerable number of men. It is recorded that the oath of allegiance had been administered to nearly a hundred and twenty men and youths who were employed on the island at that time. A year later the records reveal that a number of heads of families had become established there, accompanied by wives and children, quite a contrast with the island population today.

John William Hoffman, who was declared to be the leader of an insurrection which occured among the newly formed settlement of Lunenburg in 1753, knew George's Island as his prison home. Settlers there, embittered by treatment accorded by the Government, showed such expression of their feeling, that those in authority had to seek protection in the blockhouse. The disorders proved of little duration for Governor Lawrence dispatched a force of two hundred soldiers, and on their arrival the blockhouse was handed over to Colonel Monckton, who was the leader of the succouring force.

With exception of the ringleaders, the others who took part, were pardoned at once, but Hoffman was brought to Halifax to face a charge of being the main instigator in the mutiny. While he was held a prisoner on George's Island, Governor Lawrence ordered that Hoffman should not be allowed to converse with anybody. It was such a strict

edict that the prisoner was not even to be allowed the use
of pen, ink or paper.

When several months had elapsed Hoffman was taken
before the general court, and at first was indicted of high
treason. But the required number of witnesses could not
be found to make that serious charge stick, and later he was
found guilty of only some of the lesser charges that had been
preferred against him. A heavy fine was ordered, and
apparently there went along with this a period of imprison-
ment for two years. So Hoffman returned to George's Island
to serve out his punishment. Governor Lawrence looked
upon Hoffman, to quote his words, as a "mischievous fellow"
and feared that liberation would only be destructive to the
harmony and industry which had developed in Lunenburg.
So the frequent appeals for pardon, which came from Hoffman to the mainland, failed to win their desired effect.

Hoffman is said to have been living in Halifax in July,
1752, and had occupied the rôle of a Justice of the Peace here,
before he came into his troublesome times in inciting the
insurrection at Lunenburg. What happened to him later I
do not know.

It is set down in the annals of Halifax that by the Autumn
of 1754, a new battery had been erected on the northwest
part of the island, consisting of twenty-four pounders. It
would be somewhat above the site of the present lighthouse.
In its position it would have been able to give a hot time to
any warships of enemy powers striving to attack the settlement. Of course there were other batteries occupying other
vantage points.

Opening of the war with France in 1756 brought a new
page in the history of the little island, for nine French prisoners, who were captured on the Pontchartrain were placed on
the island in prison cells. It is interesting to note that the
names of all these who were taken as French prisoners of war
apparently bore names of German origin. French Nationals
who were evacuated from the Cape Sable district were
brought to Halifax and also placed on George's Island prior

to their expulsion from the country. During the Summer and Autumn of 1759 they remained on the island, but in November the fifty-six men, forty-six women and forty-nine children were placed aboard the ship *Mary the Fourth* and these Acadians were deported under convoy to England.

When England declared war against Spain in 1762, the natural anxiety occasioned by that move caused the defences on George's Island to be strengthened and put in the best possible repair, and the personnel of the armed forces on the island was increased to meet any eventuality. The work was spurred on by the capture of Saint John's, Newfoundland, by the French, but when later it was recaptured, the anxiety lessened and some of the work was not pressed.

George's Island was considered the pivotal point of the fortifications of Halifax in those early times and additional batteries were erected there in 1774.

The island also came in for another use. There was considerable distrust at this time developed against quite a number of prominent citizens and it was said to be found necessary to remove military stores to George's Island as a measure to assure their safe keeping.

Governor Legge saw the possibility of personal gain in securing a grant of a part of the Island for himself, and his desire also embraced considerable other tracts, even some of the slopes of Citadel Hill. He wanted to use the lands for cultivation, but in his request to the authorities, said he would readily turn them back at any time if they were needed for purpose of becoming sites for fortifications. Legge's ambitions were never realized, for his request was not granted.

The growing intercourse with the revolting New England colonies also heightened the importance of George's Island to the town. When Captain Thomas Beamish was appointed Port Warden, a notice was published in 1782 to the effect that "This is to give notice that after the last of March, no vessel or boat will be allowed to pass George's Island in the night-time, nor to depart from the harbour, without sending their boat on shore to the island, and producing a pass from Mr. Beamish the Port Warden, expressing the number of people on board; and all vessels coming in will be hailed from the island, and directed to send their boat on shore to Frederick's wharf to be examined before they attempt to land at any other part of the town." By the way, Frederick's wharf later became known to Halifax as the Market Wharf, which is at the foot of George Street. There the office of the Port Warden was located.

George's Island also had the grim honour—if such it can be termed—of being a place of execution. There in September, 1785, M. Buckley and Belitham Taylor were hanged for the crime of piracy, after running away with the schooner *John Miller* of 'Chedabucto and her cargo.

Yes, George's Island has had a varied history and is indelibly stamped upon the memory of every seafaring man who has entered Halifax Harbour during the past two hundred years. Its history of fortification or neglect of upkeep runs parallel to the Citadel in every detail.

V

BEDFORD BASIN

Whence Weird Tales are Told

It is said that Halifax has the world's third largest harbour. Whether this is an actual statement of fact or not matters little. One fact, however, cannot be disputed, and that is that Halifax Harbour with its inner harbour, known as Bedford Basin, was the finest haven for hundreds of sea-going vessels at a time, during the great wars of every generation.

During the Great World Wars, it was no uncommon sight to see over one hundred large vessels, liners and warships anchored in Bedford Basin at one time, and as fast as one convoy would sail, their places would be taken by incoming ships. Bedford Basin has played an important part in history, even before the establishment of the "Warden of the Honour of the North."

Every person who has visited Halifax by automobile is familiar with the Bedford Road, that beautiful wide concrete main artery that leads directly into the heart of the city, and which no doubt in these post-war years, will be further beautified from Bedford to the Arm Bridge as fitting the main entrance of the modern and up-to-date city of Halifax.

For years this main artery has been used by traffic of all kinds—the coaches of olden days, farmers with their carts overflowing with produce of all kinds for the Garrison and population of His Majesty's Township of Halifax.

In other days the old road twisted and turned up hill and down dale, where inns for the comfort of man and beast were to be found every few miles, along its winding course at the edge of Bedford Basin, before the days of automobiles. Mystery and story of romance and adventure can be told of happenings along the Bedford Road down through the years.

In the lands back of Birch Cove were to be found a number of mounds which appeared to be orderly graves, and stone walls surrounding a large tract of uncultivated land back of the Cove properties, give one reason to wonder why these walls were erected and who was responsible for their erection. Stories of treasure-seeking in the waters of Bedford Basin and on the hills back of Rockingham and Birch Cove add to the romantic past of Bedford Road. The beauty and charm of this area have been recognized since the founding of Halifax by our forefathers, not the least of whom was Edward Augustus, Duke of Kent, who declared that it was the most beautiful spot outside of England, that he had found in North America.

One could tell many tales of happenings along the Bedford Road since that day in June, 1749, when the Honourable Edward Cornwallis arrived with twenty-five hundred settlers to found the township of Halifax and firmly plant the Union Jack of England on the Citadel. However, there is a tale of an event connected with the area now known as Bedford Basin and part of the Bedford Road, when it was only an Indian trail, some few years before the founding of Halifax, that is worth relating.

One of the most remarkable reverses in the battle between the English and the French for the supremacy of North America, was that inflicted upon the French at Louisburg, when an untrained army of New Englanders under that Boston merchant Pepperell, captured this stronghold of French power in 1745.

As was to be expected, the French immediately made plans to recover their great loss of territory and prestige in Nova Scotia.

A few miles out the Bedford Road from Halifax, as one approaches Rockingham, can be seen a stone cairn, marking the site of an encampment of what was left of a great French expedition, that tells of one of the most tragic failures in French records.

A mighty French Armada consisting of sixty-three ships left France on June 22, 1746, under command of the Duc D'Anville, with Vice-Admiral D'Estournel as second in command. Its mission was to recapture Louisburg and Annapolis Royal, to burn Boston, ravage the New England Coast and sweep the West Indies. Misfortune haunted the undertaking. At the beginning there was discontent among the officers. The faster ships had to wait for laggards. The fleet was becalmed. One ship was struck by lightning and six men killed. A stores ship was burned. A plague broke out and 1,200 men died. A storm arose, and a transport collided with a ship of the line, and sank with all on board. Two ships were driven to the West Indies by the force of the wind, and another returned to France. Several transports were wrecked on Sable Island. Finally, with only two ships of the line and four transports D'Anville sailed into Bedford

Basin, which was then known as part of Chebucto Bay or Harbour.

An encampment was made on the shores until the end of October when the troops re-embarked, but so many had died that there were not sufficient to man the few ships, so some were scuttled or burned. Their blackened hulls could be seen under the waters of Bedford Basin for many years after, grim relics of the ill-fated D'Anville expedition which was not only intended to recapture Louisburg, but also Nova Scotia, and to carry destruction to all the settlements and towns of New England. This fleet was under the command of M. de Rochefoucauld, Duc D'Anville, who was born in the early years of the century, being at the time of the expedition about forty years of age. It consisted of eleven ships of the line, twenty frigates, and thirty-four other vessels being transports, fire ships, etc. The soldiers on board this fleet were 3,150 in number and a great abundance of arms, ammunition and provisions were sent with them. The quality of the food and supplies sent with this expedition was apparently of the poorest possible kind. Much sickness broke out aboard every ship within a matter of days after sailing and much of the flour was dumped overboard as unfit for use. Sick men and cattle were crowded together between decks and it was apparently one of the most mismanaged Naval expeditions ever to leave France. The instructions to the duke were to proceed to Louisburg and recapture it, and then to dismantle the fort. He was next to go to Annapolis, take it and leave a garrison there; thence he was to go to Boston, which he was to burn, and afterwards to annoy and distress the English on the American coast, and finally to pay a visit to the English sugar islands in the West Indies.

According to historical records, immediately after having sailed, they met with contrary winds and storms, particularly a storm on September 13th near the isle of Sable, when four ships of the line and a transport were left in distress, and not afterwards heard from, and the squadron scattered and dispersed. The *Mars* and *Alcide*, sixty-four-gun ships, bore off for the West Indies; and the *Ardent*, sixty-four guns, put back on the 15th of September for Brest. The *Ardent* was burned and the *Mars* captured on the French coast by the English ships *Nottingham* and *Exeter*.

On the 20th of September, the Duke D'Anville arrived at Chibouctou, in Acadie, in the *Northumberland* with the *Renommée*, and three or four transports. Here he found only one of his fleet, which had got in three days before him. He had some time before detached M. Conflans with three ships of the line and one frigate to convoy the trade to Hispaniola, and then rejoin the fleet. They called at Chibouctou, as ordered, but eventually sailed for France, without meeting with the rest of the fleet. On September 27th three transports arrived at Chibouctou, and on that day the Duke D'Anville died, but whether of apoplexy, sickness or poison, is not known. No doubt the knowledge of so many of his crews having died on the way over and the great number of sick men on his hands, incapable of handling their ships, whose illness was caused by the poor quality of the food supplied by the authorities at home, must have driven him to distraction. He was buried next day, on a small island at the entrance of the harbour, said to be George's Island. In the afternoon of the same day the Vice-Admiral D'Estournelle, with three ships of the line, came into Chibouctou. Monsieur de la Jonquière, the Governor of Canada, was on board of the *Northumberland*. He had been declared senior civil officer of the expedition after the fleet left France, and was then next in command to the Vice-Admiral D'Estournelle.

In a council of war held on board the *Trident*, September 29th, the Vice-Admiral proposed that they should return to France. They were deprived of four of their ships of the line, namely the *Ardent, Caribou, Mars* and *Alcide* and the *Argonaute*, fire-ship. They had no news of Conflans and his ships; so that only seven ships of importance remained. Many of the land forces, were in the missing ships, and those in the harbour were in a sickly state. From 1,200 to 1,300 of the French are said to have died at sea, and 1,130 at Chibouctou, on the shores of what is now called Bedford Basin in Halifax Harbour. They suffered from scorbutic fever and dysentery. The Indians also caught the disease from them and died in numbers. D'Estournelle's proposition was debated for seven or eight hours. Jonquière and all the land and sea officers were opposed to it, thinking themselves bound in honour to make some attack upon the English, and supposing they could at least conquer Annapolis and recover Nova Scotia, and then winter at Casco Bay in Maine or return to France. The sick, by the supply of fresh provisions from the Acadians, were recovering. The Vice-Admiral not prevailing in his motion, became agitated, fevered and delirious, and was found in his apartment fallen on his sword. According to most historical accounts previously read, it was stated that D'Estournelle died in great distress a few hours after he was found.

This would not appear to be correct, as an account published in French by Monsieur Vovard dealing with "L'Expedition du Duc D'Enville" from documents on file in the Archives of the Minister of Marine in France states that "D'Estournelle did not die from his wounds as stated by most historians. He returned to France with the Squadron. When he landed at Brest his health was much better. Thereupon he requested permission to continue in the service and pointed out his forty years service with the navy. He was allowed to maintain his appointment as an officer, on the active list, with full pay, but never went to sea again. He lived for some years in his native France. Nevertheless D'Estournelle's attempt at taking his own life at Chibucto rendered him incapable of carrying on, therefore, the command devolved on M. la Jonquière, Admiral D'Estournelle officially handing over to him, signing documents to this effect from his sick bed, aboard ship in Bedford Basin, where he lay recovering from his wound. He was apparently thoroughly sick at heart of the whole affair, and 'tis said that he declared it was better to have tried to take his own life than to continue to command such an ill-prepared expedition.

On the morning of the 24th of October, the squadron sailed from Chibouctou. There were but seven vessels of the line remaining, and five of the ships were used as hospitals, there being now not above 1,000 men of the army in an efficient condition.

The squadron bore for Cape Sable, with the design of attacking Annapolis; but when near the Cape, meeting severe storms, they consulted on their position and abandoned the enterprise. Two of the ships are said to have gone as far as Annapolis Basin, but to have withdrawn on finding men-of-war there.

The presence of this formidable fleet was calculated to agitate and alarm all the English colonies, especially those of New England. Boston was reinforced in consequence by 6,400 militia from the interior of the Province of Massachusetts; and when the fact was known that this mighty armament, intended to destroy the British power in these regions, had been dispersed and overwhelmed by storms, sickness and multiplied disasters, so that it not only failed to accomplish any part of the designs entertained by the French, but that hardly a ship returned to Europe, the joy and gratitude to God felt and expressed in New England was almost unbounded. Sermons were preached, and printed on this subject and troops were voted to protect Nova Scotia.

Three years later, after Louisburg and Cape Breton were handed back to France by Treaty, and England decided to strengthen her hold on the mainland of Nova Scotia and established the town of Halifax. The settlers who came found many skeletons of the French and Indians among the trees at Rockingham, their muskets beside them, grim relics of the ill-fated D'Anville expedition of 1746.

It is only natural that Bedford Basin area has had many legends or tales told about it and that ghost stories about former occupants have abounded.

Of all the ghost yarns, two would appear to have been most often told down through the years.

One concerns a ghostly form which was said to appear wrapped in a military cloak on certain nights, pacing to and fro along the shore where the railway now runs, as if awaiting someone. Evidently the railway has interrupted the ghost's occasional stroll, as the last time this yarn was given any credence was as far back as 1888. The other ghostly yarn which is hard to beat, and which years ago was often trotted out for local consumption, concerned a group of seamen, perhaps members of D'Anville's expedition, who kept watch over treasure buried on Stevens Island, across the basin, where the hulks of several of his smaller ships were sunk, and whose timbers could be seen at low tide, 'tis said, for many years.

The subject of the first ghost yarn met his fate in 1798, after a reception held by His Royal Highness, Prince Edward, the Duke of Kent, at his residence along the shores of Bedford Basin.

The Prince's Lodge, it appears on this evening in July of 1798, presented a brilliant and most attractive picture. A great reception was being held by Madame St. Laurent, the lady who ruled the Prince's household and was his constant companion for twenty-seven years. The reception was being held partly in honour of a distinguished visitor, an European nobleman who was a remote connection of the Prince and who having visited Canada, was now returning to his native land across the sea, by a frigate which was anchored off the Dockyard in Halifax, and partly to show Madame's brilliance on such occasions when invitations were issued to everyone of prominence excepting a few who had taken exception to her assumed position of leader of society in His Majesty's township of Halifax. Surrounded by a group of pretty women, the majority of them wives and daughters of officers of the garrison, Madame did the honours with an ease born of Continental surroundings. The fact that certain Halifax ladies were not present seemed not to detract any from her influence or her confidence in her efforts to please on this particular evening. Possessed of a magnificent figure, and being gowned in the latest of fashion which she carried with every grace, and with a complexion the fairest imaginable, eyes of the softest blue, Madame could well support the reputation for some years held before the acquaintance with the Prince, of being the most beautiful woman in the set in which she moved. The Prince being a young and brilliantly uniformed Field-Marshall in his early thirties, and possessed of an easy expression of good nature, made everyone about him happy. The company was a distinguished one. The presence of the Prince in Halifax coupled with the large number of Officers stationed in the garrison, had attracted a number of noblemen who were conveyed from England to Halifax in the Men-of-War and who after a short or long sojourn returned in the same way to Britain. 'Tis said there were in the vicinity of three hundred officers and guests on the grounds this particular evening enjoying the hospitality of the Prince. The lodge and grounds were in every way worthy of the Company. The old Mansion formerly occupied by Governor Wentworth had been replaced by an elegant residence, the Reception Rooms and Corridors of which fairly blazed with the wealth of decorations which had been lavished on them. Scarcely a Man-of-War had arrived during the sojourn of the Prince, but which had brought some precious consignment for the Lodge in the shape of pictures, ornaments or tapestries. The grounds under the organization of a staff of Engineers, with the labour of over two thousand men and under the eye of one of the most celebrated landscape gardeners of England, presented a combination of art and nature not to be found elsewhere in North America. The Duke had said that this was the most beautiful spot he knew outside of England, and no expense was spared to make it so.

The lawns and side paths under the hemlock trees were made brilliant by hundreds of lanterns between the Lodge and shore of the Basin. The band house occupied by a band selected from the regiments in garrison, flooded the air with music. While the fragrance of thousands of plants perfuming the atmosphere made altogether a gorgeous combination of music and flowers, long to be remembered by those present.

A tragic occurrence connected with this occasion, caused every guest to remember it well, and also made it the Duke's last reception at the Lodge. In the retinue of the Prince was a Colonel, one of the accomplished swordsmen and noted duelists of the time. An affair of honour, which had terminated fatally for an opponent had recently banished him from England to Nova Scotia.

At the end of the eighteenth century the duel was fashionable, pistols and coffee before breakfast was a most ordinary occurrence, no gentlemen's outfit was complete without a pair of swords, foils, and long barrelled pistols. Therefore the Colonel's reputation by no means suffered in society, by reason of his antecedents, but his tendency to sudden quarrel, spoiled an otherwise well balanced temperament, and although kindly disposed, misfortune in the shape of hostile meetings appeared to follow him wherever he went. The well known repugnance of the Commander-in-Chief to the duel and the severity with which several participants had been visited, had deterred him from transgressing, and this evening seemed far from furnishing elements of trouble, but trouble comes without invitation at even such an exclusive affair.

The evening progressed to midnight, the brilliant reception had closed, The King's Health had been duly honoured, and the main occupation of all such assemblages of the times began. Card tables were placed everywhere. Footmen in numbers were serving wine to numerous guests. Ladies and gentlemen partook freely of the Clarets, Madeira and Burgundies furnished, while the rattle of dice, the shuffle of cards and bidding of hands resounded all over the rooms and grounds.

Fully two hundred of the guests surrounded tables placed

under hanging lights in secluded spots near the lawn, the beauty and warmth of the summer night having made the outside preferable to the lodge. In an alcove at a table were seated the Colonel, along with a Nobleman on a visit to Nova Scotia, the Captain of one of His Majesty's ships anchored in mid basin, and an Aide-de-Camp of the Duke. The play was in full swing, all were wealthy, also full of wine and apparently good natured, with no thoughts of sudden trouble in such a company.

About one hour after midnight play had not slackened, and to make a night of it, appeared the determination of all. Just about this time trouble commenced. Heated with wine, a quarrel began, and before one hour had elapsed, hostile words were exchanged between the Colonel and the Naval officer, while all witnesses to the affair, to ward off suspicion of coming trouble and to keep the affair from the ears of H.R.H., went on unconcernedly with play. Nevertheless, the die was cast and next morning at sunrise set as the hour for satisfaction.

After two o'clock, the great company had separated, all but the principals in the argument, with their seconds, the Aide-de-Camp and the Nobleman who sauntered on in the moonlight to the outpost guardroom at the cove, where, providing themselves with rapiers from the Commander of the post, they both made memos for the guidance of their executors, in the event of the meeting proving fatal.

An hour later a shaft of light penetrated the eastern horizon, and simultaneously the boom of the morning gun summoned the party to the rendezvous. One by one they wended their way to an eminence south of the Round House, from which there is an unobstructed view of the entire surroundings. The dim outlines of the warships as they rested on the placid waters of Bedford Basin were just discernible, everything partook of a peaceful serenity, in striking contrast with the orgies of the past night and the dreadful tragedy about to be enacted. Presently the sun, peeping above the horizon, bathed sea rock and wood in lines of crimson and gold. The combatants came forward, took up their positions, and placed their swords "hilt to hilt." In another instant the ring and rapid flashing of steel told of the earnestness of the encounter. Full of wine and eager for the meeting, an important item in a combat had been forgotten, they had come unaccompanied by a surgeon. In the case of the death of either or both it would be murder. With a surgeon along, it would be a fully equipped meeting and only a result of honour. The duel proved a desperate one, both were splendid swordsmen, and both were dreadfully wounded before a fatal stroke given by the Naval Officer stretched the Colonel dead on the lawn. The seconds leaving the body, helped the Captain to the very alcove where the quarrel began, where he also expired before help could be procured. The seconds at once proceeded to town and gave themselves up in confidence as accessories to the duel. A most profound sensation was produced at the time, but as both principals in the affair were well connected, the matter became after the usual nine days wonder, a thing of the past.

The Prince, however, to mark his signal displeasure at the occurrence, ordered that the Colonel's body should be buried without military honours where he fell. Some years ago, 'tis said his grave could be faintly traced on the rising ground close to the railway.

The sad catastrophe marked the closing and most brilliant reception of the Duke of Kent at the Prince's Lodge. Before another month had elapsed, an accident occurred to the Prince by his being thrown from his horse and as his injured leg did not seem to respond to local treatment, it was decided that a visit to the old country and His Majesty's Surgeon-in-Chief was necessary. The Lodge was vacated forthwith, the Prince and Madame St. Laurent were soon on their way to England, but the brilliant finale to the receptions at the Lodge was long remembered, and also the tragic duel which terminated the lives of two gallant officers of His Majesty, George the Third.

For many a year the story of this reception and duel were recounted along with the fact that on certain moonlight nights a ghostly form wrapped in a military cloak could be seen pacing to and fro with solemn tread, to the south of the bandstand where now the railway track is laid. Evidently the ghost of the Colonel was like the Colonel alive, still on the warpath for many years, but with the oncoming of the railway decided it was no place for even a ghost to walk, as it is now over sixty years since anyone has reminded us in print or reported on his nocturnal wanderings.

Now let us deal with the supposed activities of not just one ghost, but a whole crew of them, who have made yarns of this type famous in years gone by around Bedford Basin, particularly in the vicinity of Steven's Island, which is located directly across the Basin, on the East side, opposite the spot where the monument is erected on the West side, to mark the landing place of the twelve hundred odd Frenchmen who died on these shores in 1746.

No ghost story of the district can outdo the supposed adventure of a midshipman of His Majesty's Royal Navy at Halifax in 1825.

It's a tale of Steven's Island in Bedford Basin and the ghostly crew which took turns to watch over buried treasure on the Island, each man being alloted the unheard of watch of forty years' span.

Steven's Island in Bedford Basin lies not far from the Naval Magazine and at times has been known as Glassey's Island and Navy Island. This tale reminds one of the traditional procedure of pirates who made it a practice, 'tis said, of murdering one of their number when burying treasure so that it would not be disturbed by other members of the crew, who would be afraid of meeting the ghost of the man they had murdered.

I leave it to you, as to the authenticity of this yarn, which was brought to my attention some years ago, when I came across a small four-page monthly newspaper which had been published around 1888, and was known as the *Rockingham*

Sentinel. It only survived four issues as far as I can ascertain. No doubt it is the basis of many ghost yarns of Bedford Basin that have been told down through the years. I cannot give you the name of the midshipman concerned or the name of his ship or other detailed information in this condensed version of what was reported as an actual happening, but here are the main facts.

It would appear that Halifax Harbour, on a particular afternoon in July, 1825, presented a scene of placid beauty and stillness. Not a breeze disturbed its waters, and the three or four of His Majesty's Men-of-War lying at their moorings off the Dockyard appeared to have fallen asleep that particular hot afternoon, making up, perhaps, for storms and perils experienced in getting there.

The flagship, stately and grand with her tiers of guns looked like a sleeping lioness, her decks scrubbed and bright, showing the care and attention of a well-disciplined crew.

From her quarter deck, looking north, the Basin glowed like a mirror with its glassy surface, but pleasing glimpses of deep woods on the Dartmouth shores, relieved the scene, making it a tempting excursion to any who had energy sufficient for the enterprise.

A young midshipman off duty was tempted to ask permission from the officer of the watch for three hours leave of absence in the Dinghy, to go to Navy Island and return.

The Lieutenant on duty readily gave the necessary permission and warned the midshipman to take care of the fog, as it was banked outside the light, on McNab's Island and he felt it would enter the harbour proper with the incoming tide. As the dinghy backed from the ship, the youth responded with a cheerful "Aye, aye, Sir," and pulled leisurely away.

Little did he realize what a story he'd have to tell before he returned.

The island to which he turned his boat had an old-time history, shrouded with grim memories and romantic interest. European seafarers of various nations, particularly French, as well as native Indians had successively occupied its shores. Pirates, buccaneers, and other salt water free lances had for three centuries sought its shelter. The ruins of an old wooden defence tower erected by former occupants of a previous century showed picturesquely through the thick copse on the south point, and the remains of an ancient Indian grave-yard could still be traced on the rising slope in the centre. It was a spot around which rude tradition had woven some queer tales, none of which troubled the midshipman. As he approached the north beach of the Island, he rested on his oars for a short time before landing. The heat of the after-noon, and the steady pull he had indulged in since leaving the ship, combined to produce an instantaneous drowsiness and while glancing at the shore, it gradually faded away, and infinite peace stole upon him. The vast expanse of the Basin, unbroken by a ripple, appeared covered by a luminous liquid haze, and as if to be in keeping with the surrounding calm of nature, he fell fast asleep in the stern sheets.

A gentle eddy carried the dinghy in shore, until at last it was completely grounded under the lee of the south point.

Toward nightfall the sea fog which had slept in the sun outside the lighthouse all day, crept softly up into the har-bour, gradually obliterating both shores, concealing one ship after the other and silently covering the Narrows, spread itself like a dense pall over the island and expanse of Bed-ford Basin.

How long the midshipman slept he knew not; several hours, he felt confident, must have elapsed, but when he awoke the sunshine and warmth had departed. It was very cold; the insiduous fog had saturated his jacket and sitting up he gazed almost despairingly around in his endeavour to locate his whereabouts.

This unexpected termination to an afternoon's excursion was rather annoying, but confident that before long the fog would lift sufficiently to show his surroundings, and gratified at being on shore instead of floating on the sea, he prepared to explore the point on which he had grounded.

Drawing the dinghy further up the beach, he groped his way over rock and knoll in the direction of the ruins of the old defence post, but had not gone many steps when he was startled by a loud halloo! which seemed to proceed from the direction of the Narrows. Thinking it might be the cry of some boatman lost like himself in the fog, he replied loudly, "Here ahoy!" and walked to the edge of the point, vainly endeavouring to catch a glimpse of the party hailing, but the thick veil that covered the Basin and shore rendered all objects perfectly indistinguishable. He heard, however, the regular strokes of oars rising and falling in dull echo on the water. After a pause, the halloo was re-echoed from the water. He was clearing his throat to reply, when to his surprise an answer came apparently from the ruins to which he was making his way. Turning hastily to the sound which now seemed so close, he was amazed on reaching the ruin to find a fire burning in a corner, and a seaman busy warming himself by the blaze. A very strange looking seaman, unlike any he had ever seen before.

Stepping back, the midshipman took a good look at the stranger. He was an elderly man with a ghostly hollow face, but the oddity of his dress was even more surprising than his unearthly countenance. Although it was summer, his legs were clothed in enormously wide trousers, descending to the knee, where they met long, sealskin boots. A pea-jacket, with exaggerated cuffs almost as large as the breeches, covered his chest and around his waist a monstrous belt, with a large buckle, on which was supported two wide-mouthed pistols and a curved dagger. A long queue descended half way down his back. The apparition appeared intent on warming himself and drying his costume, occasionally rolling a huge quid in the cavernous recesses of his jaws. Most strange of all was the fact that as this strange character moved past the fire, the flames could be seen through what should have been the most solid part of his body. No doubt in his mind but he was face to face with a spirit of bygone days.

Meanwhile, the nearer splash of oars indicated the approach of the unseen boat and behind a corner of the ruins, a number of uncouth-looking figures clambered up the knoll from the boat, bearing with them a small keg. Filing in about the fire, they silently ranged themselves around their ghostly host, as he on welcoming them, announced to them that the night of selecting one of their number to watch the treasures for the next forty years was on hand.

The young officer's horror on hearing this announcement disclosing and confirming his suspicions of the unearthly character and business of this crew of phantoms, can better be imagined than described. All the strange stories which he had heard connected with this island now came trooping through his brain.

This was doubtless the very spot where quantities of ill-gotten booty lay hidden, protected by such evil agencies, that made honest seamen shudder. Very real became the many tales he had heard from old salts of the Navy, of the shadowy ship, which at times was seen above the Narrows, standing off and on toward this island, or when fogs encompassed the Basin, of the sound of oars rising and falling in their rowlocks that could be heard approaching the shore he was now on. But mere tales all faded before the horrible reality to which he now was a witness.

While he stood entranced with curiosity and terror, catching indistinctly orders given by the leader in such quaint terms that they could scarcely be understood, suddenly a movement of all from the fire which they had hitherto surrounded, took place toward a corner of the ruin, and all present appeared tugging at a particular stone, rolling it aside sufficiently to allow a figure dressed much like themselves to emerge.

The one appointed for the next almost half century watch silently took his place. Back went the rock, a faint "All's well" from the one who had taken up watch, was heard. It was evident that the ceremonies were over, and the ghostly crew all turned toward the shore as if about to take their departure.

Now thoroughly scared, with an uncontrollable impulse, the midshipman started from his hiding place towards his boat, but, stumbling over the bank, he landed on the beach below, striking his head as he fell. How long he remained there he could not tell. When he awoke to consciousness, he was in the stern sheets of the captains gig, with his familiar crew rowing toward the *Flagship.*

The prolonged absence of the midshipman and the fear of his being lost in the fog, having prompted the officers to send a boat's crew in search of him.

His queer recital of the scenes of the previous night was listened to by the boat's crew with close attention. The officer in charge of the boat as well as the first lieutenant did not help his peace of mind by their sarcastic remarks about officers and gentlemen and the use of strong liquor by midshipmen on leave. The fact, however, ever remained with him that "This was no tale to excuse his overstaying his leave," but that he actually was witness to the phantom change of watch over the buried treasures of Steven's Island in Bedford Basin.

Believe it or leave it, my friends, there you have a yarn which was repeated as fact by our grandfathers, and great grandfathers, on many an occasion.

The ghostly crew, if by chance they still carry out their watch, must have been somewhat disturbed when the naval magazine blew up in 1945. Perhaps they were again changing the guard. Remember it was in July. Probably by this time, they have departed for more peaceful locations than Steven's Island in Bedford Basin, which is too near the modern storage place of high explosives, for even a ghost to enjoy.

At any rate, I don't expect to ever hear any more of their so-called watching activities on Steven's Island or elsewhere in Bedford Basin. On the other hand—perhaps you believe in ghosts!

VI

THE DUKE OF KENT'S RENDEZVOUS

Prince's Lodge

IT is surprising the number of newcomers to Halifax who ask about that circular building, with the round dome for a roof, which they see a few miles before arriving in the city, if they come by the main highway or by train. It is not so surprising on the part of those whose advent to Halifax is by means of a motor road, but the more fleeting view that arrivals by train experience, does not give them equal opportunity to have the structure impress itself on their minds. Yet, many of them note it, and a number express curiosity about its unique design.

Of course, it would be difficult to find a Haligonian who

does not know of Prince's Lodge, and who does not boast at least a smattering of its history. But even a number of regular residents do not know much about the building perched high on the hill, overlooking Bedford Basin on one side, and with the cutting of the C.N.R. track providing a minor precipice on the other.

The same royal person who was instrumental in the erection of the historic clock on the slope of Citadel Hill likewise caused the erection of this other building. But, where the town clock stands in isolation, the other one was once part of an extensive group of buildings which formed the home of Prince Edward, Duke of Kent, during his sojourn at this post.

True, it was separated by a little distance from the main buildings of the estate, but was a part of it. The rotunda provided the place from which the band on frequent occasions in those colourful days, disgorged sweet music for the entertainment of Edward and his guests. Legend has it that the Duke utilized the Maroons, coloured men who were shipped here from Jamaica, in his operations of building, and it is said that the rotunda was on occasions used as a kind of temple in which these Maroons practised their rites.

It was after Edward's arrival here from the West Indies in May, 1794, that this beautiful section of the Basin's shore took on its very important rôle in local history. While guest of Governor Wentworth, Edward, who had been named head of the British troops in Nova Scotia and New Brunswick, was taken to the Governor's summer home these few miles from Halifax, which Wentworth had given the name of "Friar Lawrence's Cell."

Dr. Clara Dennis, in her much read book, *Down in Nova Scotia*, says "The Governor could not know that it was destined to be the setting for a real Romeo and Juliet, whose romance would also end in tragedy, although unlike the tragedy of the imaginary Romeo and Juliet from whose story the Governor had taken the Friar Lawrence's Cell as the name for his modest summer home."

Edward found this spot, to use his own words, "better than any spot outside England," and the obliging Governor gave over his place to his royal guest. From then on, it gained its new name of Prince's Lodge.

Services of the leading landscape artist of the day in England were sought by the enthusiastic builder, and the natural beauty of the surroundings soon took on new glory as the development proceeded.

It is recalled that myriad pathways were directed through the woods, and each path was so designed that it formed a letter of the alphabet. Grottos abounded. Chinese pagodas were speedily erected where commanding views of the Basin could be secured.

It was fitting that such a place, and with such a history to be written in the brief period of its glory, should have a special pathway which boasted the designation of "Lover's Lane." What happy hours for those ill-fated lovers of history, Edward and the beautiful Julie St. Laurent who won his affections, the young widow who was Edward's constant companion until expediency of the ways of state made it necessary for him to choose a royal bride.

It was with Madame St. Laurent as the charming and beautiful hostess, that the then leaders of Halifax social world wended their way to the retreat on the Basin's shores for the gay festivities. Many a titled visitor from other climes had his good opinion of Halifax greatly increased by the happy hours spent as an honoured guest at the Lodge.

Let us imagine that we have together travelled out the Bedford Road, past Mount St. Vincent, through Rockingham, beyond Birch Cove, and but a little beyond we see the rotunda, with the tracks between it and our highway. It was up the pathway from opposite the music room that we travel to reach the site of the main parts of the Lodge.

Arriving at the site, which has lost almost every line with the past but the rotunda, we will have to close our eyes and try to picture what it must have looked like at the end of the eighteenth century.

Records tell us that the main residence was a two-storey house of Italian style, with wings at each end and the grand hall and reception room in the centre. To the rear was a church-like structure said to house the offices and kitchens, for no cooking was actually done in the main building, a subterranean passage leading to that very necessary department. What rich repasts must have been carried along its artificially-lighted course.

Near enough to the house to give ready access was the library, stocked with books which were brought at great difficulty, for it is said that seven times through piracy or shipwreck, Edward lost his household goods and books, including thousands of volumes at Sable Island.

It was a self sufficient little community that dwelt amid all this beauty, for it had its stables, forge and a variety of other outbuildings to meet its requirements. There was even a barracks there for the guards over such an important person, and this structure was said to have been just a small space north of the still standing rotunda.

But even if able to get along quite well alone, it still was considered necessary to have a link with the city. It was not as simple a matter as today, with the telephone—so on a high elevation was the observatory and signal station. From it, signals were relayed through Fort Needham, at the north end of Halifax, on to Fort George on the summit of Citadel Hill.

Expense was not spared by Edward in meeting his own whims, or those of his beauteous companion, and it is said that when His Royal Highness finally quit this section, to meet the call of state elsewhere, he left the trifling amount of $800,000 in debts in Nova Scotia.

Dr. Clara Dennis tells us that behind all these scenes of pomp and gaiety dwelt a lonely hermit in his cell. He was furnished with rich food from the Lodge, but rejected all but the plainest of scraps never leaving his cell but at nights.

His grave is said to be somewhere about, at a place selected by Madame St. Laurent, and in keeping with his habits during life, he was laid to rest in the darkness of night. We could spend many moments here merely pondering what lay behind his selection of such a strange way of life.

There is another hidden grave hereabouts, according to stories that have been handed down. It is that of the Prince's favourite charger. He would have no horse but the best, and it is said that this favourite stumbled but once, but even that was sufficient for a royal decree that he be shot.

There is still a little lake to be seen. If we travel up over the hill we find a small artificial lake. Once this was heart-shaped, made for Julie by her lover, but its shores are now unkempt. Where once stood well-kept buildings, are now but rough board structures used for picnic purpose, and a few new houses built since the war.

For years the property was used as the centre for organized outings from the city. Many of us in Halifax recall with thrilling memories the travels up the Basin in some small steamboat, to be disgorged at a wharf by the rotunda, and then to proceed on to the open parts above, where the fun of the picnic was experienced. Then at day's end, as the shades of night started to make the eastern shore indistinct, we travelled down the slope again on tired and begrimed legs for the climaxing thrill, the boat trip back to the city.

What a contrast to those days of royal parties, with bowling on the green—Prince's Lodge, the name given to the section, is today counted as a residential suburb of Halifax. But a few short years ago it was the place where the more fortunate people of the city had summer homes, to be boarded up and deserted with the arrival of the colder months. Today it has a variety of attractive year-round residences, and people who make their homes there travel to and from the city in a matter of a comparatively few minutes, where once it was a journey of hours by horse-drawn vehicles, or by water up the harbour, through the narrows and to the western shore of the Basin.

There are still to be found traces of the paths leading back of the summer homes, the paths once trod by Edward and Julie, in the days before that fateful 1818, when it became advisable that Edward's marriage to the Princess of Leningen take place. Madame St. Laurent first learned of this plan from a newspaper, and heart broken she retired to a convent, death ending her career, which knew both so much happiness and sadness, in 1832. This romance, which is said to have included a marriage of Edward and Julie at Gibraltar, but which was not recognized by his royal father, George the Third, was doomed to unkind fate at the last.

But as a result of Edward's union with the Princess, the British Empire was given its great Queen Victoria.

If you have time and wish to hold a session with the past, so to speak, then by all means visit this historic place. See the lake, which still to a measure holds to its heart shape. Don't delay for years, or it will be too late, for the area has been sub-divided for building lots. Up to recent years traces of the old foundation could be seen, but many of the rocks were more recently trucked away. Even the Gray house that succeeded the Prince's Lodge, on the name site, is now a thing of the past.

Today the rotunda is owned by Mrs. Mary Karas, Morris Street; who occupies it as a summer home; and hopes to follow that practice for years to come, and finds the unusual design of the rooms of her Bedford shore home very intriguing.

At times efforts have been spoken of to gain possession of the place as an historic shrine, but so far no successful project has been launched. Those who would preserve historic sites and who have the tourist in mind, certainly would like to see the unique building owned by the Province and to see the iron bridge across the railway cutting restored. What an ideal tourist information bureau it would make.

It is my good fortune to reside at Prince's Lodge, near Halifax, on the very grounds the great, great grandfather of our King liked so well.

Prince's Lodge takes its name because of the fact that Prince Edward, Duke of Kent, father of the late Queen Victoria built his residence there, which he occupied. He formerly lived in his town house on the south side of Cogswell Street, where the military gymnasium is now located, but even before building his own residence, was a frequent visitor to the summer residence of the Governor on the shores of Bedford Basin.

The land was originally granted to Captain William Foy, first Provost Marshall of Nova Scotia, who came to Halifax with the Hon. Edward Cornwallis, in the transport *Canning*. Captain Foy obtained the grant of land, on the western shore of Bedford Basin, on July 20, 1752. He passed away in Halifax in 1774 and this property was then obtained by John Willis, who also was well-known in Halifax, as the proprietor of the Great Pontack Inn.

Prince's Lodge property eventually fell into the hands of John Wentworth, Lieutenant-Governor of Nova Scotia and former Governor of New Hampshire. He built a small summer residence on what is now known as Prince's Lodge, but which he called "Friar Lawrence Cell."

The Rotunda, or music room, on the opposite side of the road, next the water, was surrounded by a rich foliage of beech groves, and the large white ball on the top of the building was gilded. This ball, flashing in the sunlight presented a beautiful and picturesque appearance on the approach to the Lodge. The Prince's Lodge was built altogether of wood, consisting of a centre of two stories containing the hall and staircase, with a flat roof. There were two wings containing the Duke's apartments. In the rear was a narrow wooden building with pointed gothic windows, resembling a chapel, containing the kitchen and offices, which extended some distance southward beyond the main building. The grouping of the beech and birch trees in the lawn and around the house was well arranged. The beautiful hemlock trees today are admired by all who come to visit in this historic spot, where once His Royal Highness and Madame Saint Laurent and their guests walked and enjoyed the same scenery.

The rooms of the Lodge were not spacious, and the ceilings low, which appears to have been the fashion of building in Halifax at that time.

Bridle paths, traversed walks and in several places carriage roads with views of the Basin and resting places with little wooden seats were made. Even imitation Chinese pagodas were erected. Several of these were said to be still in existence around 1830. In fact, on my own property I have discovered a foundation of one of them in the woods close to the road. Just recently the old roads on the Northern end of the property, where the Lodge stood, have been repaired, that area has been surveyed into half acre lots for development as a residential section.

The Duke erected a range of low buildings on the edge of the Basin a little to the north of the Rotunda, which were occupied by two companies of his Regiment, the Royal Fusiliers and contained the Guard Room and a Mess Room for the officers. The building was afterwards known as the "Rockingham Inn." It became a favourite resort in summer where tea and ginger beer were to be had under the piazza which ran along the edge of the water. This Inn acquired the name of Rockingham, where, for a long time after the Prince's departure, the Rockingham Club met. The Rockingham Club was partly literary and partly social. It was composed of Governor Wentworth, the members of His Majesty's Council, the Admiral of the Station, several of the principal military officers, and a number of the leading citizens of Halifax. Dr. Stanser, rector of Saint Paul's was one of its members, also the Hon. Andrew Belcher, both of whom had summer homes. Dr. Stanser's being located at Sherwood, outside of the village of Rockingham, and Mr. Belcher at Birch Cove.

The Rockingham Club was given its name in compliment to Sir John Wentworth, the head of whose family the Marquis of Rockingham, was about that time in the British

Ministry. The large room which extended along the south-west wing of the building, east and west, with the end by the water, was hung with the portraits of many of the members of the Club, painted by a gentleman named Field, a celebrated portrait painter who resided in Halifax at that time. It is said that most of these portraits are still in existence. In fact, I have seen two of them on the walls of the Halifax Club on Hollis Street.

The original grant of land comprised about two hundred and thirty acres.

In imagination one can easily picture that once famous estate which was called into being by the feudal rule of this young son of George the Third, with its bowling green, heart-shaped lake, cricket fields, etc., in those historic acres now being sub-divided for residential purposes.

While the Duke lived in this pleasant Lodge, many a picturesque, eighteenth-century frigate dropped anchor in Bedford Basin, at rest after chasing the seas in search of French prizes, in the same manner as the modern ships of war and merchantmen used the Basin as a place of haven during both Great Wars.

Summer and winter alike, the Duke lived at Prince's Lodge, for the English soldiers kept the six miles of road from Halifax cleared of snow, and from the nearby hilltop at the back of my property, where an anti-aircraft battery was located during the war just ended, the Duke's signallers wig-wagged his orders to Fort Needham to be relayed to Fort George at the Citadel. During his years in British North America, especially at Halifax, the Duke spent probably the happiest time of his life.

King George the Third had a family of seven sons and eight daughters, of which Edward, Duke of Kent, was considered the most capable son but who for some reason or other saw very little of his parents, in fact from childhood he was kept away from England. As a lad he was sent to Germany to be trained for the profession of Arms. While his tutors were sent a thousand pounds a year, for his needs, he was lucky to get a pound a week, after they had taken their fees. It would seem the Prince was destined to be in debt most of his life, never did he have enough money to pay the cost of living in the style and manner to which he was expected to keep up, and which he did in the many appointments he was assigned to, on foreign service in his Father's Empire.

At the conclusion of his military training, at the age of twenty-three, he was appointed to the Command of the Seventh Royal Fusiliers, at Gibraltar. At the Rock, the young Royal Prince very soon became the centre of a storm, in military circles.

In addition to the strict discipline which he had learned so well on the continent, he was determined to curb the drunkenness of the men, to reform and smarten up his Regiment, which had been stationed at Gibraltar for some time, and to use an army term, they were just about fed up with conditions, when their Royal Commanding Officer took over with his new ideas. His severity and reform plans almost brought the men to a state of mutiny, and the home Government wisely decided to move them from that station, lest the discontent should spread to the rest of the garrison. ·

It was not many weeks before the Royal Fusiliers found themselves marching from Rosea Barracks down to the quay, to a waiting troopship for services in America. After some weeks, they were enjoying the scenery of the St. Lawrence, as the ship made its way up to Quebec.

Early in the summer of 1791, Prince Edward, a tall, smart-looking British Officer, marched ahead of his Regiment as they made their way into barracks at Quebec for a term of service there, as all eyes were upon the young twenty-five-year-old battalion Commander.

At Quebec City, he made life-long friends, in particular the de Salaberry family, for whom he did many favours. Charles Michael de Salaberry, who later became the hero of Chateauguay, first entered the army as a protégé of the Duke, as did his brothers, and throughout their early Army careers, their royal friend took particular interest in their welfare. Many young French 'Canadians were started off with commissions in His Majesty's Service through his efforts and the Duke kept up personal correspondence with their parents for years. Nothing was too good for anyone he liked no matter what their station in life. He never forgot a kindly or friendly act. His residence on Saint Louis Street was the centre of the social swirl and the Governor's residence, at Montmorency Falls, was favoured by his presence on every week-end possible, where he loved to go to get away from the crowded city streets, to be with his special friends.

When, a few years later, in 1794, after active service in the West Indies, he was transferred to Halifax as Commander of the Garrison, he found to his delight that the Governor, just like the Governor of Quebec, had a summer residence just a few miles outside the city, and he immediately made it a point to drive out to this delightful spot whenever he could get away from his official duties.

His Royal Hightness, Edward, Duke of Kent, was as a matter of fact a good soldier, whose military ability would have been recognized had he not had his true worth overshadowed by the glamour of his Royal rank as the son of the King.

The building of the fortifications of the important outpost of the Empire, at Halifax and the personal supervision which he gave to the defences in his time, was no mean accomplishment, which any commanding General would have been glad to have had to his credit. He deserves to be remembered with graver consideration of his services as a soldier, and less as a Royal Prince, at the necessary entertaining which he was perforce obliged to carry out on occasions at Prince's Lodge.

Halifax might well have fallen prey to the King's enemies if he had not restored and strengthened the defences of the Port of Halifax, which, on his arrival, were totally inadequate and on his departure and in subsequent years through his initiative, were made of such strength that none dared to attack.

The Duke was the exact opposite to the playboy which the popular legend would have one assume. On his arrival in Halifax he found a brilliant but frivolous set, of dancing, card-playing and pleasure-loving society, which were delighted at the arrival of a Royal Prince in their midst.

Great must have been their surprise, when he promptly ordered Sunday card parties and all night carousals to cease among the officers of the Garrison, and when he ordered the unheard of parades of regiments, officers included, at such hours as five o'clock in the morning and was there himself to see his instructions were carried out.

While as a mere battalion Commander in Gibraltar, his ideas of discipline and soldierly conduct caused him to be removed to another station, now as General Officer Commanding he had the authority and determination to do what he considered was his duty to his King and Country. He had no use for inefficiency or laziness in officers or men. He was honest in his determination to have the defences in both materials and men, as clean, smart and efficient as possible and while we today could not understand or countenance the floggings, and other punishments handed out, nevertheless the practices of those days should be judged in the light of what was considered the right and proper method of stamping out vice and insubordination in the eighteen century mind, rather than present day practice.

The Duke had a certain goal ahead and by hard work and sheer ability he proved he was worthy of the promotion which came to him when he was made Commander-in-Chief of His Majesty's Forces in North America. One of the first duties he carried out in Nova Scotia was to personally inspect every possible unit of his command, and early in 1794 he passed through Kentville, which was later named after him, on a visit to Annapolis Royal, making the journey on horseback.

With this promotion, and the increased allowances and authority, he was able to carry out constructions of not only Martello towers and fortifications so essential for the proper defence of the forces under his command, but other useful buildings with which his name is linked for ever in the old Garrison City.

In the very heart of the city he ordered to be built on the side of Citadel Hill, the familiar Round Old Town Clock tower. Punctuality was of first importance with the Duke of Kent, as the troops and others of Happy-go-lucky Halifax soon found out. The clock tower was one of his devices for speeding up the life of the town, although he never actually saw it erected, as he was ordered back to England for other duties of state before the clock arrived aboard H.M.S. *Dart* from the English builders.

He had a particular fondness for round buildings, as is evidenced by the Music Room, still standing at Prince's Lodge, the Old Town Clock and that delightful Round Church, Saint George's, so full of old traditions and old memories.

Originally this church was completely round, but in later years the chancel was extended to the west, and an entry built on the eastern Brunswick Street side. But it is still the Round Church to all Haligonians, who are proud of its unusual architecture.

The church dates back to the very start of the last century and the Duke of Kent was one of the prime movers in its construction.   Subscriptions making its erection possible, included two hundred pounds from George III, and gifts of five hundred pounds each from the Home Government and the Provincial Arms Fund, as well as varying amounts from private purses on both sides of the Atlantic.

Laying of the cornerstone took place on April 10, 1800, and fifteen months later construction had progressed to a degree where it could be used for divine service.   The Duke of Kent left Halifax so history books tell, in the summer of 1800, so he never saw the completion of the church in which he had taken such a personal interest.   It was on July 19, 1801, that the first service was held within the hallowed walls.

To climb up the steps of the succeeding galleries of the church is to take oneself back in fancy over a century. First, we come to the main gallery, which boasts the original pews, next in our climb we come to two smaller galleries on the eastern side and here the students of the early Sunday School sat, restlessly probably, through the long services of the other days. The pegs are still there where the boys placed their hats. Still higher, under the very dome, itself, are openings where sailors from the men-of-war sat on hard, backless benches that encircled the whole dome. From this point of vantage the men looked down the main body of the congregation far below. These openings have been blocked off, but some spaces have been left from which it is still possible to get a view of the church's interior.

"The sailors were noted for their good behaviour as they sat up there," declared the late Rev. Canon H. W. Cunningham, who until recent years was rector of St. George's over a great period. This praise will be heard with gratification by present members of the Senior Service. It may be an experience for them to write back to folks at home, when on an actual visit to St. George's they sit for a moment on the circular bench and ponder back on the men who helped build the fine traditions of the British Navy. From windows a fine view of that section of the city can be obtained, and by means of a ladder, an even higher point of vantage can be gained.

In cubbyholes of the false dome and under the roof, there have been secreted for many years antique iron, rope-handled fire buckets, a wooden bier upon which earlier Haligonians were carried when they went to their last rest. Oh, yes, old St. George's has much to tell us of this earlier Halifax.

Intermural burials were the custom for many years after the round church was built and among the colonial celebrities buried in its vaults is that interesting old man, who doubtless related many of his tales to Kent himself—Governor Desbarres, who died in 1824, at the reputed age of a hundred and three. Desbarres fought with distinction at Louisburg, and was Aide-de-Camp to Wolfe, at Quebec. He was, as his memorial states, "Cartographer, engineer and administrator, and also preceptor of Captain Cook, the circumnavigator." He founded Sydney, Cape Breton, while he was the Island Governor, and he was also Governor of Prince Edward Island, named for the Duke of Kent, when he was eighty years of age. He lived long after Kent was dead and gone, until Kent's little daugher was five years old.

When, during the summer of 1800, his Royal Highness the Duke of Kent took his final departure from Halifax, the usual addresses were presented by the House of Assembly, His Majesty's Council and the people of the town. He embarked on H.M.S. *Assistance* on the 3rd of August, and sailed on the 4th. His embarkation was attended with full ceremony, the troops lining the streets. His Royal Highness, accompanied by the Governor and Council, and the principal Naval and Military Officers, proceeded on foot through the avenue formed by the troops to the King's Wharf, whence he reached the ship under salutes from the batteries, the artillery corps and the ships of war. For years afterwards old inhabitants who recollected the scene, would proudly describe the feelings evinced by the townspeople on the occasion.

According to historians of that era, his tall, commanding figure in full military uniform, his hat surmounted by the lofty white plume then worn by the Fusiliers, could be seen above the heads of the surrounding crowd as he walked down the line, with a smile of recognition for his friends on passing them, amidst the plaudits of the crowd. Though the Duke exhibited on all occasions the most kind temper in civil life and his manner and conversation with those he liked almost amounted to familiarity, yet his sternness in military affairs never forsook him. Eleven soldiers had been sentenced to death for mutiny and desertion, and had been left by the Duke for execution, which was carried into effect under his orders a few days after he left our shores. On the 7th August, those unfortunates were brought out on the Common, dressed in white, with their coffins, accompanied by the

Rev. George Wright, the Garrison Chaplain, and Doctor Burke, the Roman Catholic clergyman, in the presence of the whole Garrison. Eight of them were reprieved under the gallows, and the three who belonged to the Newfoundland Regiment were hanged. Public feeling was against the Duke in this affair. It was thought that on the eve of his departure he should have granted a remission of the death sentence, which, as General Commanding, he had power to do, until the King's pleasure should be known. Three executions only a day or two after his departure produced a disagreeable impression of His Royal Highness in the minds of the people of Halifax, who had just taken leave of him with so much kind feeling.

Just twenty years after leaving Halifax, Prince Edward died in England, on January 22, 1820, at the age of fifty-three, just one week before his father, George III. After the reigns of his brothers, George IV and William IV, his baby daughter Victoria, was destined to become Queen of England in 1837.

After the Prince's departure, Governor Wentworth occupied the Lodge on the Basin, which had been built on his land. He resided there for some years after retiring from the Governorship of Nova Scotia. By strange coincidence, Sir John Wentworth, died a few weeks after the Duke of Kent, in the spring of 1820, at the age of eighty-four.

No man has left his mark more indelibly inscribed in the annals of Nova Scotia than His Royal Highness, Edward, Duke of Kent, whose former residential site on the side of Bedford Basin is officially known far and wide as Prince's Lodge, and after whom the lovely town of Kentville was named in 1826, just six years after his death, and thirty-two years after he visited what was then the hamlet or village of Horton Corner. Kentville and Prince's Lodge were named after a truly great soldier, administrator and builder of his day.

VII

E MARI MERCES

Wealth from the Sea

UNDER the Crest or Coat of Arms of the City of Halifax are written the following Latin words: *E Mari Merces.* How appropriate!

Once upon a time the Old Town Clock looked down at a waterfront that bristled with tapering spars which pointed upward from staunch wooden hulls. Those who love a long fine curve in the hull of a boat would have delighted in the wind ships of Nova Scotia which gave the Province wide fame. The years from 1840 to 1886 were the palmy days of wooden ship-building in Nova Scotia. The Province

103

abounded, and still abounds in timber excellent for shipbuilding purposes, and Bluenose vessels were renowned for their
buoyancy, a quality which at times was often lacking in
ships built elsewhere. The tang of the sea permeates Nova
Scotia, and from the sea the Bluenose-breed have learned
the largeness of vision, the freedom of thought and action
and the spirit of adventurous daring, that is so much a part
of a maritime country.

They have that sense that comprehends the sea.

In these days of oil and coal fed ships, we seldom think
of the staunch wooden craft that have been built on Nova
Scotia's shores, in days when sailormen relied on sail for
power. True, war-time conditions caused the remaining
shipyards along the shores of the Province to spring into
renewed activity. Not only that, but new yards carried out
a variety of works, with construction of barges, landing
craft—any number of new types of vessels demanded by a
country at war.

These wooden craft of modern times are a far cry from
the graceful lines of Nova Scotia's famous windships of the
past. They were designed to meet the special needs of the
war services. We, who have Nova Scotia blood in our veins,
or who from living here long, have gained a great love of the
salty sea, cannot but feel a nostalgic pull at the heart strings
when we think of those graceful queens of the sea. Those
were the craft of the days of wooden ships and iron men.
Nova Scotia's seamen of today are still men of iron—they live
up well to their rich heritage. They have been tried in the
testing furnace of battle and emerged with full glory.

With days long since gone when the waterfront of Halifax was a forest of masts, then at the many harbour docks
largely owned by private firms, hundreds of sailing ships
called each year with rich cargoes from all parts of the world.

In the memory of the older folk, this massing of tall
tapering spars against the skyline of Halifax shore was a
familiar sight. Then, it was no novelty to see three, four
and even more masts with sails set, carrying some staunch

ship out from Halifax, past Maugher's Beach light and away on a foreign cruise. There were sailing craft flying the flags of many nations in this port in those days of the past. But a surprising number of those ships flew flags that identified them with our own people, and were sailed by Nova Scotian crews, and bore names that had special significance to the people of this Province—for one can hardly go into any small port along our shores, where the older inhabitants cannot point out a smooth sloping section of shoreline as the place where vessels were built. Take Hubbards for instance. Recently, gathering material for a broadcast on that popular resort, the fact was made known that big ships were constructed there in years gone by. Yes, and Chester, beauty spot of Mahone Bay, had its busy shipyards where big boats were once built. I have travelled to different places along Old Fundy's shore, and while today no trace remains, the old folk have thrilled me with tales of impressive launchings of their prized wooden ships. In most of these places it has been long years since the sound of the caulker's maul has been heard. Stories are told of this and that—and its record for fast time—and the names of Bluenose skippers have come up for discussion, skippers who commanded or sailed on these boats which were home products.

John W. Regan, who has spent so many years in delving into things historic about Nova Scotia, tells us in his *First Things in Acadia* that English Harbour (Louisbourg) can technically lay claim to being the site of the first ship building in Canada and New England. It was away back in the summer of 1604, that two French Captains, Pontgravé and Morell, constructed a coasting craft. It is said that ships commanded by these mariners were units in an expedition which was directed by Sieur de Monts. The expedition was sent to this side of the Atlantic to locate and establish French settlements over a wide area.

It was only two years later according to historic records, that shipbuilding in somewhat limited form was carried out at Port Royal. There Pontgravé headed up the work of building a long boat, a skiff and a pinnace.

While it was many years later that Halifax saw its first shipbuilding venture, it was but a short time after the establishment of the settlement that has grown into our city of today. It was in 1751 that 'Captain John Goreham, employing slave labour, built a brig, which was launched into the waters of the harbour. The site where the vessel was built, was given the name of Goreham's Point. In a few years' time the point and some adjoining lands were expropriated and became the start of His Majesty's Dockyard.

It is interesting to note that the Dockyard is adjoining to the site of the present Halifax shipyards, which in the First Great War turned out merchantmen of steel and in the second great conflict added fighting craft to Canada's fleet of destroyers.

Today the building of wooden ships is not an industry of Halifax, although the skill of shipbuilders has not been lost. We find proof of this in the construction of the ferry steamer *Governor Cornwallis* which was built on the Dartmouth shore and launched in the fall of 1941 and put into service late in 1942. It was built by Hugh Weagle, well-known Dartmouth shipbuilder, and was a craft of 150 feet in length.

When we speak of the glory days of Nova Scotia's sailing shipbuilding, we naturally turn in memory to Maitland. That Hants County port has seen many famous ships slide into the water, but none of them, it would see, can lay claim to greater fame than the noted *W. D. Lawrence.* This massive craft was the largest full-rigged ship ever built in Canada. It was a craft of 2,459 tons. It is difficult to give a fitting word picture that will convey the proportions and the lines of this fine product of the Nova Scotia builders' art. I would suggest to those who wish to delve deeper into the subject, that they visit the Archives Building at Studley. There they will see oil paintings and line drawings which will convey the real romance and glory of this great vessel. The *Lawrence* is said to have cost several thousand over the hundred thousand dollar mark and took to the waters in 1874.

While the *Lawrence* was the largest full-rigged ship built in Canada, she was not the largest sailing ship in the world. The craft to win that distinction was the *Great Republic,* which had a capacity of 6,000 tons, was 325 feet in length and carried over fifteen and a half thousand feet of canvas. Nova Scotia had special interest in the feat of producing such a mammoth ship, for it was Donald McKay who sent that craft into the water—and McKay was a native of Shelburne in this Province.

The *Great Republic* was a product of the United States workmen, but we can well imagine that McKay drew many of his most skilled men from his native Province, for he knew well their capabilities. It was this same McKay who built the most famous of all clippers—the *Flying Cloud*—a name that has been immortalized in sagas of the sea. It was the *Flying Cloud* which set the unbeatable record of eighty-nine days and eight hours on a trip from New York to San Francisco.

Today at Castle Island in Boston, there stands a granite obelisk, which has a height of fifty-two feet, and which was unveiled in 1933 to McKay, acclaimed as master builder of the "world's fastest ships," but it took many years after his death in 1880 before this recognition came to a son of Nova Scotia, who in his day had made such a noteworthy contribution to marine transportation.

When we think of the Nova Scotia builder's skill, we naturally recall that famous "Queen of the Atlantic," the fishing schooner *Bluenose,* which won undying fame in the international schooner races. The *Bluenose,* as a fisherman and racer, has passed from the scene. We can't forget her, but it does always seem a pity that she could not have been kept in home waters, where once she was acclaimed as a queen. The *Bluenose,* designed by William Roue, was superb.

Haligonians have watched many famous ships. From the

largest to the smallest of ocean-going vessels, no ship was more graceful or beautiful to the eye as she moved on the broad expanse of Halifax Harbour, on her way to the open sea, than our own Nova Scotian fishing schooner, the *Bluenose*.

It was with regret that on January 30, 1946, the news was received that this internationally known vessel had gone to Davy Jones' locker.

It's history now, that the once graceful and triumphant "Queen of the North Atlantic" is no more . . . that the International Champion racing schooner *Bluenose* went to her doom on January 29, 1946, on the jagged reefs of the Haitian Coast. We can give thanks that none of her crew was lost. . . . Yes, the *Bluenose* is gone. . . .

She had to go sometime; the life of a wooden vessel is limited to a comparatively brief span—but it is sad to see her end her days and career far from her home waters and under an alien flag, twenty-five years after the keel of this noble old Champion was laid at Lunenburg. She came into being and did her first fishing and racing in 1921.

And not only was she never defeated in an official series of contests (local or international), but she was the greatest fishing schooner of them all.

She could go where any of them could go, she could carry what any of them could carry—and she could beat them all to windward in a fisherman's chance.

· The *Bluenose* was the most authentically Nova Scotian thing we had in this Province. She never should have left Nova Scotia. The nation should have acquired her and kept her here in her home. She could not last forever in a working life. She was bound, sooner or later, to meet her end at sea. Her end was a melancholy finish of a grand and glorious career.

We cannot speak of Lunenburg without conjuring up a picture of a harbour, which at certain seasons, is a home haven for many staunch craft—the boats of the fishing fleet. But even there, the numbers of masts have dwindled, not only because of fewer boats, but the change in design which has come with adoption of engines. Desbrisay tells us in his *History of Lunenburg County* that it is recalled that in August, 1787, a handsome brig, built at Lunenburg won much attention as she arrived in Halifax Harbour. Over a century ago, to be exact in 1829, Lunenburg had upwards of a hundred vessels engaged in foreign trade coasting and fishing. In the year 1838, records reveal that Lunenburg had seventeen square-rigged vessels, plus a variety of other craft.

These days, excluding such craft as government tugs and smaller boats, there are generally only a couple of fishermen launched from Lunenburg yards. But in 1860 it was a different story. In that year it is recorded twenty-two vessels were launched at that port, and at one time in the following year there were eighteen vessels on the stocks at the same time. Such sailing vessels as the *Geneva* and the *Ocean Belle,* built at Lunenburg and sent around the Horn, gained the distinction of being credited with being among the fastest vessels ever to operate on the Pacific coast.

There is the story of a notable launching feat at Mahone Bay. At Clearlands, some three-quarters of a mile from the water, many, many years ago, Frederick Hiltz built the three-masted schooner *James William*. It is told that twenty-six pair of oxen were attached to a giant sled constructed for the purpose. Hauled along on this by the straining oxen, the great vessel was safely conveyed to salt water. Then there are such famous old timers as the *Scotia* and *St. Kilda,* built at Bridgewater, and which gained fame for their ability to break records on voyages . . . and so the story could go on, for we have only skimmed the surface for interesting shipbuilding notes and stories, and touched only a few of the counties, all of which could contribute their share to a picture of wooden shipbuilding in Nova Scotia.

The Halifax Waterfront ever holds a fascination. On different occasions we have visited it together in fancy . . . and always found much there to hold interest.

I've often recommended it to my friends—who want real relaxation. There's no place I know where one can get more real rest than on the sunbaked end of a wooden wharf. Yes, just relax with your back against the sun-warmed boards of a warehouse, and enjoy a quiet smoke. Watch the boats— those busy little harbour craft—skittering about on the waters of Chebucto at their daily and varied tasks. Perhaps you'll see a grey form of one of Canada's staunch warcraft, such as the modern aircraft carrier *Magnificent,* heading out for some appointed task. These days we give thanks that men aboard are not heading out to face the rigors of battle against a deadly U-Boat. But even today, Canada's Navy has tasks to do and the grey clad warships move in and out of the port. It may be a grimy looking tramp freighter that next catches your eye, as she slowly moves up to wend her way into a pier, there to disgorge a welcomed cargo—a shipment that may have come from the ends of the earth.

Yes, a visit to the Halifax waterfront offers much. When the waves are pounding the pilings of our Halifax wharves, and the smaller craft are bobbing like corks at their dock moorings, there is special fascination along the waterfront.

We move along Lower Water Street . . . and as fancy directs, make side trips out on the various wharves. We are never sure what we'll find at each one. Some may be bare of merchandise . . . or without any craft moored in the dock. But in most, we find a quota of boats, tied there to carry on the business of this great port—a great variety of small craft have to be at hand.

Most of them are painted grey, with spreading cabins that give a top heavy look. But our boat builders know their work—and these sometimes cumbersome-looking watercraft meet the elements well. It is interesting to watch, as one heads out from the comparative peace of a sheltered dock. Probably it's bound with a mission to one of the ships anchored in the stream. As it rounds the end of the wharf and strikes out into the unsheltered waters, it takes the full force of wave and wind. But there's not a break in its forward pace—even if waves slap against the side and go half up the side of the cabin.

It's not only the boats that catch my fancy. The buildings themselves are of a variety to set one dreaming. We move down the roadway leading to one wharf. On each side are towering warehouses of dark rock and with windows and doorways framed wtih granite, grown greyer in the passing of years. Today these warehouses may hold a variety of merchandise—perhaps modern fish stores or steel casks of oil. Perhaps in other days they were filled to the roof with great puncheons and smaller kegs of rum—for we recall that Halifax's consumption of that beverage in days gone by reached a staggering figure—and I make no play on words in this.

We think of Enos Collins, the merchant prince of early Halifax, as we pass that building which still has the word "Bank" cut in the stone top casing of its front doorway. The building is today far back from the point of the modern pier which juts to the east. There was a time, as we know, when boats could come right up to the building itself. There was— and still is—a high pulley wheel in existence, which allowed the puncheons and other bulky articles to be hauled from the waterfront entrance to the upper floors for storage in the days of that merchant prince, Collins—a name that has loomed so large in the mercantile history of Nova Scotia, of this Province's daring days of privateering ventures.

In this storied old city—and on its waterfront which has contributed so much to the prosperity through the decades— we find these grim and forbidding warehouses of stone, brushing shoulders with modern office buildings. We may go down a wharfway which is a visit into the past, with these drab storehouses bordering our paths, only to find a modern wooden frame building attached to the waterside end, and with modern fluorescent lighting aiding a busy office staff of men and women at work.

There is one spot on the Halifax waterfront which was for years an historic landmark, and which has changed its appearance by the removal of its old time piece. I am thinking of the famous old Ordnance Wharf, at the foot of Buckingham Street, which since being taken over by the Navy is now known as the Central Victualling Depot.

Changing times saw the Ordnance property lose most of its picturesque old stone buildings. There was a keen sense of loss among the older citizens of Halifax. It was decreed that the old Ordnance Clock must pass out of the picture, for a time at least. So it was that on April 7 in the year 1937 the Halifax *Mail* published a large picture showing workmen demolishing parts of the building at the base of the clock, and starting the work of taking the clock itself apart for storage.

In the albums of many Halifax people who take interest in collecting views of the city, as well as in museum and archives, among the most striking pictures that link us with Halifax of the past, are scenes photographed through the Gun Wharf gate. There, between the pillars of stone, which edged the opening in the imposing and high stone wall, the old clock was framed. The top of the frame was completed by gracefully arched metal frames, surmounted by the equally familiar lantern. In the days that were, this picture was frequently used to illustrate tourist booklets, and unquestionably it aided in impressing upon these would-be visitors a part of the lure of historic environment to be found here.

The clock which was mounted on the building used for general artillery stores at the Gun Wharf, had a name for dependability. This timepiece, while of some ten years later date than that on the Citadel Slope, is still of great historic interest because of its age. Records show that the clock was made in Clerkenwall, England, by John Thwaites and Company in 1813, and it is presumed that it was brought to the city within a year, although there are no actual records to show when it was erected here.

To wind it, the keeper of the clock had to expend considerable muscle, for by turning a crank he raised three heavy weights a distance, to draw them up to the bottom of the clock in its tower. The three weights did not have the actual task of running the mechanism of the clock. Only one weight ran this part of the machinery. The other two provided the incentive for the old clock to musically chime out the passing time. It was so arranged that one bell would strike on the hours, and two others of different tone, struck the quarter, half and three-quarter hours.

At one time, it is recalled, a local jewellery firm had a contract for winding the clock, but in the more recent years prior to its removal, it was a task of one of the men at the wharf.

True to its task, day in and day out, it ticked off the minutes in its service to Halifax until the Great Explosion of December 6, 1917. When the fatal blast occurred, as did many other public timepieces of that era, it stopped at once. Several months went by until it was completely repaired— and then it took up its important duties again, to keep faithfully at them until the time of its removal.

It is known that the old gun yard dates back to the city's earliest days. Halifax was founded in 1749, and history tells us that six years later Governor Charles Lawrence advised the authorities in Britain he was erecting a ten-gun battery on the spot to help guard any incursion by the French from the direction of Louisbourg, or possibly, by those subjects of France dwelling on the shores of the Bay of Fundy.

But it was not until some years later that the buildings of the Gun Wharf, which were known to Haligonians until their comparatively recent removal, were erected. Some of them went up around 1800, and in more modern times, their interiors offered strange background for the modern lathes used in dealing with armaments. The original stone fireplaces of the smithy were able to be operated up to the last.

Fortunately some of the majestic trees still remain. May modern progress see fit that they be not touched.

The whole waterfront gives us food for thought on the matter of contrast. Contrasts apparent from the varied types of architecture of eras spanned by long periods of time—contrasts in the boats found docked there today, with ones seen moored there in the past, when windships alone carried on the commerce of Halifax. Think what a contrast there is between the modern seagoing ships and the *Sphinx* which came here in 1749 when Cornwallis arrived to found Halifax. Every boat we find along the waterfront of our stroll sets a chain of thought running.

There are the names on the bows and sterns of any number of craft. There are too many for us to consider in detail. But each probably has its story behind it, which prompted the owner to give the identifying name to his craft. We see bobbing at one dock, a staunch looking grey motor launch. Its name sign reads *Half Brothers*—seemingly a strange name for a boat.

Ships do not have to be giants to be classed as famous in our way of reckoning. In fact, the smaller ships more than hold their own in our memories. We must not forget ships like the *Hector* on which the ancestors of many Nova Scotians came from Scotland, and we could go on and on naming ships which have made history and are connected with Nova Scotia in one way or another—such as the *Mary Celeste*, the ship that was found at sea, with sails set and nobody aboard, or the *James Stewart*, on board which Captain Kenny had such adventures in the South Seas, or the *Ancona* on which Captain Ellis had a visit from cannibals and who left when they discovered the Captain had a Bible, and then presented him with a very rare sea shell. Then there comes to mind the three master, *The Maid of France*, which was resurrected from the mud flats of Lunenburg Harbour to go to sea again under the name of *The A. S. Publicover*. Others I can think of are the four master *The James E. Newsome, The Lillian E. Kerr* and that remarkable fast tern schooner, *The Edyth*, which was skippered by Captain Benjamin Ham of Mahone Bay and sailed from New York to Halifax in forty-six hours. The mention of the *City of Boston* will bring sad memories to many of our elder citizens. This ship left Halifax and was never heard of again and no reason was ever given for her loss.

We cannot overlook such ships as the gallant Yarmouth barque *Sarah* on which Captain Cook did such gallant rescue work and won Lloyd's Silver Medal. There was also the *Milton* of Maitland, whose skipper, Captain Henry McArthur, with his twenty-five-hundred-mile trip in an open boat won fame which rivals that of Captain Bligh of the *Bounty*. We cannot pass by the famous old *Niobe* of the Royal Canadian Navy, which did splendid work in the early part of the first world war in capturing German prizes along the North Atlantic, and our list as far as naval vessels is concerned, will be a long and honourable one when the ships of the second great war are added to it. There are also names of ships too long to list at this time, that have made history for Halifax and Nova Scotia, such as the famous Allan liners and the White Star and Cunarders, the Furness Withy boats and the different cable ships which have made Halifax their home port for a number of years.

Many will remember just a few years back when the harbour would be full of sailing ships anchored in the stream, which attained fame for a few years, such as the one called *I'm Alone*. It is an interesting subject to wonder about, how some of the better known Nova Scotian ships got their names. I suppose the *I'm Alone* earned that from her trade of rum running, in which no doubt she sailed very much alone.

How would you account for a ship having a name like *Essence of Peppermint?* She was a Yarmouth schooner launched somewhere around 1880.

And what about the Hantsport ship called *Happy Home*? She didn't turn out to be a happy home, and would have been better named like a St. John full rigger *The Hard Times*.

Then there was another ship which hailed from Yarmouth called *Better Luck Still*.

If a person took the trouble to look up the names of our Nova Scotian ships, they would find plenty of odd names. There used to be two *Jenny Linds*, one of them out of Newport, just outside Windsor.

Then with a musical taste we had the *Mozart* and the *Beethoven*.

New Glasgow had a ship evidently named by someone fond of geometry. It was called the *Euclid*.

The builders must have stayed awake at night thinking up names in the old days. There was one with the most unromantic name of *Maggot*, out of Yarmouth. The builder must have been an apple man.

There was also one called the *Germ*.

Other out-of-the-ordinary names to be found include the *Chart* and *Fiddle*, and *Pam-Be-Civil*. Then there was the *Dusty Miller* and the *Great Deceiver*.

Jeddore and Saint John seem to have selected the strangest of the lot with the *Can't Help It*, and the *Go Ask Her*.

With such names, no wonder ships make such an interesting topic.

Today there are comparatively few wooden vessels to be found along the Halifax water-front. Instead we have the less graceful steel hulls rubbing against the pilings on the docks, or more properly in many cases, surging up and down with the swell, against the buffers that protect them from the hard surface of the concrete wharves.

The Halifax waterfront itself has seen many changes. Where once there were only the wooden wharves of the individual merchants or companies, these have given way in large measure to the great concrete piers, many of them Federally owned.

We may sigh for the romance of the days of the "Wooden Ships and Iron Men," but nevertheless, we have to acknowledge the fact that the need for faster modern mode of travel has been met by the great giants of the ocean highways, or the sturdy tramps that pound their way around the world, bringing the spices from the Orient, let us say, then heading out with the products of this Canada of ours, serving the markets of the world. Yes, Halifax has so much to offer a person who likes to poke about among ships and old wharves looking for the things that capture the fancy.

There's always something to be seen in such a place. The bigger ships moving about the harbour, or even the tiny harbour launches, each importantly bent on its own mission, chugging along its way. What port does that begrimmed, and rather rusty-sided tramp freighter hail from? Close by your wharf may pass a little single cylinder power dory, its "gunnels," to your shore-man's eye, close to the lapping waves. In it may be seated a whole family group, the father, his face browned by the sea air and fogs, at the tiller, mother and the youngsters, and even a few of the neighbours. The rest of available space will be filled with bundles that constitute stores for their own seaside home, as well as those which neighbourly kindness has prompted them to buy on request for others living near them. It is always a source of amazement to me how these people dare to do things they do in their small boats, which even in an automobile age, travel from shore fishing villages or nearby islands, to give the family an outing in the city or to get the much needed supplies. But the men folk know the sea and know the handling and capabilities of their boats.

You will be in luck if you pick up conversation with some talkative seafaring man, who may chat with you from the deck of his ship, or perhaps is stretching his sea legs on the wharf and will be glad for a chance of companionship and opportunity to try your tobacco. From my knowledge of the sea you may not want to make it an exchange and try his, for it is apt to be black and powerful—too strong for your landlubber taste.

Your chance acquaintance may be one who can tell you of trips to the seven seas; who can tell you of happenings in his career that would vie with the pages of Stevenson in their thrilling appeal. Who knows your luck?

Let's hope that it will be your luck to meet such a one who will match the stories that were spun by one, met in a reminiscent mood, and who was not adverse to telling some of his career of more than fifty years—one who had seen the day of sail give way to the era of steam and other means of marine propulsion.

He recalled his first voyage made after leaving his home in Ireland, aboard a rigger Orient-bound at first, and from there to the Port of Saint John with tea and silk. The very nature of the cargo immediately catches your fancy—tea and silk, products of far lands that have come to mean so much to our comforts and pleasures. Two members of the crew and part of the staunch ship's rigging formed the toll taken in making passage around the Horn.

You may meet up with a man such as this one old chap, who could spin you a yarn of a visit to Madras forty years ago, when a Hindu holy man came aboard his ship, carrying a wooden container the size of a cigar box. Placing it on the deck he muttered a few unintelligible words and then raised the lid. To the amazement of onlookers a tree commenced to sprout, reaching a height of about six feet. "Seein's believin'," said my new-found friend—it happened before his very own eyes.

It takes men of the sea to spin you these yarns. On another occasion he said he saw another holy man of the Far East toss two peas into the air, and before his eyes they were transformed into two live pigeons. Suggestion that they might have been concealed in his clothing brings a snort— "That man hadn't nothin' on but a loin cloth."

Tales of ghostly ships passed in the China Seas, like the fabled *Flying Dutchman* came up in conversation. You may doubt his veracity, perhaps, but you certainly do not grow tired of his tales.

That's the kind of man you meet on your pilgrimage to the waterfront, if good fortune is with you. Mind, I don't promise you such an experience, but on various occasions such good fortune has been mine. I've heard stories of treasure quests, mutiny and any one of a hundred things that capture the fancy of a landsman.

Your chances of meeting the "Iron Men" of the era of

"Wooden Ships" that sailed to all parts of the globe are not so good as a few years ago, but on hunts like this you never know your luck.

You may meet one who will spin you a yarn about the ocean-sealed mystery of the brigantine *Brazil,* the Halifax-owned ship which vanished forever almost in sight of her own port. That happened about sixty years ago. The vessel was owned by R. I. Hart and Company and plied between this port and Pernambuco.

It was dusk on that evening in winter of the early 'eighties when the *Brazil* reached harbour limits, on her homeward voyage from the south. A pilot was said to have boarded the ship. His course was shifted toward "Maugher's Beach" light when heavy snow squalls swept in from the North Atlantic. Through this blanketing mass of snow, which lifted momentarily at times, the vessel was seen to be beating her way through the storm-tossed waters of the outer harbour. Then came an end to the storm later in the night. A brilliant moon shone on the still white-crested water, but no trace of the *Brazil* could be seen. She was gone.

What was her fate? It is not known. But ask some of the old time sailormen, who have more than a bit of super-stition in their makeup and they will shake their heads and mutter something about the *Brazil* being doomed from the day of her launching. Didn't the bow of the *Brazil* strike the waters on her launching day and point at the setting sun? What but a weird fate could await such a vessel, they will ask. That boded ill for the vessel, according to ancient sea lore, they maintained. The *Brazil* went to her doom and the sea has kept well its secret.

Such stories that you get from some of the old-time sailor-men fairly drip with the tang of the sea. You may not have the good fortune to encounter such a yarn-spinner on your trip to the harbour front, but you will be well repaid just by contemplating the scene before you.

There is rich reward in living in a community on the shores of one of the busiest of the many great harbours of our Empire. There is much to see, much to stir the imagination. Yes! the waterfront calls and is ever in my thoughts when I want relaxation.

Because the old wooden ships are few and far between these days, there must be a thrill in the heart of any true Haligonian, when he sees the towering sticks of a sailing ship high on the skyline, etched against the blue, as it rests in some local wharf. We still do find them, these fine veterans of the sea, which still carry on the traditions and provide quite an imposing sight.

All the ships one sees along the waterfront are of never-ending interest be they large or small. Having seen the largest ships in the world to the small coastal schooners at different times, I can truthfully say that I know of no more interesting place than the waterfront.

The sound of the lapping of the waves against the weeded piling is music of a soothing nature, and the ever changing scene, with the fresh tang of the sea is ever calling. It's meat and drink to Bluenoses, and Halifax has every reason to carry on its coat of arms the motto *E Mari Merces*— "Wealth from the Sea."

VIII

THE NORTH WEST ARM

A Playground Extraordinary

NATURE has been kind indeed, to the little man of Halifax, the Haligonian who with his family can, in a matter of ten to fifteen minutes, find a place for a picnic by the salt water.

The place where thousands of Haligonians spend many holiday outings is known as the North West Arm.

During the past fifty years many new homes have been located along its shores, but thanks to the forethought of one former citizen, Sir Sanford Fleming, a large tract of land, along this famous expanse of water, has been preserved for John Q. Public.

No finer gift was ever left to any city.

It is not until May 24th that, what is considered the

121

official opening of the Arm's season takes place, but long before that time, some of the more venturesome are indulging in plunges into its waters. Mind you, I'm not referring to the "Polar Bear" gentry, who delight in cutting holes in the ice and enjoying—if the term enjoying can really be used—a mid-winter dip. I'm referring to just the ordinary citizen who likes a little chance to boast to his friends that "I was in the Arm yesterday," just a bit in advance of the real bathing season. Then, too, the owners of small pleasure craft will be out in force, giving attention to overhaul jobs on yachts, dinghys, launches, rowboats or canoes—a new bit of canvas here, some splicing rope, a fresh coat of paint all round.

When once the spirit of the North West Arm gets in the blood, there's no getting away from it, and those citizens who have fallen under its spell spend the happiest hours of their lives on its glittering surface, or breasting its waters or even just comfortably seated, with the back resting against the warm sheeting of a boathouse, while they talk over the past performances or future prospects of some of the club crews.

In the earlier maps of the settlement that has grown into the city of Halifax, we find the North West Arm marked out as Sandwich River. It was when the first settlers came up the wide waters of Halifax Harbour in 1749 to found their new homes, that they noticed the mouth of a watercourse branching off to the North West. What was more natural than for them to consider it as a river? They named the towering point at the mouth of this body of water Sandwich and the body of water itself was called the Sandwich River. Sandwich was the name of a statesman who had a prominent rôle in the Councils of King George the Second.

However, the Indians who had lived here long before, and knew the waterway so well, had given it the name of Waegwoltic—which translated, stands for "end of the water." These redmen were well aware that it was no river, although it had then, and still has, a small rivulet flowing into its very peak. In those earlier days, the shores of the Arm were still far outside the protective palisades—to venture there was to tempt death and the subsequent loss of the scalp to the Indians lurking on the outskirts of the new settlement. It is said that it was some time after the treaty signed with the Indians in 1760 that land allotments were taken up on the Eastern shore of the Arm to any extent.

By the way, Sandwich was not the only name bestowed on the beautiful sheet of water, for some earlier military maps also refer to it as Hawke River. But that was also at the very start of the settlement. For, as early as 1752, there is a record of a grant of land to William Russell at Purcell's Cove, and in that grant, part of the description refers to the land in relation to the North West Arm, according to the late John W. Regan; who was so well versed on the history of the section in particular—"The North West Arm itself"—and that would seem to be so, for it is such a fitting name—so descriptive.

However, to many of us perhaps, the name bestowed by the Indian might seem more tongue attracting—"Waegwoltic." We do have, however, as most of us know, a certain retention of that name, for there is the Waegwoltic Club on the shore.

Through the years the North West Arm has been the beloved dwelling place of many men whose names have loomed large in history. It was on its shores that the great leader Joseph Howe was born at "Emscote"—and I could go on and on recounting the names of many others. Surely the shores of the Arm have seen an illustrious band of citizens in its days.

If any of these former dwellers, now departed, could have the chance to return to the place they loved so well while on earth, I can think of none who would more willingly make the pilgrimage than Sir Sanford Fleming. No one would have a better right to possess a desire to return and see the Arm as it exists today—for it was Sir Sanford who made possible the existence of the memorial park which today bears his name—Fleming Park, which is on the shore about opposite where South Street has its western termination.

Sir Sanford lived at what was known as the Dingle, which in its main portion, just to the north of the section today set out as the public park, bears his name. We have every right to often think of this man and his benefaction, a gift which has brought untold happiness to thousands of permanent residents and transients during the years. However, the Dingle property as a whole at one time extended from Melville Island property on the North to Jollimore village south of Tower Point. The land was originally granted to a William McGrannigan. Purchase of the property was made by Fleming from several owners and their heirs.

The section known as Tower Point, and on which the great tower of stone now stands, was at one time the property of William Cunard, who lived at Oaklands on the city side of the Arm. In those days Oaklands ran from Robie Street clear through to the Arm, embracing much of the territory through which the modern residential street Oakland Road, now is laid out. As many may know, the little cove by Tower Point, where many people bathe today when they visit Fleming Park, is known as Fairy Cove.

Sir Sanford made his gift of land for a park, conditional—that a tower be erected there in connection with the hundred and fiftieth anniversary of the establishment of representative government in Nova Scotia. It was his contention that Halifax was the constitutional birthplace of the outward British Empire. All other overseas territories included in the British Empire secured their elective assemblies later than Nova Scotia, which too, was the first Province in Canada. We have much to be proud of in this distinction, and Sir Sanford desired that we accord our heritage suitable recognition.

Today the Memorial Tower stands on its place of prominence on Tower Point and can be seen clearly from the most remote ends of the North West Arm.

There's much to be seen of interest along the North West

Arm, places of beauty and places about which strange tales are told.

If one is bent on sight seeing, after arriving at the Arm bridge, at the Junction of Quinpool and the Dutch Village roads, and crossing the bridge, one should move along to the left, taking the road to Melville Cove. There at the Cove can be found the site of the grave of John Dixon close by the shores of Dead Man's Cove. But it would be a fruitless quest unless you knew just where to look—and then, there might well be a question in the mind if a grave actually exists where once stood the wooden slab supposedly over the last resting place of a man.

It's rather a confusing story.

In the Provincial Museum in the Nova Scotia Technical College Building, there is a wooden tombstone, which bears the painted inscription "Sacred to the Memory of John Dixon, of Sydney, C.B., who died the 6th of August, 1817, aged twenty-one years. Erected by the VIII Kings." For many years the wooden slab stood close to the now crumbling dance hall at Dead Man's Cove, which is close to Melville Cove.

The slab was given to the Provincial Museum by C. F. Longley, who formerly owned about two hundred acres in the district, and who erected the dance hall, in 1909 or thereabout, as he says, in the hopes of making it a highly prosperous resort for the people of Halifax. But prosperity did not follow in the wake of his ambitious move, he will tell you today, and "Kealoha," the name he gave to the dance hall, proved a severe drain on his finances. He presented the grave marking to Mr. Piers, the late curator of the museum, feeling that it should be preserved and not lost.

But even to this day controversy arises about the grave at Dead Man's Cove. Mr. Longley believes that there never was a body interred at the point so marked. He recalls that some person, in quest of treasure, which it was rumoured had been buried there, had at one time dug deep at the place

marked, their shovels going down to solid rock, but no trace
of bones had been found there.

However, the right of the little cove to its rather grue-
some name of Dead Man's Cove can hardly be challenged,
for there is a real maze of graves in the hillside above the
cove, and slightly higher than the one where Dixon was supposed to have slept his last sleep. Many skulls, and other
bones have been found during excavation work in the
vicinity, or even in gardening. "I suppose many of them were
French prisoners-of-war who had died years before in the
old Melville Island Military Prison," says Mr. Longley.

On one occasion, in preparing a berry patch, he found
three skulls. He unearthed them, cleaned them off and put
them on a rafter in the basement of the dance hall and said
to himself, "There, that will keep people from coming down
in here." But in no time at all they disappeared. Who took
them? He doesn't know!

One story told about the grave was that it was the burial
place of a young soldier, who had become enamoured of the
daughter of the commanding officer of his regiment.

When the officer discovered the romance, he was said to
have been enraged, and on a trumped-up charge, had the
man placed in the military prison. There, despondent over
his plight and the fruitlessness of his love to win through
over such obstacles, it was said he had taken his own life in
the waters by the island prison. Burial was said to have
been made close to the scene and succeeding military units on
duty in the district accepted, as a duty, the care of the grave.
Up until a few decades ago the grave, neatly enclosed,
presented a well kept appearance.

But with changing times it became neglected, and today
it is difficult to place the spot with a great degree of cer-
tainty. The late Mr. Piers, who made a study of the area,
at the time of securing the grave marking from Mr. Longley,
included a diagram in the accession book at the museum,
showing where the grave was supposed to be.

Alfred F. Johnson, who for a decade lived within a few

yards of the place where the grave was supposed to be, was unable to point to the exact spot. He knew of the various stories told about Dixon, but time has erased traces of the once well kept little lot.

The story of Dixon, as recorded by the late Mr. Piers and accepted by him as the proper one, was more prosaic than the story of the hopeless lover taking his own life.

Dixon was a mariner, who saw his start of life on the shores of the North West Arm at Sydney and who, strangely enough, came to his end on the shores of North West Arm at Halifax, reputedly at the comparatively early age of twenty-one years. The young sailor was said to have fallen a victim to a deadly fever while here aboard a brigantine, and either died aboard that craft or in a house close to the shore.

But Mr. Longley's report that persons had searched the supposed place of the grave and found no trace of a body having rested there, gives an added twist to the situation, which provides a real touch of mystery.

There is still the mystery as to why the various units stationed in the vicinity assumed it as a duty to look after this one grave, while the many others scattered about the hillside went neglected. Probably a share of these were victims of fever, who found a last resting place far from their scattered homelands, many of them on the other side of the world.

Even the slab resting in the museum aids in adding to the complexity, for Curator Piers stated that the date given as that of death, 1817, was in error. After some years of delving into contemporary records, the late curator was convinced that the original date on the slab was 1847, and that in renovations undertaken from time to time, the figure four had been overlooked, allowing it eventually to appear as the figure one.

Today people know of Dead Man's Cove, but the lonely grave is lost to the eyes of the casual visitor. The area is speedily becoming the year-round residential area for many families, where once occasional summer cottages stood.

The most interesting spot on the North West Arm, from the historical point of view is Melville Island, which was for years known as the military prison. The history of Melville Island, goes back almost to the very founding of the settlement of Halifax. One of the earliest records we have, referring to this section on the western side of the North West Arm, is the signing of a deed on April 27, 1784, by which John Butler Kelly conveyed to James Kavanagh what was termed "an undivided moiety of a tract of land," which later became known as "Melville Island."

There is a generally accepted belief, that with the transfer coming so soon after the founding of the settlement, that Kelly must have been the first owner. However, on the other hand, there is a current of opinion, which I cannot support by any evidence, that even earlier, a man by the name of Cowie had possession of the tract.

Kavanagh had a purpose in securing ownership of the island, for upon it he erected his home. He also built storehouses in which to protect his boats and his harvest of the Arm waters, for he was a fisherman. As a result of his ownership, the Island for a time was given the name of "Kavanaghs."

In the passage of nine years, a rather momentous occasion took place, and one which later, left its mark in the history of the once peaceful little island. When an expedition, outfitted in Halifax, directed its attention on the little French Island of St. Pierre, and on its return to Halifax brought with it not only the Governor of the French Island but also some seven hundred prisoners.

There was no great problem concerned in disposing of the Governor, for a man in his station could readily be placed on parole, and this course was followed. The prisoners in such numbers, however, did provide a major problem. At first it appeared that Kavanagh's Island would immediately enter into the rôle which was later to be its lot. Governor Wentworth contracted to rent the island from its owner at a rate of sixty pounds a year. However, the General Officer

Commanding the forces, who at that time was General Ogilvie, did not fall in with this proposal. He decided instead that the several hundred Frenchmen be placed in Cornwallis Barracks. This latter course was adopted, and the prisoners were held in the barracks until they were later transferred to Guernsey, in July, 1794.

Wentworth's idea did have merit, it appeared, for with arrival of French prisoners in greater numbers, with the problem they created, the Island eventually came into use for the purpose originally intended.

The first guard was mounted there, on August 24, 1803. This was composed of a Sergeant and five privates from the Twenty-Ninth Regiment, with two corporals and four privates from the Fifth Battalion of the Sixtieth Regiment. Their tour of duty, on the then isolated island, was set at one month's duration.

In less than a month it was deemed necessary to place the guard under a subaltern and to increase the number of men assigned to duty at the Island and on different occasions later, the numbers were again increased. Fort Clarence, which was located at Imperoyal, was also called into use as a place for internment of the steady flow of French prisoners, but even in the face of this relief, the prisoner population of Melville Island continued steadily to expand.

It proved a profitable time for Kavanagh, who collected rental for the island which came into his possession. Later, on July 27, 1804, there was a deed signed by Mr. and Mrs. Kavanagh, which conveyed the island property to His Majesty the King. In return for the sale of their island, Mr. and Mrs. Kavanagh received what was then—and in fact would still prove so today—the considerable sum of a thousand pounds of "current money of Nova Scotia."

Naturally, with the change of ownership, the Authorities felt that with the section under Admiralty Control, the name should be a rather more impressive one than merely that of the previous owner. Sometime between October 9 and December 4, 1804, the name of "Melville" was adopted. In bestowing the new name, which has since been in use, the then First Lord, Viscount Melville was honoured. Just as a matter of record, it might be mentioned here, Melville was impeached two years later, but was subsequently acquitted.

It was a bleak prospect that prisoners faced when they were sent to Melville Island, for the buildings were not kept in proper repair and the severity of the winter imposed much suffering. The members of the guard did not face a happy lot either, for they eventually complained and gained some relief. Major-General Hunter graciously granted an additional halfroom's supply of fuel for their kitchen. But that did not assist the poor prisoners, who continued to shiver as before.

It is recorded that in 1808, the Admiralty decided to embark on a more permanent type of structure for their Island Prison. The cornerstone of a large wooden structure was then laid. This was to serve as the main prison building, but was not intended for the accommodation of the prisoners themselves—that is, their regular quarter. At the same time, the house on the hill at the Arm side of the Island was erected as living quarters for the Chief Warder.

Leniency was at first extended to the French Prisoners, in regards to restrictions of freedom and they were allowed to leave the island and roam the nearby woodlands. Five managed to escape. This led to a certain tightening. Then turbulence broke out in rather troublesome form. A party bringing fuel to the Island was pelted by the prisoners, and in the flying of missiles, some of the windows in the officers' quarters were shattered. A definite order that they must remain on the island was the sequel.

It was found that a practice was growing up for outsiders to buy from the prisoners certain articles, and a threat was made of a general court martial for any person suspected of carrying out this type of what was then considered to be an offence.

Those were days of hard discipline. When any man returned drunk from escorting prisoners from the island to the settlement of Halifax, he might expect to have his back pay for his spree, by coming under no less than five hundred to seven hundred lashes.

An officer who was convicted in a court martial for having been drunk while in charge of the Guard at Melville Island was cashiered for his dereliction of duty.

However, while sale of any form of supplies might be frowned upon, there was a type of commerce which did flourish. When sightseers came on Sundays and holidays to visit the prison, they frequently bought ornamental articles carved in wood and bone. These articles were the work of prisoners, who, finding time heavily hanging on their hands, achieved remarkable results in their handiwork. If you visit the main display room of the Nova Scotia Archives at Studley, you will see in one of the cases a handsome little warcraft of the days of windships, which was carved by a prisoner at Melville Island. For years it occupied a place of honour on the librarian's counter at Dalhousie University, in the days of the late Dr. Archibald MacMechan, until later transferred to the Archives collection.

With the fall of Napoleon in 1814, the French were able to bid farewell to Melville Island, probably with no feeling of regret. It was not only the French who came to look upon Melville Island, set in a scene of such natural beauty, with feeling of distaste. With the outbreak of the war with America in 1812, it is said that many Americans were added to the overcrowded quarters, and in the current novel *Grand Parade*, which has its scene laid in and about Halifax, we find a description of the scene there woven into the story. When a number of the Negroes who had flocked north in quest of freedom were placed on Melville Island, after smallpox broke out in Halifax in 1815, they wore the green uniforms of the American Rangers which had been disbanded, and the uniforms turned to the practical purpose of protecting these poor coloured people from the cold which they felt so keenly.

In the early days of Halifax, discipline was hard and

records show of privates in the armed forces here, being
ordered to bear as many as fifteen hundred lashes for the
offence of desertion. In May, 1847, the military prison was
opened in a small space in the Citadel. It was not a satisfactory solution, as the following years proved.

In May, 1856, a letter was sent to the proper authorities
suggesting use of Melville Island as the site for the Military
prison for the garrison. On October 23rd of that year, Major
General LeMarchant was instructed by the War Office to
take steps to obtain possession of Melville Island from the
Admiralty Department. On November 10th, the document
of transfer was signed and the order for the transfer of the
prison to its new Island home was issued the following day.
There were two main buildings then on the island. There
was one well on the island, some smaller buildings, such as
stable shed, cook-house and wash-house. On the mainland,
immediately across the connecting bridge, were two more
wells and a guard house also stood there. At first the local
representative of the Admiralty set down a rule that use of
the Island did not entail use of the well—but fortunately after
certain formal representations, that matter was ironed out.
There later developed one of those inter-department disputes
which are not unknown today under the "red-tape" systems,
but whether the ownership of the Island was finally confirmed or not really mattered little, for the Army was in possession of the Island from 1856 onward.

Not only was it a place of incarceration, but also provided
some form of training. Records show that in 1857, James
Simpson was appointed provisionally as Senior Warder and
School Master. He was not satisfactory and was removed,
and his successor was also not long in tenure, for it was found
he could not engage in teaching.

In January, 1858, Mr. Draper took over the duties of
School Master, Warder and Clerk, and later became the
Chief Warder, a position he long held and members of his
family still reside in Halifax. Earlier in its history, under its
rôle of a military prison, Melville Island had only taken court

martial cases. Later men sentenced by the officer in command of their unit for lesser offences were given a vacation at the Island Prison.

Even though the Navy lost possession of the island, under special arrangements, sailors and marines were also later incarcerated there along with the Army offenders for many years.

And so the story could go on and on. There is so much of interest that could be detailed about an institution which has had such a colourful history, and frequently a tragic one. During the First Great War, it had many guests for periods of twenty-eight days and over. With the Second Great War, it ceased to be used as a military prison, and has been much in the limelight, as to its future use.

Whatever the future of Melville Island, which some few years ago was robbed of some of its buildings by fire, it may serve a more useful purpose, but never have a more colourful life, than in its storied past. At present under special lease it is the headquarters of a very active organization, the Armdale Yacht Club. No city has been favoured with a finer recreational centre than Halifax with its North West Arm.

IX

THE NARROWS BRIDGE

Which Twice Was Wrecked

Three times a bridge o'er
These waters shall rise
Built by the white man
So strong and wise;
Three times shall fall,
Like a dying breath,
In Storm—in Silence—and
Last in Death.

(An old Indian legend sent to the author by Mrs. P. E. Cooper of Schumacher, Ontario, formerly of Dartmouth.)

. . . .

The following item appeared in the Halifax Press on Tuesday, October 5, 1943:

URGES BRIDGE BE BUILT AFTER WAR

A recommendation that a bridge be constructed across Halifax Harbour after the war is one of the main points of a brief to be presented to the Royal Commission on Post-War Planning today by Mayor L. J. Isnor, of Dartmouth. The brief was presented at last night's meeting of the town council for review by members of the council. Mayor Isnor, who is also chairman of the Dartmouth Ferry Commission points out in his brief that a bridge would serve the heavy traffic while the ferry could be used exclusively for pedestrians.

This news item, coming at this time when definite plans are being suggested to keep men busy after the war is most interesting and time worthy, because older Haligonians remember when there was a bridge. In fact, just over fifty years ago, the second bridge to span the harbour passed out of existence.

The first bridge which stood for some years of service at what is known as the "Narrows" was destroyed in a storm on the night of September 7, 1891.

The *Acadian Recorder* in its issue of September 8, 1891, described the disaster as follows:

THE BIGGEST STORM YET CAUSES HUNDREDS OF DOLLARS DAMAGE—DESTRUCTION OF THE NARROWS BRIDGE AND THE ELEVATOR GRAIN CHUTE — DEMORALIZATION OF SHIP-CRAFT OF VARIOUS KINDS — A GALE THAT IN INTENSITY RIVALLED SAXBY'S.

Yesterday, September 7, 1891, there was nothing particular in the atmosphere conditions. It rained heavily and steadily, wind W.S.W., and the barometer showed 29.10, an ordinary reading; while the thermometer stood for seventy-six, for the highest. Even toward evening there was no sign of a disturbance. At six o'clock the wind suddenly backed to E.S.E. indicating that a cyclone was at hand, as these

visitors nearly always back against the wind in a half circle
(and vessels leaving just before such a storm are not affected
by it).

About nine o'clock there were fitful blows with a deluge.
At eleven, there was a young hurricane. At twelve there
was chaos—the wind was terrific, the fire alarm and electric
wires clashed, and the tolling of the former and the tingling
of the latter added to the confusion. The light current was
cut off. People who had retired, arose and redressed themselves, and from the impossibility of ascertaining how matters
outside stood, a great deal of fear was engendered. Sheets
of rain swept along through the darkness with the rapidity
of at least forty miles an hour; while every little while crashes
were heard, indicating disasters close at hand. The trees
bowed themselves to the ground; the harbour waters lashed
themselves into a fury; the sky was of inky darkness; and all
the storm forces of nature seemed to have got loose and to
be chasing each other around.

Still, Cogswell thinks the storm may not have come from
very far beyond the harbour, and it is quite possible was not
experienced to a very disastrous extent outside. (This was
the case in the Saxby storm, where a full rigged barque
under full sail knew nothing of the storm until she arrived
at the mouth of the harbour, and then was carried irresistibly
up as far as Bedford and ashore there, presenting a picture
that added to the terrors of the storm, as she drove violently
along.)

About twelve o'clock the Narrows Bridge structure went
overboard, or at least one thousand of the fifteen hundred
yards of which is was composed. As is well known, it was
built with a concave, the convex towards the Narrows, down
which the ice-slides came in spring; and it was thought that
this form would help it, the ice would come against the
curved back of the bridge, and instead of weakening tend to
strengthen it. But this was just what proved fatal to it last
night; the tremendous sweep of the wind up the Narrows
caught the concave, and destroyed it from within two hun-

dred feet of the Halifax side to the "draw," which is three-quarters of the way across to Dartmouth. This morning there was open waterspace over this distance, except where some broken timbers fastened at the bottom, were sticking up. The sections were built of piers with "pockets" in them which held twenty tons ballast; but this was not sufficient to resist the force of the gale. The "draw" is built on a solid foundation, and therefore did not suffer; neither did the piece of the bridge on the shallow Dartmouth side.

The paper went on to say:

The loss will be very great; certainly, $50,000 will not cover it. Communication with Dartmouth by rail is shut off for months, and cars over there will have to remain, unless they can be lightered over in any way. The breaking of the bridge will cause great inconvenience, as quite a trade had grown up because of it. Lighters will have to be called into requisition. Some people talk of not rebuilding the bridge, but going back to the other plan of branching off at the head of the Basin and thus bringing in the railway. A great deal of the broken timber floated down the harbour. The break was seen, when it took place, by very few people. One man on the Dartmouth side said he got up to secure a scow, the bridge was there then, and while he looked it disappeared. The force of the break twisted the rails in the air on the remaining piece.

Commenting further on, the paper said:

The debris of the broken bridge was allowed to drift about the harbour, some stranded by the heavy weights attached to them. Quite a quantity was in the way of navigation. Whenever anything untoward happens in this locality in connection with Government railway matters, there is apparently no jurisdiction to do anything, everything drifts until word is received from Moncton or somewhere else.

So nothing was done in the way of clearing the harbour. Tons of material, in big masses, drifted on to Commercial wharf, and clung there, hundreds of feet out in the harbour until morning. The Dartmouth ferry boat that night collided with a huge pile, and broke her floats, consequently there was only one boat on in the early morning.

D. Cronan's schooner, *Ellie*, Captain Mundy, arrived from Porto Rico next morning. She had pilot John Hayes on board. Tacking up unsuspicious of anything wrong, the remains of the bridge confronted her, barring access to the wharf. A light twinkled on the outer edge of it, but nobody on board could make out what the trouble was. Halifax through the haze, appeared all right; the "golden galleons of the west" were calmly reposing at the wharves; the tall chimneys on both sides of the harbour loomed up, but here was a barrier not laid down in the charts. Another tack was made; cautiously the mass was skirted, and finally the wharf was reached from the opposite side, the schooner sustaining some slight damage.

Next morning, Jim McCormack, the janitor of the Queen Building commenced the job of taking away the wreckage. Lines were made fast to it, and to a tug, and away it went up to its old home, the remnants of the once gallant bridge, which curiously enough, almost everybody who was heard to remark on it on the Halifax side, said "ought not be rebuilt." But the Dartmouth people had a right to a very important say in this matter.

The paper commented further:

By the way it should be ascertained at an early date whether the bridge fell during the storm, or after it, so as to form a basis for future calculation.

After considerable argument between the authorities and the Town Council of Dartmouth, a new bridge was built at the same site, the "Narrows," joining Halifax and Dartmouth, but it was not to have a very long life, in fact it was not two years old when disaster overcame it on July 23, 1893.

The *Acadian Recorder*, in its issue of July 24, 1893, described its collapse as follows:

THE NARROWS BRIDGE COLLAPSES A SECOND TIME. IT DISAPPEARS IN THE NIGHT

The Narrows Bridge became a complete wreck early yesterday morning. Trains passed over as usual Saturday night; and when Sunday dawned, residents, in the vicinity saw that the larger half of the bridge was gone, deals were floating about, but the greater portion of the wreckage had taken a trip up the Basin. The collapse is supposed to have occurred about 2.00 a.m. It is the western end, which is by far the largest portion, from near the draw to the Halifax side, that was carried away.

It is fortunate for the Government that there were no lives lost, because there have been many serious expressed misgivings from time to time—especially when it was carried away in September, 1891—about the safety of the bridge. As the *Herald* remarks: "How flimsy the structure was, is shown by the collapse, for it has come down in less than two years with hardly a breath of wind moving."

The Dartmouth Town Council in 1891 remonstrated against the rebuilding of the bridge. In the letter sent to Ottawa, it was stated "the difficulties of a reconstruction of the bridge on a secure basis have been increased by the failure of the late construction, which has greatly deteriorated the holding powers of the ground for pile-driving." It was suggested that the necessary outlay would be more effective in bringing the railway into Dartmouth on firm ground from near Windsor Junction.

A brief reply was received to this remonstrance, to the effect that "it was not deemed advisable."

Reporting further the next day, July 25, 1893, the paper said:

An explanation of the breaking away of the Narrows Bridge is that the piles were worm-eaten almost through between high-water and low-water mark. When the last train went over on Saturday evening it is supposed that these rotten supports gave way, and rested on the surface, the bridge actually sinking to that extent, or being upheld very frailly. Then, when the tide rose, sometime after midnight, these broken timbers were lifted, sagged, and the whole thing swept away. The danger of loss of life may therefore be seen. Death was lying in wait, but his ambush was happily escaped. "The deep water terminus will go the same way," was the comment of one who appeared to pretty well understand the position.

There were thirty-four freight, box and coal cars stranded on the Dartmouth side—nineteen at the Refinery, and the others on sidings. Seven cars belonged to the G.T.R. and C.P.R., the others to the I.C.R.

The Halifax Narrows Bridge was first built in 1884. Duncan Waddell was the first man to make preparations for building. He had the contract for the stone pier on which rested the swing section of the bridge. The public knowing the class of work that Mr. Waddell was capable of doing, felt assured that a bridge would be constructed which would be a credit to the contractor and the Government.

It was very soon learned that Mr. Waddell only had the contract for the stone pier. He had piles driven in about thirty feet of water at low tide; these piles were driven in a gravel bottom to a depth of about five feet, and were used as a framework or guide for building the pier. This stone pier stood perfectly firm, and is in its original position today.

The woodwork of the bridge was done by parties imported by the Government. Cribs were built to a height of about eight feet, filled with stone ballast and laid on the bottom, about eight or nine feet between each crib. On these cribs were fastened iron knees, the piles which had to carry the weight of the bridge. The first piles came just above low water. The section of timber was placed on these piles and trestle work built from the stringers to the height of the bridge.

No braces were driven in the bottom to prevent the bridge from swinging north or south with the action of the current, or pressure of trains passing over, the latter having a very great pressure at the curve, having a tendency to throw the bridge northward. It cannot now be determined whether this was the fault of the contractor or of the engineer, but it is presumable there were defects in the plans. However, outside of this, it was such a ginger-bread constructed piece of work that in a very short time it showed signs of weakness.

Several months before its first collapse, the dangerous condition of the bridge was brought to the notice of the authorities. No action was taken; fortunately no lives were lost at the first collapse.

The second bridge was even more flimsy than the first. Piles were driven through the old cribs. The water in the channel was seventy feet; the piles were about eighty-five feet in length; some of them were spliced with two splices; the splices were protected with eight-inch deals, fastened on with spikes. It is not unlikely that these spikes were broken in driving the piles.

Persons of practical knowledge at the time claimed that such unsubstantial splicing of piles was not calculated to bear the pressure of trains passing over, and that the piles should have been spliced with timber, of at least eight by eight, to lap the joints at least five feet, and placed on four sides of the pile, fastened through both timbers and piles with screw bolts.

This second bridge, like the first one, was not braced by piles driven in the bottom. The critics of the new bridge claimed that it should have been properly braced with piles driven in the bottom and fastened to timbers at, or about, low water mark, the piles having an angle of about one in three, their length would have been sufficient to resist the action of the current, and brace piles of same proportion fastened to top of bridge would have resisted the pressure of passing trains. Instead of brace piles, anchors of railroad iron and wire rope were fastened to top of bridge. This was not sufficient to prevent the bridge being thrown north by pressure of trains; and having no support from the action of current at or about low water mark the bridge, being thrown so far out of its original position, drew the piles out of the bottom, and these piles were carried away by pressure of the current.

After the debris of the second bridge was cleared away, in 1893, the Dartmouth Town Council met to consider the matter, there being present: Mayor Oland, Councillors Young, Anderson, MacLean, Cunningham and Johnson.

The following requisition was read:

J. C. Oland, Esq., Mayor of Dartmouth: The undersigned citizens of Dartmouth request you to call a meeting of the ratepayers at the earliest possible date to consider the advisability of memorializing the Dominion Government and requesting them not to rebuild the Narrows Bridge, but to build a branch road to Windsor Junction.

And so the "Narrows" Bridge passed into history, just over fifty years ago.

The suggestion to build a bridge again, coming from the present Mayor and Council of Dartmouth, is most interesting. It certainly would be a welcome post-war scheme with modern engineering ability.

X

THE SHUBENACADIE CANAL
1794-1870

A Short Route to the Bay of Fundy

WHEN you stand by the Old Town Clock on the Citadel Hill and gaze across the Harbour, to the town of Dartmouth, you will notice that the town is settled mostly in a valley between the hills. On one side is the high ground on which the golf links are located and on the other high hill is the site of the lovely home of H. R. Silver. On this hill I first saw the light of day. It was then known as Evan's Farm. Between these high places the famous Dartmouth lakes are located, and they empty out to the Harbour of Halifax, down a controlled waterway of the Starr Manufacturing Company, and the rolling mill in Dartmouth Cove. The Dartmouth lakes where I spent my boyhood and the famous Shubenacadie Canal, which was built with the idea of a commercial waterway from Halifax Harbour to the Bay of Fundy, are of interest to visitors, who come across the famous granite locks at the head of the Lakes.

The Dartmouth lakes which now bear the name of Lake MicMac and Lake Banook, were for years known simply as First and Second Lakes. When I was a boy, living alongside First Lake with grandparents, there were only one or two rowboats and the odd steam launch on the lakes, whose chief reason for existence seemed to me, to be as a place where next summer's ice could be obtained by my old friend Sam Chittick, but with McPhee's Boat House, and the establishment of the Banook Canoe Club and later the MicMac Rowing Club, the scene completely changed.

The Dartmouth lakes became the playground of Dartmouth, and there is nothing finer anywhere. Today instead of just half a dozen houses at the foot of the lake on Prince Albert Road, and two or three on the other side of the lake, one finds some of the nicest residential sections, particularly on the north side, and all along the Waverley road lovely homes are springing up, where a few years ago only summer camps were to be found.

To the Dartmouth lakes on Natal Day, goes practically every Dartmouthian and thousands of Haligonians, for the regatta and fireworks display, which outstrips anything in the way of celebration that takes place in the Province.

To those who did not own a boat or canoe, McPhee's boathouse for years proved a blessing. Here one could hire a boat and row up First Lake, through the tittle and on up Second Lake to Port Wallis Locks, where family picnics would take place.

When this beauty spot was discovered, and after the usual romping around had been done and the family had settled down to eat on the banks of the canal leading to the locks, nearly every small boy asked his parents what the big granite walls were for, and no doubt many parents in Dartmouth have had to explain for their boys and girls the reasons for this structure, which is part of the Shubenacadie Canal, with which it was proposed to join the Harbour with the Dartmouth Lakes and then make a Canal joining other lakes until the Shubenacadie River was reached as a waterway into the Minas Basin. The history of the Shubenacadie Canal covers a period from 1794 to 1870, nearly one hundred years, and ended in complete failure, as far as a commercial enterprise is considered. Now it is nothing more than a magnificent scenic waterway, over which adventurous youths sometimes in summer spend a couple of weeks in a canoe trip with several small portages between lakes; the locks long ago having fallen into disrepair. A great many members of the Banook Canoe Club will tell you of trips they have taken over this route, during the summer holidays.

At a very early period, the importance of obtaining easy access to that part of the Province lying on the shore of the Basin of Minas, by making a canal between the Dartmouth and Shubenacadie Lakes and Rivers, attracted general attention. Sir John Wentworth in a letter to Colonel Small, dated May 27, 1794, says: "Your territory at Kennetcook will be much improved by my plan of rendering the Shubenacadie navigable, and a communication thence to Dartmouth by a chain of lakes. This great work I hope to get completed, if we are not interrupted by hostilities."

Lake Charles, near the first Shubenacadie Lake, is three-and-a-half miles from Halifax. From the southern end of this lake there is a descent through the Dartmouth Lakes to the harbour of Halifax, of ninety-one feet; and from its northern extremity, a gradual descent through several beautiful lakes into the great Shubenacadie, thence in the channel of the river for a distance of about thirty miles to the junction with the waters of the Bay of Fundy. The lakes on this chain are the First and Second Dartmouth Lakes, Lake Charles, Lake William, Lake Thomas, Fletcher's Lake, and Grand Lake.

In the year 1797, the matter of the canal was brought before the legislature. The House appropriated the sum of two hundred and fifty pounds, and appointed a committee to institute inquiry into everything connected with the construction of a canal from Dartmouth Cove across the Province to the mouth of the Shubenacadie River, where it falls into the Basin of Minas. This committee employed Mr. Isaac Hildreth, a civil engineer, who made a survey and reported to the commissioners. The report was dated November 15, 1797. He estimated the cost of a four-foot canal suitable for navigation would be £3,202 17s. 6d.

In the session of 1798, a Bill was brought before the legislature, for incorporating a company to complete the canal. A petition praying for legislative assistance had previously been introduced and signed by William Forsyth, Andrew Belcher, and Richard Kidston. The governor of the Province, Sir John Wentworth, being very friendly to the undertaking, addressed a letter dated July 16, 1798, to the gentlemen who proposed to form the company for constructing the canal. He stated that the House of Assembly had addressed him, requesting that a patent might be issued toward carrying into effect the purposes intended in the said petition, and that he would give the necessary orders to expedite that patent for the advice and consent of His Majesty's Council.

He goes on to say, that he is persuaded that the greatest benefit will be derived from the execution of the plan, "to the revenue and morals of the country, by making it the interest and convenience of numerous and increasing inhabitants to purchase of the fair trader in or through Halifax; whence the frauds, lying, violences, and prejudices attendant on illicit commerce will naturally vanish." Evidently bootleggers were in existence in those days.

Notwithstanding all this, the Bill did not pass. The subject of a canal was therefore in abeyance until 1814. About this time the opinion was held by certain promoters of the scheme, that communication could be made between Lake William and the Harbour via Bedford Basin. A competent engineer, however, who was authorized to examine this line, disapproved of the proposal and gave his adherence to the original route. Further sums of money were then voted at the solicitation of Mr. Sabatier, and expended under his direction by Mr. Valentine Gill, a civil engineer.

About this time a small amount of money voted by the Assembly was expended by Mr. Gill in removing obstructions from the river near Fletcher's Bridge, and rendering that point accessible during spring and autumn for large boats from the bay shore.

On opening the session of 1820, Lord Dalhousie, who was then Governor, deemed the matter worthy of being included among the suggestions for the improvement of the Province. He said it promised great public advantages, and he suggested the employment of competent engineers to ascertain the extent of its difficulties. The House replied that it would carefully consider the interesting subject. Two hundred pounds were accordingly voted for a more particular survey but this sum being found to be inadequate, further proceedings were delayed until 1824, when an additional sum of three hundred pounds was appropriated to secure the services of a gentleman of competent ability for the execution of the important task.

In order to encourage and facilitate the formation of an association to construct the canal, an Act to authorize the incorporation of such a company was passed by the Assembly in 1824. At the close of the session, His Excellency Sir James Kempt said, "The internal communications of a country tend so manifestly to its improvement and to increase the productive industry of its population, that I shall lose no time in employing the means which you have placed at my disposal, to ascertain the practicability and expense of forming a canal to unite the water of the Basin of Minas with the Harbour of Halifax."

The Shubenacadie Canal Company was incorporated by letters patent dated June 1, 1826. On Tuesday, July 25th, of the same year, the ceremony of commencing the canal took place. Sir James Kempt, the Governor of the Province, attended by a large escort of the military and naval force, with artillery and rifle bands, also the officers of the Grand Lodge, the Royal Albion, and the Lodges Nos. 4, 8, 188 and 265 of Free and Accepted Masons turned out, together with a large number of spectators, to do honour to the occasion. They proceeded to Port Wallis, three miles from Dartmouth, at the pass between the Second Dartmouth Lake and Lake Charles; and there ground was first broken by Lord Dalhousie who was visiting Halifax at the time.

The funds of the Company were increased by the sale of stocks in England to the amount of twenty-seven hundred pounds sterling, and also by a loan of twenty thousand pounds sterling by the Lords Commissioners of the Treasury. In consideration of this loan, the Lords Commissioners of the Treasury received a mortgage of the canal. The total expenditure of the Company up to December, 1835, was in currency eighty-seven thousand eight hundred and thirty pounds.

Notwithstanding Mr. Hall's abilities and attention, and the approval of his designs by Thomas Telford, the consulting engineer, the works in the locks and dams proved very faulty. Every winter the frost did great damage. The contractors declared their inability to proceed with and complete their work. The Company itself undertook to make good the damages, but with no better result. The dam broke at the northern end of Lake Charles, and immediately the costly works at Fletcher's Lake and at the Grand Lake were destroyed by the great rush of water. This disaster proved a death-blow to the Shubenacadie Canal Company.

While the work had been going on, Dartmouth had profited materially by the enterprise. From the beginning, it had been difficult to procure suitable workmen, and a vessel called the *Corsair* was accordingly chartered by Mr. Kidd, who proceeded to Scotland and returned in the spring of 1827 with about forty stone-cutters and masons with their families. These men laboured at the locks for two or three years. They were industrious and skilful artisans, and infused a spirit of emulation in their fellow-labourers, which has long borne good fruit in Nova Scotia.

After the unfortunate disaster caused by the breaking of the dam at Lake Charles, the works were inspected. And in the years 1835 and 1836, a most elaborate survey, with plans, estimates and report, was made to the order of Charles R. Fairbanks, Esq. It was estimated that the cost of the works would be four hundred and eighty-seven thousand three hundred and seventy-five pounds.

The mortgage made by the Company to the British Government was now foreclosed, and by a deed in Chancery it was conveyed to the Province of Nova Scotia on June 11, 1851. The properties not covered by the mortgage were sold in the following year to satisfy judgment, and the whole was purchased for the Province by Hon. James McNab as trustee.

In 1853, the Inland Navigation Company was incorporated, having a capital of thirty thousand pounds. It purchased from the government of Nova Scotia the property and works of the late Shubenacadie Canal Company. The opening of the canal was again proceeded with, under the direct supervision of the new company's engineer, Charles William Fairbanks, Esq. All their cash, twenty thousand pounds, having been expended, the Company was obliged to borrow money by mortgage of all their property. The canal progressed very slowly, but in 1861 it opened for business throughout. A steam vessel of sixty tons, the *Avery,* named after the president of the company, Dr. James F. Avery, having cleared at the Custom House, Halifax, reported, via the canal, at Maitland, and returned again to Halifax Harbour.

On June 11, 1862, the whole property and works were sold by the sheriff. They were purchased by a company called, The Lake and River Navigation Company. No boats were provided by this company, but private individuals placed on the canal three steam-boats and twelve scows, together with one eighty-ton barge. Consequently some business was done. A large quantity of timber was delivered at Halifax, also many thousand cords of wood, with building materials. Coal and supplies for the gold mines were transported from Halifax. The Canal was thus worked at a small profit by the Lake and River Navigation Company, until they sold the property in February, 1870, for $50,000. Lewis Piers Fairbanks, Esq., was the purchaser. It was again doomed to go to destruction. Gold was discovered at the summit reservoir, and the Mines Department, without any regard to the rights of the owner of the canal-lands there, disputed Mr. Fairbanks' title, and the effect of the Provincial Government deed made by the Hon. James McNab, trustee for the Province, in 1875. One thousand dollars damages were awarded to Mr. Fairbanks, against the government for trespass. While this matter was under consideration, the drawbridge at Waverley was removed by the provincial authorities, and a fixed bridge erected in its place. This was a bar against all passage. The Dominion Railway or Public Works Department removed the bridge at Enfield, and replaced it by another bridge, whose girders were so low as to prevent the passage of a boat on the River Station. The owner, harassed by persons opulent and in high places, was obliged to realize the fact, that the completion of this inland river communication did not fulfil in any degree the expectations so earnestly expressed by Sir John Wentworth in regard to the great improvement to the "revenue and morals" of the country.

And that's the story of the Shubenacadie Canal. Perhaps it's just as well. If the Dartmouth Lakes had become a commercial waterway, thousands of people would have lost one of the finest playgrounds—camping sites and residential sections. And my only hope is, that the town fathers will see to it that it is kept beautiful, and that a large section will always be available for John Q. Public and his family to enjoy themselves in God's fresh air amidst such gorgeous scenery.

XI

HISTORIC HOUSES OF HALIFAX

Monuments of Early Days

To every visitor Down East there are three historic Halifax "houses" which should be seen. They are Province House, Government House and Admiralty House.

There's a door in Halifax that intrigues me more than almost any other. It's a very plain appearing door. There's nothing much about it, to tell of that which will be found within, when it swings open. There's no large-lettered sign to give a hint of that which lies behind. It has a slot for letters. It has a modern gadget at its top, which prevents it from slamming. That's an invention of an age far different from the one in which it was first hung on its hinges.

Where is this door? It's in our Province House. For that matter, almost any door in that historic building can lead to a period of speculation on the past. Each room in the storied building has its own individual story to tell, but the one door, above all the others, which catches my fancy most is that leading into the Provincial Library, a room with character, with individuality. Its proportions and fittings leave nothing to be desired. It's in keeping with the building that harbours it. I suppose there may come a time when some person with a mania for change will want to modernize it. Let's hope no such person will ever have any authority who should feel impelled to remodel the Province House Library. Enter this mystic portal of the Provincial Library and you leave the rush of the outside world behind. Busy, bustling, commercial Halifax is left without. Auto horns and exhausts are not entirely obliterated. The muted clatter of street cars can still be heard. But they seem to take on a subdued tone. They can't rob this charming room of its quiet and its atmosphere.

Glance through the books on hand and you will realize that this is no cluttered library that only deals with the past. The most modern volumes have their place. Then, too, there are books that go back to the very foundation of this Province. There are the annals of this New Scotland.

The heart of the man who designed the stairways leading gracefully upward to the gallery, which also boasts orderly rows of books, must have been that of a poet. To ever think of their removal would be an act of desecration. Just to sit and contemplate their harmonious lines is restful. All of the books in sight are by no means the contents of the library. The rooms above are also part and parcel of the library and contain still more of the valuable printed materials. Once upon a time, these upper rooms were used as the quarters of the caretaker of the building. Presumably the library needs more space. Time is at hand when steps will have to be taken to provide it. I believe there is a room to the south that might serve. When the time for change does come, let's hope there will be careful thought. Provide the space, yes, but in so doing, don't for a moment destroy the proportions of the present library room itself. That would be tragedy.

Who uses this library? Well, primarily, it is for the Members of Nova Scotia's Legislature, as well as members of the Nova Scotia Historical Society. Yes, and judges of our courts also are permitted, among others, the courtesy of its use. But they are not the only visitors. Practically all who visit the Province House are conducted there. It is a room worthy of their attention. They are well repaid for their visit. Its charm is engaging. The paintings that line its gallery rails speak from the pages of history.

Before we delve into the history of this particular room, let's stop to pay a tribute to Miss Annie Donahue, the Librarian. For a number of years she has presided there, providing a type of charming service that cannot be described in mere words. It is a service that desires to be helpful in every respect. It is a service that bespeaks a thorough knowledge of the books within her charge. Ask any member of the Legislature of the things which he recalls with particular pleasure of his periods of residence in Halifax. Unquestionably among them will be the smile, service and welcome of Miss Donahue. She is friendly to all, proud of her trust and with particular pride in her library and its important functions.

We'll have to call a halt on the library itself, but we'll return again, for I must give a brief idea of the events of great importance that have transpired within its four walls. However, for a moment, let us learn a little of the building itself.

The late Doctor MacMechan, a Dean among historians, tells us that the Province House took eight years to build and cost much money. He is right when he says that it "is a stately monument to the pride and taste of our ancestors."

It stands in the middle of the Lower Parade on the historic site of Old Government House.

There is no longer any mystery as to who designed this stately building. In the office of A. S. Barnstead, Provincial Secretary-Treasurer, there is a small portrait of John Merrick. He is recognized as the designer of this building. His was a feat that was not small. Today architects come to study it from afar. It is recognized of perfect proportions. And this Merrick, its designer, was Master Painter at the Dockyard. It was a matter of surprise to MacMechan that a man in such a post could have produced such a masterpiece of architecture. Today, Mr. Barnstead tells me that other claims of its design have been swept aside and to John Merrick is ascribed the sole credit. He has earned a debt of gratitude from us. He has given us a building that, for centuries to come, will serve us well. Across the street we have the modern, blocklike Provincial Building. In it are housed the many offices needed in our modern concept of what a Province must provide for its people. Comparatively few offices remain in the Province House proper. The new building, with all its modernity, cannot hope for a moment to compete with the effectual charm of its older sire on the western side of Hollis Street.

Others have written in detail of the technical details that go to make up this building. I do not propose to deal with those, for if you care to, you can consult the volumes that deal with that phase.

It's well over a century ago that Halifax gathered to witness the laying of the cornerstone of this momentous building. Momentous it must have been to those Nova Scotians of early days. It still arrays itself in that category, for it is widely acclaimed for its symmetrical proportions.

We have, many of us, gone into the chamber of the House of Assembly. We have taken our places, with backs against the high board seats of the gallery. We look down at our elected legislators below. They are seated in a form that allows the Speaker's chair to be at the north end of the chamber. How many of us know that originally the House of Assembly was so laid out that the seats ranged east and west, instead of north and south.

Today, we have no Legislative Council or Upper House, as it was considered. But we still have our Legislative Council Chamber, which it is still called. We keep it in tip-top repair, mundane as that term may sound. It would be a sad commentary upon us if we did not. Few rooms within the whole Empire can compare with it for sheer beauty. Others may be larger, but ours is something apart—distinctive. Today it is largely relegated to the reception of visiting personages of real moment. It was within these walls that the Province of Nova Scotia gave official welcome to our beloved sovereigns, King George the Sixth and his gracious Queen Elizabeth. Never has this beautiful old chamber had a happier time.

Lovers of Dickens' writings take pride in the fact that he knew our Council Chamber. It was on a winter's day in 1842 that he was present at the opening of the House and declared it was like seeing Westminster through the wrong end of the telescope. It impressed him as being in every way akin to the scenes he has witnessed at home, except, naturally, in numbers.

In this same room of the Province Building is an item of real interest. That historic table in the Council Chamber. There it rests serenely today. But what other days it has seen. To the uninitiated, those who do not know its history, and fail to study the brass plate in its centre, it might be just another table. But study that plate.

It says "Around this table sat His Majesty's Council for the Province of Nova Scotia, July 14, 1749, on board the *Beaufort*, Transport. Present: His Excellency, the Governor, the Honourable Edward Cornwallis (whom we all recall as the founder of Halifax). With him were Paul Mascarene, Esquire; John Gorham, Esquire; John Salisbury, Esquire; Edward Howe, Esquire; Benjamin Green, Esquire; and Hugh Davidson, Esquire; the Secretary." You can, at will, enter this building and there rest your elbows upon the selfsame table where the founders of this historic city once rested theirs. There's no roped off space. That is not roped off in strictest sense. There are brass posts and corded ropes. But, under the friendly eye of an attendant, you too can take your place at the board. You can vision a distant time when this table rested in the cabin of the historic *Beaufort*. You can, if you have imagination, pretend that you were a member of the august company. What was said? What planning went on? Go there, and see if you, too, don't feel the presence of these pioneers of the beloved Halifax to be.

By the way, every door casing is ornamental in Province House. Each door has carved upon the top corners an eagle. On close examination one will note that someone has cut off the heads of each one. It is said it was done by some super patriot who felt they were too American in appearance, when Province House was first built.

To get further atmosphere of the historic past, let's descend the well-worn stairs of stone of the Province House. It is amazing how they have been worn by the tread of people through the centuries. What famous footsteps you can well imagine. We move past the tablet to Cartier, and on to the first printing press, just a little way removed from this site, that brought the printed page to this continent.

Let's halt for a moment to visit the present Premier's office. In the same room where that great leader of Nova Scotia, Joseph Howe, once laboured. The present premier can sit at his desk and, close at hand through the window, see the statue of Howe, with upraised hand.

In the lower lobby of the Province House, we find the colours encased there of the 193rd and the 219th Highlanders of Nova Scotia, proud battalions of the First Great War. On the outside, at the east entrance, at each side of the stone platform where the Lieutenant-Governor takes the salute at House openings, we see two metal light standards. They speak of the past too. They are from the old Waterloo

Bridge in London, England, and were donated by Freeman I. Davidson of Falmouth and erected in 1938.

Around the grounds to the north, near the base of the South African campaign monument, we find two old cannon, far removed in appearance from the modern type of armament. One bears this inscription on its side. "Tradition saith that this cannon was used in the historic sea fight between the *Chesapeake* and *Shannon,* June 1, 1813." It was used as noon and evening gun of Halifax between the years 1882 and 1905. There's so much about our Province House to tell, but let's return to consider that room which houses the library. Once it was the court room for this, the new-born land. On Wednesday, July 28, 1819, handsome Richard John Uniacke, the younger, was tried for his life. A week previous he had shot and killed William Bowie in a duel. It was outcome of something Bowie was supposed, and probably did, say at a trial in which Uniacke was acting. The father of the accused, then Attorney-General, accompanied arm and arm, his son to the scene of trial. He handed him over. But the code of honour, and duelling held sway. Uniacke was acquitted. Within these walls Howe so ably defended himself against the charge that he had attacked the junta of wealthy merchants for pocketing the taxes. Howe, the journalist upheld his position. His tongue prevailed.

The trial of the Saladin pirates, with all its pomp, took place here.

Do you wonder I find this room of greater interest than all others. That's why I spend so much time delving into the pages of the past. That's why I say, visit the Province House.

Strange as it seems, Halifax has a building where the back door is used as the main entrance. Seldom indeed do its occupants, or visitors, enter or leave through the front of the building. This house is Government House, one of Halifax's most imposing structures. It is a house of real history.

Within its high ceilinged rooms, through the decades, have taken place many of the city's most brilliant social functions.

The New Year's levees were traditional ceremonies dear to the hearts of loyal old Halifax. On that first day of the year, when such events were held, our people by hundreds passed through the entrance. There they moved in regular line through the stately room to pay their respects to their sovereign's representative, the Lieutenant-Governor.

There are varied views as to the proper and fitting future for Government House. Some hold to the view that it should cease to function as residence of the Lieutenant-Governor and his family. They advance the opinion that it is an expense that could be dispensed with. They feel a residence of ordinary proportions could well serve the purpose. They suggest that Government House could be put to some use where it would serve the general public, say as a library, a museum or a gallery for display of art. In times of war suggestion has been advanced that its spacious interior might readily be adapted as a centre for use of the services. No matter to which shade of opinion we may give allegiance, we can be as one in hope that everything will be done to safeguard the permanence of the structure itself. The presence of scaffolding about its walls, seen in recent years, is a matter of gratification. It shows care is being taken to preserve this impressive and historic pile of masonry.

We can give thanks that far-sighted Dr. D. C. Harvey, Provincial Archivist, who saw fit to direct the compiling of an interesting pamphlet on *The Romance of Government House*. This was prepared by the late Dr. J. S. Martell, of the Archives staff. Dr. Martell was a gifted writer, as well as one who delved into the past with a thoroughness that provides us with much of interest. When Their Majesties King George and Queen Elizabeth visited the Government House on June 15, 1939, they were presented by the Government of Nova Scotia with two especially bound copies of this interesting booklet.

In telling sentences Dr. Martell painted for us a glowing picture of words that made us seemingly present at the cornerstone laying. This event took place in the year 1800.

It can be imagined that few of any age in Halifax who could move about on that momentous day failed to witness the ceremony.

Then the Government House site was not practically in the heart of business Halifax. In fact, its so-called remoteness from the very centre of things, led to its final selection for the purpose it was to serve.

The first residences of the Governor were on the site of the present Province House, in vicinity of the Lower Parade. The lot on which the Government House stands today, between Barrington Street, where it faces St. Paul's Cemetery and Hollis Street, was originally purchased for a Province House. This led to a protest from many Haligonians. They held that it was too far out of town to make it suitable for public offices. This lot was then in what was known as the south suburbs of Halifax. The field on the other side of Barrington Street, earlier known as Pleasant Street, up to Spring Garden Road, is still known as Governor's Field. It is that section to the rear of Technical College and south of St. Paul's Cemetery. It was then the Governor's South Farm. The Government House garage today stands on the narrow strip of land leading to that field.

Sir John Wentworth gave Halifax its present Government House. Perhaps "gave" is hardly the word. It was his continued pressure that brought about its erection. In fact, before it was completed, the cost involved ran so far above the estimate, that protests were frequently voiced. Sir John, and his charming lady were accustomed to luxurious surroundings, and he stuck to his guns. The old, or second Government House, which he occupied was far from his liking. So he kept up his campaign and saw it meet with success.

It is chronicled that the only regret expressed at the colourful ceremony of laying of the cornerstone was that the Duke of Kent was absent. By Royal order, which directed him to a new station of duties in Great Britain, His Highness was forced to sail shortly before the ceremony. This sorrow was hardly allowed to detract from the celebration. The workmen were well supplied with food and drink. After the parchment was placed by Governor Wentworth, and the stone well and truly laid, and Reverend Mr. Stanser, Rector of St. Paul's, had offered prayer, privileged members of society repaired to old Government House. There they enjoyed the well-known hospitality of Sir John and his lady.

Many there were at this cornerstone laying who had seen the erection of the first Government House. This was hastily erected by Cornwallis the first summer of the new settlement. It was but a one-storey affair. This was followed by a second one at the same site, but this time boasting another storey. It continued to be the place of residence of the Governor until 1805. It had an appearance that was deceptive. It appeared to be constructed of freestone. In reality, it was a wooden building painted to give that effect.

John Parr who became Governor in 1782 seemed well pleased with housing accommodation provided. In fact, the revenue provided him by the farm lands at his disposal, and the house itself won his surprised praise. Included in the things which he wrote to a friend, that made him well satisfied with his lot, was the well stocked cellar. In it were plentiful supplies of port, claret, Madeira, rum; and Bowood strong beer, etcetera.

When Wentworth took over in 1792 we find him informing the Legislature that the whole structure was in danger of falling into the cellar. There is a strong suspicion that Sir John rather overemphasized conditions. It is likely that he was prompted to a strong choice of words. Used to luxurious surroundings and stately residences, he wanted a new Government House and set about getting it.

While, in personal correspondence, he often decried living in an old, decayed house as harmful to health, he probably took a different tack in driving home his point to the minds of local legislators. He could stress the added proof this would give of loyalty to the Crown in those troublesome times. A fine new Government House, second to none on this continent, would speak in no uncertain terms of this feeling toward the Monarchy. His campaign was well laid. In 1799 the legislators declared that the old Government House was in so ruinous a condition as to be unfit for the residence of the Governor or Commander-in-Chief of the Province.

Dr. Martell explained to us how this harmony of view between Wentworth and the worthy legislators of Nova Scotia did not last. The House of Assembly had willingly voted 10,500 Pounds for the Governor's residence. This they did, prompted in part probably by promise of increased grants for roads and bridges in their country districts.

Construction costs speedily mounted. Charges of illegality and incompetence were said to have been hurled at Wentworth and the Honourable Michael Wallace, the Chief Commissioner of the building. Increased grants had to be forthcoming, or, as Wentworth pointed out, all previously spent would be only counted as lost money. The story from the Archives records that, when Wentworth retired in 1808, more than twice the estimated amount had been expended. The furnishings, and changes made by his successors to complete the building, must have cost easily thirty thousand pounds. This represented more than a tidy sum of money in those days. In fact, it is no mean amount today.

Nova Scotia had a Government House of which it could well be proud. Indeed, it was second to none. So imposing was it considered, that when Sir George Prevost came to take over his duties, he took one look at the imposing mass and promptly demanded an increase in salary.

To consider all of the details of the building would be too lengthy a task. It is familiar to most of us, situated as it is on the city's main thoroughfare, just on the edge of the principal commercial section. It is interesting to note that the building is said to belong to the closing period of the Renaissance architecture. It followed the Gothic age. It provided a return to the classic principles.

The original front faced the east, but usage has made

the Barrington side to be considered as the front of the structure.

The ground floor is largely devoted to rooms that serve official purposes, the ball room, with artistic Greek columns, being to the north, with offices in the central section and drawing and dining-room to the south. The second storey provides the private apartment for the Governor and his family.

The Maroons who dwelt at Preston between the time they were removed from Jamaica to Nova Scotia and later sent to Sierra Leone, along with soldiers were engaged to carry out the earlier work of excavating. The actual building was largely done by local tradesmen. Isaac Hildrith was the architecture in charge of construction and John Henderson, a Scot, was chief mason, receiving seven shillings a day. The masons under him received five or six shillings, each according to his skill. The head carpenter was paid on the same scale as Henderson, but the man under him never received more than five shillings and six pence a day. These were among the higher paid tradesmen on the job.

Government House is largely a home product. Pictou, Antigonish and Cape Breton provided source of the freestone, Lunenburg and Lockeport yielded the building stone. From Antigonish came red flagstone, blue rubble from Bedford Basin, flat stone from the North West Arm. In the woods used, red pine came from Annapolis and Tatamagouche; white and yellow pine from Cornwallis. Sand was brought from Shelburne, Eastern Passage and McNamara's Island. Bricks were purchased in large quantities from Dartmouth. In addition to footing the bills, practically all parts of our Province have still a greater interest in our picturesque Government House. Even in those early days fire-proof construction was an aim. These precautions proved effective for in 1854 the local fire fighters battled three hours with flames there. Only the central part of the roof and the attic were destroyed, thanks to early precautions.

Wentworth saw his ambitions realized, but he had only

little more than two years' residence within its coveted walls before he retired in 1808. Even then workmen were still about the place, for he had been so anxious, he moved in before the place was entirely completed.

Government House stands in its impressiveness today, in the eyes of all. To pass it, if one has imagination, can cause speculation as to past scenes. History of varied type has been written within its walls. Grave conferences of state have taken place there. Royalty has often been entertained. Gay levees and balls have taken place on innumerable occasions. Invitations to these affairs were keenly coveted. Government House offers much material for speculation and stories of the romantic past of Halifax.

Amid the many new buildings erected for the Royal Canadian Navy during the Second Great War stands the old Admiralty House on Gottingen Street. Never in the history of Halifax has there been greater activity at Admiralty House than at this time, it would seem. Of course, there are the crowded days when it served as the centre for the Massachusetts-Halifax Relief Commission, in the wake of the Halifax Explosion of 1917, but that was only an interlude. It was not then associated with the life of the navy, for which the building was primarily constructed.

To be truthful, even today's chapter in the life of the imposing grey stone building is apart from the original scheme of things at the time of its construction. Then it was built for the purpose of being a place of residence for the British Admiral on the station. It was not remotely pictured as a mess for all officers of the Royal Canadian Navy. Commissioned Naval Officers of lesser rank than flag rank could not hope to walk freely in and out through its artistically proportioned portals. For men of such rank to dine there would be an unusual favour and distinction. Today they consider it their "home away from home." During the war, at the hour of mid-day dinner, they were served in seven sittings. In the spacious dining hall, where once the Admiral and his guests would leisurely sit through course after course, these diners did not tarry too long. Others were ready in successive order to occupy the chairs. In fact this applies not to the dining-room alone, it goes also for the lengthy table which had been set in the glass enclosed porch on the east side of the building.

But the Admiralty House of today—or as it is more informally refered to, "Ad. House"—is not a place for dining alone. It has its recreation rooms, in which the officers can gather to talk and play cards. It has its reading room, its billiard room, yes and even its small but popular music room complete with piano. Then, when opportunity offers, on a pleasant summer evening, there is no more delightful place than its upper eastern verandah. With signal flags draped about as protection from the breeze, and with soft lights shining from its tall windows, it affords unsurpassed surroundings for an informal reception. Here it is that many Halifax people are privileged to make acquaintance with new arrivals among our Naval Officers ordered here for duty.

Let's delve back a bit into the history of this building, which in appearance speaks to us of a Halifax of other days. It speaks to us of the time when only Royal Navy ships were here. It carries us to the days before the Royal Canadian Navy came into being. We always welcome our friends of the Royal Navy to this port which has known it so well and favourably in the days gone by. Nowadays, we also take pride in the growing sea strength of our own Dominion, and we have every reason for pride in the brilliancy and daring of many of its exploits and the efficient way in which it is carrying out, day in and day out, the many tasks that fall to its lot.

Admiralty House is a familiar sight to all Haligonians. It stands just east of Gottingen Street, a little north of North Street. We have all viewed it often. We have seen it standing there, framed by the entrance gates that provide a break in the high wall. Before it is the circular greenness of its well-kept lawn. This lawn is now adorned with the memorial which recalls the heroic battle of H.M.S. *Shannon* and victory over the *Chesapeake*. No need to repeat that story. It is known to us all, of how the *Shannon* led her prize into the harbour, under the command of Lieutenant Wallis, after having defeated her in a short but fierce encounter off Boston, and how the United States commander was fatally wounded and the British Commander Broke also severely wounded.

Records tell us that Admiralty House was begun in 1814, but was not completed for a few years after that. I have been told that there was really a predecessor of this Admiralty House in the 1760's, but which was destroyed by fire. In any event we are concerned with the present structure.

Aikens, that well versed Halifax historian, tells us that in the spring of 1814, it was decided that a fitting residence for the British Admiral on the station should be erected. The British Parliament granted three thousand pounds for the purpose. But this amount was found to be insufficient. The House of Assembly of the Province of Nova Scotia stepped into the breach. From the treasury of Nova Scotia a further sum of fifteen hundred pounds was voted to make possible the completion of the large structure.

The site between the Naval Hospital grounds and Gottingen Street was selected and the present building known as the Admiralty House then commenced. Lacking the modern facilities for speedy construction, Aikens recalls the work was slowly progressing during the summer and autumn and completion came some time later.

He comments: "Why the local funds of the Province should have been devoted to this purpose does not clearly appear."

There is, at the building of the Nova Scotia Archives, an interesting map of Ward Six, which was printed in 1878. It shows the grounds, the stables, gardener's cottage, etc. In this map there is shown a pond from which ran a stream which apparently terminated at Barrington Street.

Originally in possession of the late Harry Piers, curator of the Provincial Museum, there are many notations on the map in his hand-writing. These give added information on "Ad. House." He records that it was the scene of a ball for Prince Alfred in 1861. It is set down that the Marquis of Lorne and Princess Louise had been guests there, making it their temporary home, while in the city in November, 1878. Mr. Piers has noted on the map's margin that the final sale of furniture at Admiralty House and the Naval Hospital took place on January 3, 1905, a time within memory of many.

Admiralty House grounds, in more recent years, was taken to mean the then vacant field to the south of the building and adjacent to the garden. Many sporting events took place there through the years. Then came its useful service as the North End Supervised Playgrounds. But all this is past now. Today the "field" is covered with permanent and temporary buildings to meet the new needs of the service. Canada's Navy has found the site an important aid in providing needed facilities here.

They had a big task at Admiralty House during the War. It's no simple matter to provide the number of meals required daily for officers who dined there. Few hotels had such a number of meals to prepare. Perhaps the wonder is much greater when you consider the size of the kitchen. Really it is not much larger in size than those found in some private residences. Yet, from this kitchen an average total of six hundred meals were served daily. For breakfast some one hundred and twenty-five hungry officers turned up. Lunch offered the biggest call on the menu. At that time three hundred meals were served. This means that diners had to turn up in some six or seven shifts and it did not allow for leisurely meals. Little time could be spent at the tables in polite conversation. For that matter, the officers of our Royal Canadian Navy would hardly have had much time away from duty for such a conventional pastime at the mid-day hour. For supper the number on hand was a bit smaller.

At that time there was an average of some two hundred diners.

The kitchen is modernly equipped with various aids to the busy cooks in the white garb of their calling. It has a tiled floor and is well lighted, for at another period in the history of the Admiralty House, the kitchen was a surgical operating room. That was the time when it was headquarters for the Massachusetts-Halifax Relief Commission. That colourful period of history came in the wake of the Halifax Explosion of 1917. The people of Massachussets responded nobly to the need for outside help. Without hesitation they sent medical and other aid. Then, from the generosity of their giving, they were able to help through the years in improving the general health of the city in the time of restoration. During those days "Ad. House" was a modernly equipped and efficiently administered health clinic. This time of warm-hearted help would in itself make a story worthy of full description, but we are more concerned today about the link with the naval service.

Admiralty House boasts possession of some handsome pieces of silverware. They all have a history. Each is worthy of individual study. We cannot give a comprehensive review. We can merely look at some of the handsome pieces that decorate the centre of the mess tables or are given places of honour on the mantels. Some of these pieces came to "Ad. House" from the familiar old H.M.C.S. *Niobe*. Halifax will always have a warm place in its heart for that staunch old warship. She had an important place in the earlier days of Canada's Navy. When her sea-going days were over, she was moored at the Dockyard and there, her lines marred by temporary superstructure, served as a naval headquarters. She was there when the explosion swept its devastating course close to her mooring place.

Some others bear inscriptions dealing with the naval ship *Dominion*, now but a memory. One was presented by the Department of Marine and Fisheries. It was in recognition of a particular service. It was aboard the Canadian ship

Dominion that the body of Minister of Fisheries PreFontaine was borne from Cherbourg, France to Halifax in 1906. There are some particularly handsome candelabra which add to the dignity of the tables.

One of the decorations that will dwell in memory of the visitor is a striking picture of one of Canada's new type of fighting craft. New, to the extent that it was developed to meet the needs of the Second World War. It is a striking scene of a Corvette at sea. It was painted by a naval man during his stay in Halifax. Sub-Lieutenant Bailey is now on another station. But he will not be forgotten by residents at "Ad. House" or visitors there. The product of his talented brush has a place of honour by the main stairway.

"Ad. House" meeting the call of the present, speaks of the past. You get an immediate feeling of years gone by when you stand in its gracefully designed lobby. You can readily picture it as the gracious home of the British Admiral. You can easily picture carriages, drawn by prancing steeds, rolling up to its entrance. From the carriages would step the ladies invited to share in some social event of moment. Its spacious, high-ceilinged rooms, speak of scenes of hospitality.

Admiralty House has so much personality and dignity. It is made of stone, but its walls are not cold looking. It seems to breathe hospitality. Its high walls seem to shut out the world. Even new construction close at hand cannot rob it of its charm; and it still has its garden filled with bright bloom to the south. Admiralty House along with Province House and Government House bespeak a grandeur of building seldom found in our age. They contribute much to Historic Halifax, and must be preserved at all costs.

XII

SAINT PAUL'S

A Venerable Landmark

No city in Canada can boast of more interesting places of
worship. Many can point to the magnificence of their church
buildings, but for historic charm, Halifax ranks as the top.
These churches of Halifax have become more than mere
buildings—they are truly venerable Canadian landmarks.

Of course, the dean of them all, is old Saint Paul's, with
its central position adjoining bustling Barrington Street, the
city's main business thoroughfare. There is the Round
Church, St. George's at the corner of Brunswick and Cornwallis Street, which gains note from its truly unique form
of architecture. Then, but a little further north on Bruns-

wick Street, at the corner of Gerrish, is the quaint picturesque little Dutch Church, standing in its tiny Garden of Sleep, where rest the bones of a number of the city's earlier settlers. On Spring Garden Road stands imposing St. Mary's Cathedral, on the site of the earlier St. Peter's, and almost opposite, on Barrington Street, is St. Matthew's.

For those who like to dig out the facts and delight in things that hold an inspiring link with our past, there are many afternoons of interest to be found in visits to any one of these. Not just a casual visit of a few minutes' duration, but more lengthy stays in which the inscriptions on tablets within, or on gravestones outside, may be read. There are the moments of speculation, in which the imaginative may build up stories in their own fancy of the lives that were lived in the Halifax of the long ago.

We cannot hope to visit all the churches of Halifax in a single jaunt.

It is fitting that a visit be paid to the first church built in Halifax, St. Paul's. We have all seen it standing there in its impressiveness, with its unusual tower, facing the Grand Parade. Go inside, and if you are wise, pick an hour when slanting rays of the sun will come through its stained glass memorial windows. It is then that the old church seems to take on a greatly added charm.

Move about, taking time to read the inscriptions on the tablets that abound, and there are few that do not give stories that fascinate, that bring up pictures from the past. So much has been written about this church of royal foundation of the time of King George the Second of England, that there is naturally a feeling of bewilderment to know on what to touch in a brief visit. However, the facts that we may learn in passing, will unquestionably whet the appetite. Then, from the interesting pamphlet available at the church, a more complete history can be gained. Many of you, may have heard me refer to old St. Paul's when I had the honour of speaking for the Maritime Provinces of Canada, on the first around-the-world British Broadcast on Christmas Day, 1932, the first occasion we heard the late King George V speak from his fireside to the Empire. On that day I referred to the service at Saint Paul's.

It is a matter of history, often recounted, that the first settlers of Halifax arrived in the Harbour of Chebucto on June 21st, in the year of our Lord 1749. The fleet containing the adventurers consisted of thirteen transports, and a sloop of war, named the *Sphinx,* on board which ship was Colonel the Hon. Edward Cornwallis, M.P., who was in command of the expedition.

According to the Reverend Doctor George W. Hill, who wrote a history of St. Paul's in 1879, "Among the names of those recorded as intending settlers are Mr. Anwyl, clergyman, John Baptiste Moreau, gentleman and schoolmaster." Shortly afterwards—probably in the month of July—the Rev. William Tutty of Emmanuel College, Cambridge, arrived at the newly formed town called Halifax, in compliment to George Montague, Earl of Halifax, then presiding over the Board of Trade and Plantations. These three gentlemen were sent out with the expedition for the purpose of establishing the Church of Christ in this new country. When the representative of the King of England raised the Royal Standard, these ambassadors of Christ were at the same time to unfurl the banner of the King of kings. These missionaries at once set about their duties, holding divine service and preaching on the old parade ground amid the felled trees and roughly made huts of the settlers. They were assisted in their work by Mr. Edward Halhead who opened a school and taught the children. The official record of the first and great missionary society of England—the Society for the Propagation of the Gospel in Foreign Parts—has the following minutes written soon after the publication of the document relative to the settlement in Nova Scotia, issued by the Lords Commissioners for Trade and Plantations:

The Society soon after appointed the Reverend Mr. Tutty and Mr. Anwyl to be their Missionaries and Mr. Halhead to

be their schoolmaster, to go with the first settlers from Great
Britain to Nova Scotia, that Mr. Tutty is fixed minister in
the first settlement, viz.: in the town of Halifax, which is
already become populous, and that Mr. Tutty behaved
very properly and is very useful in his station.   But the
Society being not so well satisfied with the conduct of Mr.
Anwyl, they have recalled him from Nova Scotia and they
have appointed Mr. Moreau, a worthy clergyman of French
extraction, to a settlement now forming, which is chiefly to
be composed of French Protestants.

The salaries of the two clergymen were seventy pounds
sterling each, and that of the schoolmaster, fifteen pounds.

They had not long been landed, when the surveyors who
accompanied the expedition were set to their work of laying
out the town, and among the directions given to them, was
that of apportioning a square or block for the site of a church.
There was difficulty in obtaining a suitable frame for such
a building as was required, and as a necessary consequence,
orders were sent to Massachusetts for it.   In a letter of
Governor Cornwallis', dated March 19, 1750, he says, "I
expect the frame of the church will be here next month, from
New England.   The plan is the same with that of Marylebone Chapel."   A few months later it is stated that "The
Church then setting up would cost one thousand pounds, by
the estimate sent from Boston."   There can, of course, be no
doubt that Governor Cornwallis was stating a fact when he
wrote respecting the plan of the church; but it cannot be
doubted that St. Paul's Church, as it was until 1812, was
identical in architecture and size, and even in the most
minute particulars, such as the size of the panes of glass, with
St. Peter's, of London.   Bishop John Inglis, D.D., son of the
Rt. Rev. Charles Inglis, first Bishop appointed to an English
Colony, was accustomed to relate that the plans for St. Paul's
were the same as those used in the construction of St. Peter's,
which was built at the expense of the British Government.
The only way by which to reconcile the statements of

Governor Cornwallis and the Bishop is that a number of Churches were built about or a little previous to, the middle of the eighteenth century, under the direction of the Bishop of London and the funds drawn out of the public exchequer; but in order to save unnecessary expenditure, one plan served for several buildings, and the Board of Trade and Plantations sent the Governor a copy of this. An observant person will see at least half a dozen churches in London which he will instantly recognize as being closely allied to St. Paul's, Halifax.

Whether the actual working plan was that on which Marylebone Chapel or St. Peter's was built, the vigorous efforts which were made, succeeded and on the second of September, 1750, the church was formally opened for divine service by the appointed minister, the Rev. William Tutty, who says in a letter subsequent to this date (October 29, 1750), that "the number of inhabitants, not including the soldiery, is four thousand, and that the church, when completed, will be a very handsome structure."

In 1758, the town having become to a certain extent, settled, it was deemed advisable to follow the examples of the old country and form a parish with all the essential features of boundary lines and a corporate body of wardens and vestrymen. This was done by an order-in-council in 1759, just ten years after the settlement of Halifax, and the name given to it was the "Parish of St. Paul." In the autumn of that year, the first vestry meeting was held, October 10th, on which occasion the ordinary custom of appointing church wardens as in England was adopted, the clergyman nominating one and the parishioners the other. The first record made runs thus: "The Rev. John Breynton and the Rev. Thomas Wood, Vicar, having nominated Richard Bulkeley, Esq., as a fit person to serve as church warden for the ensuing year, the parishioners then present made choice of William Nesbit, Esq., for the other church warden to serve for the ensuing year—and the said parishioners then present hereunto prescribed their names." At a meeting of the corporation held on April 7th, of the following year, a sum of £30 was assessed on the inhabitants of the parish "for providing church elements, paying for surplices and fencing in the New Burying Ground."

The ground here referred to was that long used and known as the "Poor House Burial Ground," situate on the north of Spring Garden Road and West of Grafton Street. This term "new" implies that there had existed another ground which had been used for the burial of the dead, and certain documents now in the Archives of St. Paul's prove beyond doubt that such ground was that which lies on the west side of Barrington Street, opposite the present Government House and Church of St. Matthew being distinctly referred to in the grant as the "old burying ground" and also so entitled on the plan attached. Why at this particular juncture a new lot should have been taken up to be used as a cemetery, it is difficult to say, though one might conjecture with some show of plausibility that the old ground being outside the picket fence which enclosed the town, it was exposed to the Indians who might do dishonour to the dead, and with whom the final treaty had not yet been made. Hence a safer place of repose was selected and used for a time, though from the dates on the monuments in the old ground it could not have been for long.

Dr. G. W. Hill, in his history of St. Paul's Church, written in 1878, says:

On the following year (1763), Mr. Breynton subscribed to the fund being raised for the purchase of an organ, and although there is no written document by which to prove it, the instrument was obtained and put up in the church sometime during the year 1765, for a minute of proceedings of the next year shows that the organ was in its place, having been erected by a Mr. Evans who, by the way, had to be paid for his services with borrowed money. There is a tradition relative to this instrument that a Spanish ship, on her way to South America, was brought into harbour as a prize, and that among the articles composing her cargo was an organ made of excellent material, having a solid mahogany frame of chaste design, on its way to a Roman Catholic Chapel. The organ, as the other goods on board, was offered for sale and the church wardens of St. Paul's became its purchasers. The instrument did good and faithful service for many years, lasting until the year 1841, when a new one was brought from England and took its place in the old frame. This remained in St. Paul's until 1873, when it was purchased by a member of the congregation and put up in Trinity Church, which had a short time before become the property of St. Paul's corporation.

An interesting and amusing item from the minutes of a vestry meeting, held some time in 1770, in reference to the organist of that period is worth repeating.

It read as follows:

(1770) Voted, that whereas also the organist discovers a light mind in the several tunes he plays, called voluntaries, to the great offence of the Congregation and tending to dis-' turb rather than promote true devotion. Therefore he be directed for the future to make a choice of such Tunes as are solemn and Fitting Divine Worship in such his Voluntaries, and that he also for the future be directed to play the Psalm Tunes in a plain familiar manner without unnecessary Graces.

It would appear that this remonstrance had the desired effect and that Mr. Viere Warner restrained his wishes to indulge in unedifying music, for his services were continued for another year.

Just before one walks inside St. Paul's, one should stand on the steps for a few moments, in the same place where the city founders met to pray for strength to meet the hardships and problems they encountered in a new land in which they were cast in the rôle of Empire builders. As one stands there, the words that so fittingly came from the pen of Arthur Wentworth Eaton about our St. Paul's are brought to mind.

Timbered in times when men built strong,
With a tower of wood grown grey,
The frame of it old, the heart, still young,
It has stood for many a day.

If one wants proof of the strength lovingly put into this early house of God, one only has to walk to the hall of the Western entrance to the church, and there proof is given. When some few years ago, it became necessary to replace certain sills and flooring, a section of the great timbers was saved, and placed there, leaving evidence of this strength. There it can be seen, with its porticoes, for spikes were not as easily securable then, and builders resorted to other practices.

The first Church of England Service was held on June 21, 1749, at the city's founding and in that year work was started on St. Paul's, which did not entirely have its present day appearance when it was opened for Divine service on September 2, 1750, for some parts were added later as needs imposed called for greater space.

Many visitors from all parts of Canada, even as far distant as the Pacific coast, may well have heard of old St. Paul's, for it bears the proud distinction of being the first Protestant Church in Canada, and earlier in its history was a Cathedral church. It is recorded that the names of some of the greatest Naval and Military heroes in the annals of the British Empire, and some of its most famous regiments are associated with St. Paul's. Just within the entry, by the great metal memorial doors, bearing names of heroes of the First Great War, and also serving as a reminder of a late rector, the Rev. Archdeacon Armitage. There, stands an historic tomb stone, removed for preservation from St. Paul's Cemetery. It is linked with the great sea incident of the *Chesapeake* and

Shannon, and will hold particular interest for the boys of the Navy.

Beneath this church built originally of pine and oak brought from Boston, are the graves of over a score of early settlers, some of them men of particular note. To list them is too exhaustive, but all are recorded in the history of the church. High in the entry is a piece of metal, driven through the wall and left as a reminder of the devasting force of the terrible Halifax explosion of December 6, 1917. There is the Governor's pew to be seen, with its coat-of-arms, and in it, have sat many royal personages.

In the west gallery is the unique "Explosion Window," also a relic of Halifax's disaster of the First Great War, the shattered glass leaving in silhouette the head of a man, and said to bear striking resemblance to one of the earlier ministers of the church.

In the clergy vestry of old Saint Paul's Church, just to the East of the chancel, there is a profusion of pictures, and in a glass case are books and other historic objects of great rarity and much interest.

At the south end of the West wall will be found the pictures of the first Rector, the Rev. John Breynton, D.D., who was appointed in 1752. It is recalled that he went to England on sick leave, and finally, after being called upon to make some intimation of his plan, sent in his resignation.

Next on the wall, immediately above is his successor, Rev. Robert Stanser, who was rector for a number of years. He later became the second Bishop of Nova Scotia, a rôle which he held for seven years. He retired from the office of Bishop, due to ill health, and this only came after he had long sought that right. During his time as Bishop he only visited the Episcopacy twice, due to the difficulty in travel. It is sad to recall that while he was rector his wife was fatally burned in a fire which damaged the rectory just across from the church on Argyle Street.

Next picture in the cycle on the wall is the Right Reverend John Inglis, who later became Bishop of the

Diocese. He, too, was first, rector of Saint Paul's, succeeding the Rev. Robert Stanser. He also succeeded him in the office of Bishop.

The fourth to occupy the post of rector of Saint Paul's next in the line of pictures on the wall, is Archdeacon Willis, who was named by the Colonial Office to take over the spiritual leadership of the parish. At the time he was Rector of Trinity Church in Saint John. The congregation had very largely placed their heart on the appointment of the curate at that time, and they sent an appeal to the Colonial Office asking that the curate be given the rectorship. But with the Colonial Office committed to the previous appointment no change was made. As a result there was a cleavage in the congregation, and quite a few seceded to the Baptist Church. They went over to Salem Church, which building was for years part of the Orpheus Theatre, and which congregation gave rise to the First Baptist Church congregation in the city today.

The fifth rector's picture is that of the Rev. George Hill, D.D., who was rector from 1865 and 1885. He was very prominent in the city and was Chaplain of the House of Assembly, and was Chancellor of Dalhousie College. His experience was exceptional for that time, in that he had been born in the parish, was christened, confirmed, ordained deacon and married in St. Paul's. The historic old church was also the one in which he saw service as curate, before later being advanced to the rôle of rector. The full length photo shows him in the gown which was then always worn in preaching. Another great preacher and outstanding pulpit orator in the person of the Rev. Charles Hole, D.D., was rector for three years, commencing his rectorship in 1886. It was during his career that he showed a somewhat mechanical turn of mind, so he had the pulpit put on wheels. It was thus possible to push it to the centre of the chancel before he mounted to deliver his sermon. In this way he was able to get a view of those seated in the gallery, which he could not do when the pulpit was placed in a stationary position at one side of the chancel. The late Doctor Savary used to tell an amusing story of the occasion when the Reverend Mr. LeMoyne, late rector of St. Mark's, was about to preach a sermon in St. Paul's in his younger days, suddenly he felt the pulpit moving across the aisle. He had not been told of the mechanical arrangement. He hung on to the pulpit rail for dear life and while he eventually discovered the sexton pushing the pulpit into its place, and recovered his composure, the congregation never did, so amused were they at his apparent alarm.

The next picture brings us down to what may be considered as fairly modern history, and is that of Rev. Dyson Hague, who became Rector in 1890 and remained as rector for seven years, later going to Toronto to become professor of Liturgy at Wycliffe College.

The last picture of the series on the wall is that of Archdeacon Armitage, who was rector of Saint Paul's for thirty-two years, having assumed the office in 1897, and gave outstanding service, which is well recalled by many members of the congregation.

With the death in 1948 of the Reverend Doctor Savary, another photograph is added to the long line of outstanding men who have served this famous church as its rectors, Doctor Savary would point with pride to this small room, which he declared was the most historic clergy vestry in Canada. Of special interest to this good man, which he always pointed out, was a picture, dedicated to the George Dunk, Earl of Halifax, and it shows Saint Paul's very prominently, along with the palisades, Government House, and soldiers drilling on the Grand Parade. The details are very fine and for the student of Halifax's past, it shows how the settlement, or that immediate part of it at least, looked in the year 1761.

At that time the two entrance doors of the church were apparently at the south end, and it was long before the present chancel was erected. The picture shows the original tower, which later had a successor.

Another picture shows Saint Paul's and part of Halifax in

1777, as viewed from Hollis and George Streets. It shows the Governor's residence, and at the extreme south, Mather's meeting house, where the Eastern Trust Building now stands. Mather's, as you will recall, was the forerunner of Saint Matthew's Church of today.

There is much detail of interest in this picture for it shows the town pump on George Street, and the cruder methods of lighting the streets in those days, with lights erected on posts about six feet high. There are the citizens to be seen moving along the street in their long coats and some using unusual types of conveyances, a far cry from the modern motor vehicles that travel our streets today.

Below the pictures of the rectors, on the west wall of the vestry, are a number of interesting framed documents. Particularly appealing is one dated September 21, 1773. It is directed to the Reverend Doctor Brynton and it reads, "The bearer, John Monagle, has applied for licence to marry Dorothea Wranford, and has gone through all the necessary forms in this office and nothing remains to prevent the marriage of the parties." It is signed as follows, "I am, Reverend Sir, Your most obedient, humble servant, Richard Bulkeley." Bulkeley was the first Provincial Secretary, and the first Church Warden and Organist of Saint Paul's Church. His home was just south of the church, where the Carleton Hotel stands today, and where the Admiralty Court was early held.

Among the interesting papers on the wall is a photostatic copy of the document which makes Saint Paul's a church of royal foundation and exempt jurisdiction. The special words of interest are these. "Whereas His Majesty has been pleased to grant lands in glebe for the endowment of the said church, and the support of the incumbents of the same, and a minister and vicar having been inducted into the said church, by virtue of His Majesty's royal instructions, and the said glebe lands being insufficient for the support and maintenance of the said incumbents according to the intention of the royal founder of such church, and the said church having become a Royal Foundation and of Exempt Jurisdiction, and the right of further endowing the said church being vested in His Majesty or the Governor of this Province" . . . it then goes on to set down details of the glebe lands, much of which are still in the possession of the church, and which from time to time, some sale is made and an endowment fund being gradually built up.

While this distinction of being of exempt jurisdiction is enjoyed by no other church outside the motherland, it has no legal bearing today, for when a bishop was appointed for this diocese, and the parish no longer considered within the Diocese of London, it lost its special privileges. It was dated on January 7th, in the thirty-third year of the reign of Our Sovereign Lord George the Second, by the Grace of God of Great Britain, France and Ireland, King Defender of the Faith, and in the year of our Lord one thousand, seven hundred and sixty. It was signed by Charles Lawrence, Governor, and Richard Bulkeley, Secretary, and by John Breynton, Rector, Thomas Wood, Vicar and William Nesbitt and Richard Bulkeley, as church wardens.

Further along the wall is another original wedding licence, and is of outstanding interest, for it was given by Frantz Karl Erdman de Seitz, Colonel of the Hessian Infantry, and "Chef" [sic], over a regiment, giving leave to Corporal Hermann Guttberlet, of Major de Schallern's "compagny," after he had paid eight dollars to the 'Charity House in Hessen, to marry Miss Anna Elizabeth Schuhard, daugher of Sergeant Schuhard.

It was written on May 20, 1780, and ends as follows: "Signed and wrote by my own hand in Halifax," and then appears the signature of the baron. And there is also a receipt bearing the signature of another officer showing that the required eight dollars had been paid. It is interesting to note that the term dollar is used, instead of the pounds then in use by the British, for the Hessians used the dollar as a form of currency at that time.

As is well known, Baron de Seitz is buried under Saint

Paul's Church, in one of the more than score of burial vaults there. He was buried with an orange clutched in his hand, which signified that he was last of his line. His memorial hatchment is on the gallery of the church at the north end.

Two other licences adorn the wall, one being dated 1784, and is apparently one of the earliest printed forms. It is given by John Parr, termed His Excellency, Captain General and Governor in and for the Province of Nova Scotia and its dependencies. It is a licence for the marriage of Titus Smith and Leddy Bartow.

The next one was issued by Sir John Harvey, His Excellency and Lieutenant-General Knight Commander of the Most Honourable Military Order of the Bath, Knight Commander of the Royal Hanoverian Guelphic Order, Lieut.-Governor, Commander, etc., and is directed to Rev. George William Hill, then rector of Saint Paul's, who is thus given the right to marry Emma Almon, and is dated September 14, 1849, and is signed by Joseph Howe, then Provincial Secretary.

Along the walls are a great number of interesting pictures, engravings of other clergy early associated with the parish, often in the rôle of vicar, which is much the same as the office of Curate today. Many of them are shown wearing the mammoth wigs affected in their periods.

The earliest of the pictures of the church's interiors which is possessed, shows it before the chancel was built, and reveals a railing across the front of where the chancel is today, with prayer desk and lectern combined, standing in the same position as the present prayer desk. It also shows the pulpit erected on a single post, and entered by stairs of a dozen or more steps on the congregation side of the church. Included in the view is the Governor's pew and the bishop's pew at the front of the respective aisles, and it is worthy to note that the governor had an armchair in which to sit with ease, but no prayer desk. While on the opposite site the bishop was provided with a prayer desk and no armchair—a distinction between church and state.

The picture also shows Archdeacon Willis, then Rector, and Rev. George Hill, the curate, and was taken between 1857 and 1865. Included in the picture are A. M. Uniacke and Mrs. Uniacke, Honourable P. C. Hill and Mrs. Hill, and Mr. Keefler, the Sexton.

There is in the vestry the Verger's staff of heavy oak, of over five and a half feet, surmounted with silver top. This was always carried before the rector when he entered the church for service, and as he left. It was used for many years and reference is made to the presence of the staff in accounts of services appearing in early services. It was not used for many years until the visit of the Archbishop of Canterbury, when it was taken from the Vestry and used in the procession.

Other pictures abound of a number of clergy who had in various capacities been connected with the life of this historic old church.

Pointing to the northeast corner of the room, the late Doctor Savary would say, "I call this my Royal Foundation Corner where there are framed pictures of King George the First, King George the Second, the Royal Founder of Saint Paul's, and George the Third who presented the Prayer Book to Bishop Inglis, and which is preserved in the bookcase in the Vestry, and King George the Fourth.

There are also pictures of Edward Duke of Kent and the Duchess of Kent, the Duke having attended services in Saint Paul's during the time he was stationed here. There is also a picture of Prince's Lodge as it appeared in the days of its splendour.

Along the east wall one finds a picture of King Edward the Seventh, who visited Halifax in 1860, George the Fifth, who worshipped in Saint Paul's many times when in command of H.M.S. *Thrush*. One of the former churchwardens has passed on the story how Prince George often came in a few minutes late, in order to escape having to proceed up to the Governor's pew, though the right place for such royalty, and would instead ask permission to slip unobtrusively into one of the rear pews.

There is an illustration from the London press, showing the arch erected in vicinity of Saint Paul's hill, and spanning Barrington Street, on the occasion of the visit of Edward, Prince of Wales, later Edward the Seventh, and it shows Saint Paul's tower, with flags fastened on the four corners. Children were massed on a series of raised seats on the Parade.

Just above, in this corner of this historic room, is what the rector calls the Bishop's section, and there appear pictures of all the bishops from the first, Charles Inglis, right up to modern times, just awaiting the addition of the present Bishop, Rt. Rev. George Frederick Kingston. There is an interesting water colour sketch of Saint Paul's Church, dated 1840. In the foreground are the different costumes worn by people of that era.

In what is called the Washington corner is included a photograph of the stone commemorating Major General Robert Ross, which stands over his last resting place in Saint Paul's Cemetery, and there is a copy of a picture of the man himself, and other pictures linked with his memory.

It was on September 29, 1814, that the burial of Ross took place. The stone tells how after having distinguished himself in all ranks as an officer in Egypt, Italy, Portugal, Spain, France and America, he was killed at the commencement of an action which terminated in the defeat and rout of the troops of the United States near Baltimore on September 12, 1814. At Ross Trevor, the seat of the family in Ireland, a monument, termed more worthy of his memory, has been erected, and a picture of that more impressive memorial also adorns the vestry wall. It is noted in the inscription that under his conduct, his force attacked and dispersed the Americans at Bladensburg on August the 24th, shortly before date of his death, and the same day victoriously entered Washington, the capital of the United States.

There is an interesting glass-covered case on the south

side of the little room, and within it are a variety of highly significant and interesting articles. One of these is a book. for direction of services, and bears the date 1852 on its bound cover. The inscription there informs that it was presented by the Lord Bishop and that the gift was made to Saint Paul's Cathedral, Halifax, Nova Scotia—in the time when Saint Paul's was the cathedral church. In fact there are a number of other highly interesting books in that display case, as well as in the vestry's bookcase. They are of great age, and have interesting stories linked with them.

Everywhere one looks in Saint Paul's can be found something of interest, something that speaks of bygone days in Halifax.

The Colours of Halifax Regiments, the Hatchments of men famous in the early history of Halifax, tablets and stained glass windows dating back to the very beginning of the town.

Saint Paul's Church, as the dean of all churches in Halifax, is truly a venerable landmark.

XIII

THE PENALTIES OF WAR

The Halifax Explosions of 1917 and 1945

To every Haligonian of about forty years of age or more, two outstanding dates, in the City's History are indelibly marked on his or her memory.

The two dates are December 6, 1917, and July 18, 1945. These are the two days on which Halifax paid the price of being Canada's chief port of export of supplies of war in two great wars.

Both conflicts have left their ugly scars on the loyal old garrison town and Haligonians, more than any other citizens in North America, know the meaning of war. Thousands of them carry scars received in the explosion of some four thousand tons of T.N.T. on that cold December day of 1917. Those who had gone through the first explosion, while spared the physical injuries, through the grace of God on the occasion of the second explosion at the conclusion of the Second

Great War, suffered mental torture for nearly twenty-four hours, such as no other group in North America has been called upon to undergo in our generation.

Many a Haligonian performed deeds of valour of which no official record or ribbon of service is witness for, nevertheless their splendid behaviour will forever remain with those who were privileged to know Haligonians and Halifax in its most tragic hours.

December 6, 1917, started off as a beautiful clear wintry Thursday morning. Not a cloud in the sky. Every Haligonian who went through that day has his or her own memory of it, and can only relate the story from one person's viewpoint. With this in mind I ask the indulgence of my fellow-citizens for any variance with their views in relation to any particular detail after a lapse of so many years.

On December 6, 1917, I was stationed in one of the out-forts, some few miles down toward the mouth of the harbour, and for this reason did not go through the horrible experience of those who were right in the city, especially the North End which got the full benefit of the blast. My location did, however, give me a view of the cloud of smoke which rose so high into the heavens that the top could not be seen. This cloud of smoke caused by the explosion of roughly four thousand tons of T.N.T. rolled and rolled, up and up it seemed for a never ending time. I also had a first hand view of the destruction, when I was ordered immediately to proceed with the troops to Campbell Road to try and clear the road through to Africville.

Early that morning among the ships that came into the harbour and proceeded up towards the North End was a French vessel painted a sombre war-time grey. She was the ammunition ship *Mont Blanc*, from New York, loaded with picric acid, benzol and T.N.T. Slowly she wended her way up the harbour and as she was going north, another ship, the *Imo*, a Belgian relief ship was outward bound from Bedford Basin. Carefully the *Mont Blanc* pilot guided the dangerous vessel up the east shore, when he sighted the

other ship approaching him, obviously headed southward
for the open sea. The pilot gave one blast on his siren to
indicate that he was going to starboard. For some unknown
reason the *Imo* came on. The *Mont Blanc* veered and
blasted wildly a second time but the *Imo* apparently misun-
derstood and steered closer still, until directly opposite Richmond, both pilots with the imminence of collision staring
them in the face, rang for reversed engines, but it was too
late. The *Imo* rammed her bow into the *Mont Blanc* amid-
ships and burst drums of benzol on deck, which immediately caught fire. Great shooting chemical-fed flames leaped
toward the sky. The crew of the *Mont Blanc*, knowing their
cargo, abandoned ship in disorder and in their boats made
for the Dartmouth shore with all dispatch. The *Imo* slid
clear and stood by. It was only a few minutes before nine
when the helpless, abandoned *Mont Blanc*, with no hand to
guide her and no voice to give desperate warning, drifted
in the prevailing current toward Pier 9 on the Halifax shore.

At this very time, office workers were making for the
centre of the city, while thousands of innocent, light-hearted
children were making their way to school, many of them to
schools within sight of the burning ship, which attracted
much attention. The Halifax fire department prepared for
action. Fire fighters with their fire fighting apparatus raced
north and took up their position on a wharf nearest the
ship to await the opportunity to help put the fire out, when
the ship might be brought within their reach. There was no
fire boat available then.

The British cruiser *Highflyer* was anchored in the stream
and sizing up the situation in a matter of minutes, a party of
these brave sailors boarded the burning ship with the idea
of taking control of her if possible and putting down the fire.
No braver men ever lived than these British sailors who must
have known they were going to almost certain death. Hardly
had they got aboard when the town clock boomed the hour
of nine, business men settled behind their desks, school bells
rang, industry hummed. The sailors worked like Trojans try-

ing to gain control. To the north the crew of the *Mont Blanc* beached their boats and made for the Dartmouth woods. The *Imo* grounded off the Dartmouth shore. On the wharf the terror-stricken attendants of the fire engine, now fully aware of impending disaster, frantically signalled for help. But Halifax was beyond human aid. At 9.06 the *Mont Blanc* gave a mighty roar, as the fire on her deck burst its confines and ignited the deadly explosives within her hold. With an ear-splitting, screeching explosion, the great ship disappeared. The devastating blast mounted unleashed, roar upon roar, mile upon mile, picked up by the vacuum-pocketed air, a mighty thunder building upon itself during what seemed an endless time, but was only a matter of seconds. Never will we forget that oily looking cloud rolling ever upward into the blue of the sky.

Hundreds of tons of shattered brick and stone, timber and metal bombarded the devastated area for blocks, and the entire north end of Halifax, some two and a half square miles, was reduced to twisted wreckage such as can be scarcely described. The gigantic blast had raised a tidal wave in the harbour which drove up over the Intercolonial tracks sweeping away to destruction loaded freight cars, passenger cars and locomotives. The North Street Railway station was a complete wreck. Where a few minutes before a fine building stood, now nothing but wreckage remained. Everywhere could be seen homes wrecked and on fire. The blast killed every man above deck on the relief ship *Imo*. Buildings choked thoroughfares, and fire burst out in all its horror to consume what little remained. To give some idea of the force let loose, reports were received of windows being badly shaken in Truro, some sixty miles away. The anchor of the *Mont Blanc* landed at Edmonds Grounds across the North West Arm, about three or four miles distant, and the gun off the stern landed in Albro's Lake about three miles in the opposite direction, its nose cut off as if by a gigantic knife.

Every conceivable variety of vehicle was pressed into

service to transport the sick and wounded. They staggered through the streets over wreckage and impediments of every description, including tons of glass blown everywhere by the concussion. Stores were forsaken, homes deserted and open spaces crowded with refugees. Troops were immediately dispatched bent on rescue work, and well do many of them marching north remember the scenes and rumours of further explosions to come from those going south, for safer regions than the devastated north end. It must be said here and now that the people were wonderful. Once they saw the troops going north, they joined in rescue work and while they did not have the advantage of organized disciplined soldiers, thousands of civilians did heroic work and saved many of their fellow citizens through the day and all that night. All day long the troops marched and worked to make a road from the Railway Station to the wharf, where the brave firemen died, and generally cleared a passage for traffic, so that some semblance of order was restored along Campbell Road, the hardest hit section. So the hours passed and grim darkness approached, the still-burning wrecks of houses appearing like so many bonfires all over the hill, which that morning had been most thickly populated. To describe the scenes of the dead and wounded at this time would serve no useful purpose, and only bring sorrow and sadness to many Haligonians. Yes, Haligonians know all about the horrors of war and what T.N.T. can do, and no person of thirty-five years of age in this city needed any coaxing to join the A.R.P. or other services during the last war. They knew how important organized relief can be in the event of an emergency. If Halifax had had an A.R.P. organization in the first war, such as they had and were so proud of, in the second world war, many, many lives might have been saved.

Word of the horrible Halifax disaster was flashed to the North American continent on one solitary telegraph wire which the explosion had not destroyed. The lone telegraph operator at Richmond died a hero's death. He stuck to his post and sent calls for help to the last moment of life. Every means of communication—telephone, road, railway and wireless—had been blasted from the face of the earth in that one awful moment. The news reached the adjoining New England city of Boston and in a space of hours a relief train was organized. Doctors, nurses, workers of every type and description volunteered and were hurriedly enlisted. Thousands of panes of glass, hundreds of pounds of putty and a small army of expert glaziers journeyed north to protect the survivors of the Halifax disaster from the cruel winter winds. Special trains simultaneously left from Moncton, Truro and Windsor, headed for the city. The Victoria General Hospital which was crowded to the roof with terribly wounded and burned survivors, resembled a war-time front-line dressing station. All public buildings, that remained standing, churches, Y.M.C.A., hospitals, schools and even private homes were hastily converted to temporary relief quarters and the army of wounded carried in.

When the morning of December 7th dawned, Halifax found itself in the throes of a blinding snowstorm, which swept the city. To make matters worse practically every building had few if any windows! Well do I remember being ordered to take many of my company back to the army huts for a rest and having to leave one of my best friends, an officer, in charge of a guard on the goods train at Fairview in this awful blizzard, which caused his death in later years. Rescue workers were forced to suspend operations and a thick pall of snow covered the blackened ruins. The destitute were protected by barriers of tar paper hastily erected in window frames. The blizzard with its chilly temperature for hours raged. Finally, after some twelve hours, the winds abated and the rescue workers of Halifax were given an opportunity to continue to save human life. Halifax licked its wounds and went right to work without a pause. Nearly two thousand were killed, thirty thousand were homeless, among them some twelve thousand wounded, and damage to property was estimated in the vicinity of thirty million dollars.

The heroic work which was carried on under the most trying circumstances by the hundreds of civilian volunteers, soldiers and sailors, can never be forgotten. Nothing was too much and no task was too great. Medical supplies were rushed in. Temporary structures were erected and hundreds of panes of glass replaced. Everyone rushed to the aid of his fellow-sufferers. In a surprisingly short time order was restored and somehow the city carried on. Carpenters, builders of all kinds arrived and temporary homes were established on the Garrison grounds and Halifax went on with its job as a great Eastern Canadian port, although they did not call it that in those days. Our friends from Massachusetts sent every kind of help and eventually the Halifax-Massachusetts Relief Commission built those stone residences so well known in the north end and the work of reconstruction went on apace.

Today one can still see several reminders of the happenings of December 6, 1917. We remember with sad recollection, the greatest explosion the world has known in a seaport town and pay tribute to the brave people of Halifax who were located here that day. Haligonians have every reason to be proud of their conduct in their hour of trial on December the 6, 1917, and the comeback they made to carry on as a great Canadian seaport.

With the end of the second world war it is now possible to talk about many happenings at this great Eastern Canadian Port, that for security reasons could not be mentioned since 1939.

When Hitler forced Britain into war in September, 1939, Canada lost no time in aligning herself alongside the Mother Country, and from that moment the broadcasting of news of Canada at war became a feature of the most importance.

CHNS, through the leased wires of both British United Press and Canadian Press news, gave almost a blow-by-blow account of the daily events, throughout the six year struggle for the survival of democracy.

The Canada which at the end became such an important cog in the allied war machine, was a far cry from the country that went to war on September 10, 1939. From the moment this nation went to war, Canadians streamed from the farms, the mines and factories to bring the armed forces to a total strength of 757,000, including nearly 34,000 women.

Canadian industry and farming matched military expansion, and in four years her industrial productive capacity was doubled.

From east to west, Canadians saw the efforts of Canada at war, and in no place was it more evident than at this great Atlantic terminus of Halifax. In two years the population had doubled. During the six-year struggle Haligonians knew and saw many things of which nothing could be told because of security reasons. Now, at long last, it can be told that the anonymous "East Coast Canadian port"—which had so often made the headlines during the war—is "Halifax." The city has probably seen more action and tasted more of the bitter fruits of war than any other port on this side of the Atlantic.

The great news gathering organization, the Canadian Press, summed up the part played by Halifax in its news dispatches sent out on its radio wires on V-E Day as follows:

Halifax was the centre of the battle of the North Atlantic —now ended officially with Germany's capitulation. In fact, it might be said Halifax was in the front line of the battle of the Atlantic, which reached the height of its fury during 1942 and 1943. During these grim days, ships were sunk at the rate of one or two a day, and convoys were attacked by treacherous undersea raiders.

Probably Halifax knew better than any other Canadian City the intensity of the Germany fury. Ten thousand survivors of torpedoed merchant ships were brought into the city and cared for. In fact, the war was almost on the doorstep of Halifax citizens. On February 23, 1942, they watched

a torpedoed tanker burning like a giant beacon on the horizon just seven miles from the port. More than once ships
were torpedoed only a few miles off the harbour mouth.

But that wasn't the worst. Late in 1943 German submarines mined the approaches to the harbour, and Canadian
Minesweepers worked night and day without rest to clear
the approaches to the port. They did their work well, for
not a single ship was lost. On another occasion a ship
loaded with explosives caught fire in Bedford Basin, and
her crew had to abandon her. (Thanks to a Naval Officer
and some naval ratings who immediately boarded her, the
ship was headed out towards the harbour mouth, and when
it was seen that they could not make it, these brave men
opened the sea cocks and ran her ashore, where she settled
down, the inrushing water putting the fire out and another
catastrophe was averted. Those sailors more than earned
their decorations.)

A serious situation for the city occurred in April, 1942.
A freighter loaded with ammunition and explosives caught
fire in the main harbour, opposite the city proper. (The fireboats and gallant city firemen unsuccessfully fought the blaze
for some hours, but were forced to abandon their efforts.)
As flames streaked skyward, gun crews aboard Canadian and
American warships took careful aim at the compartments
known to be empty of explosives. They blasted the doomed
freighter at the waterline and sank her, and one more danger
was averted. However, some shells overshot, or passed
through the blazing vessel, and splintered docks on the Halifax waterfront not fifty yards from where people were standing. (This feat was performed during the hours after midnight.) Not many Haligonians slept that night as round
after round was fired. Finally, the vessel sank in seventy or
eighty feet of water, and for months the tip of her mast
showed above the harbour surface, a reminder—if one were
needed—of how close the war came to that East Coast
Canadian Port.

Throughout the five years of war, despite many narrow
escapes, Halifax came through without a scratch or damage.

The declaration of Germany's surrender, however, instead of bringing joy and happiness to the gallant people of Halifax, was the occasion of much sadness and disappointment to a people who looked forward to peace and happiness. For the so-called celebrants of V-E Day undertook to do, and did do, what our enemies had been unable to accomplish; namely to smash up the business section of the city.

Starting with breaking into the provincial liquor stores, the riots that ensued for two days, wrecked over one hundred stores and caused damage estimated at over one million dollars.

Halifax was placed under a curfew law, and a battalion of paratroops was finally brought in to patrol the city streets and ensure that law and order would be maintained. Just short of declaring martial law, Halifax settled down to lick its wounds once more, having been made the victim of an unaccountable outbreak of rioting and looting such as was never before experienced in a Canadian city.

Some weeks later, after thousands of plate glass windows had been imported, the business district gradually began to look normal again and Haligonians again settled down, glad to forget the unfortunate celebration, despite the fact that many newspapers, without any authentic information, hundreds of miles away in other parts of Canada, did their best to blame the unfortunate victims of this outbreak, instead of extending a friendly and understanding hand in time of need.

Just two months passed, when once more Halifax was to become the victim of circumstance. What war had been unable to accomplish, the era of peace very soon did with a vengeance.

July 18, 1945, was a lovely summer day, and Haligonians, who had just finished their day's work, were sitting at their evening meals, some probably planning to spend the evening at the lovely Public Gardens or at their camps or on the incomparable North West Arm; when suddenly a terrific blast rent the air. Windows in the north end of the city and Dartmouth, and in those lovely homes along the Bedford

Road, were blasted out. Buildings for miles around felt the concussion and in less time than it takes to tell, thousands were on the streets. The Radio Station and newspaper offices were deluged with calls from anxious citizens.

A large cloud of smoke arising from the east side of Bedford Basin, from the Naval Magazine, told its own story to Haligonians, who knew immediately what had happened. To those who were old enough to remember the Halifax Explosion of 1917, it brought back all the memories of that tragic occasion. Fortunately, this time, by a miracle and God's grace, the loss of life was unbelievably small, but the happenings of the next twelve to twenty-four hours were a terrific strain on the nerves of the brave and remarkably calm people of Halifax. The first explosion was only the first shock to be received.

As metropolitan Halifax rocked and swayed to a seemingly endless series of terrific explosions all night and next morning, scores of thousands of citizens streamed from their homes to seek safety in parks, commons, open spaces of any sort and clogged the only outlets open—those along the Eastern Shore and that leading toward St. Margaret's Bay.

The tension built up, hour by hour, as the rumble of blasts, which sent shells and debris thousands of feet in the air, was interspersed by even fiercer explosions which crashed in windows and doors in a manner reminiscent of 1917. Worse than the loosing of the explosives, in lots of what appeared to be tons at a time, was the anxiety over what was to come. This was not allayed by official announcements that "worse might be expected."

Fire, which began on a wharf loaded with ammunition at the Bedford Basin Magazine about four miles from the city, and which on the first explosion scattered it and its load over the waters and countryside, was still spreading and the biggest munitions stock of all lay in its path. There was no obstacle to its progress except earthen abutments, which throughout the night had failed to block the fire. All human beings had been removed from the area to protect their lives.

Fireboats were not allowed in the area. The land fire-fighting apparatus likewise was held at bay by the explosions.

Preceded by a low rumble, as of artillery fire in the distance, the first terrific crash occurred at 6.35 p.m., smashing buildings for a wide distance around the Bedford Basin Magazine where munitions, stored in thousands of tons, began to go into the air. In the northernmost extremities of the city people were swept from their feet and in all sections, with freakish force, the concussion drove in plate glass and window glass, hitting one here and leaving others undamaged a few feet away.

Hour after hour, the explosions continued with greater or lesser intensity until eleven minutes after midnight when another explosion of first magnitude occurred. Again damage was reported throughout the northern section and spread southward. Just eleven minutes later came the third great explosion and warnings were issued then that no let-up might be expected.

At around ten minutes to four in the morning, after a period of comparative quietness, the biggest explosion of the lot occurred, followed by another about ten minutes later, both of which lighted the night with the brightness of the sun, and were heard one hundred miles away.

Haligonians, who had been evacuated from their homes to country villages twenty and thirty miles away, never expected to find any of Halifax left when they returned in the next day or two. Gradually, after the terrific four o'clock blast, the explosions became less and less, and by six-thirty that evening, just twenty-four hours after the first blast, it was officially announced that the main danger had passed, and that while more explosions might be expected, they would not cause any damage as the fire was dying down and had practically burned itself out.

Haligonians gradually began the trek back to their homes, and for the second time in two months, the stores had to replace their plate-glass windows.

It was a terrifying experience, which none of us want to

go through again, and we sincerely hope that the magazine will be removed to a less thickly populated area. Haligonians have put up with more than their share of danger. In wartime they have expected to do their part, but in peace times they deserve special consideration.

We Haligonians can all congratulate ourselves on how well we have all come out of what might have been a very serious situation. As my home is located at Prince's Lodge, directly across Bedford Basin from the Magazine, I feel that I can well marvel at the fact that outside of some broken windows and some hours of nervous anxiety, everything was as peaceful and normal as ever a few days afterwards.

While everything is now normal, nevertheless the authorities still remind us that people should not go wandering around the magazine area, and if anyone comes across an unexploded shell, they should leave it alone. Citizens are advised not to go souvenir hunting. Leave that work to the men that know what they are doing. The Provost Corps or Ordnance Depot men will remove any stray shells in the woods and the people can help most by staying at home, or at their regular occupations or amusements.

Some few days after the 1945 explosion, there appeared an editorial in the Halifax *Herald* and Halifax *Mail* which I feel everyone should know about. With the permission of my old friend, Edgar Kelley, whose editorials are always worth while, I am going to repeat it for you. Here it is. It is entitled "Their Part":

And now a word for this community and its citizens—this community or group of communities that ring the perimeter of the Halifax Harbour area and lie within range of the menace of vast quantities of explosives stored or in transit
   The City of Halifax itself, the Town of Dartmouth, Woodside, Imperoyal, Eastern Passage, Tufts Cove, Burnside, Bedford, Millview, Prince's Lodge, Birch Cove, Rockingham, Fairview, Armdale, Melville Cove, Jollimore. . . .
   These are some of the communities of the great Halifax area whose citizens, to use the words of the Mayor of Halifax,

have displayed such "steadfastness in the face of danger," not this week alone, but constantly during the war years.

It has remained for a man from another part of the Dominion to state the facts. He is E. L. Cousins, peace-time General Manager of the Toronto Harbour Commission and War-time Administrator, Canadian Atlantic Ports.

"The people of this community," Mr. Cousins tells the rest of Canada "realized exactly the risk they were running all during the war." "This," as he puts it, "is the threat under which the people of the Halifax area have been living for the last six years—and living without complaint or protest."

"The citizens of this community," Mr. Cousins reminds the rest of Canada, "were aware of this and they did not know from night to night how soon or how late a great catastrophe might occur." He adds in a published statement:

"The danger was continuous and there was no averting it, but the city, as a national port, took this in its stride. There was no complaining nor any demand that the shipments of high explosives be handled at some other isolated and less congested port. It was looked upon as a part of the war effort and that Halifax was a naval and export base, which must make this contribution to the efficiency of ships and munitions movements."

"But let me emphasize again," Mr. Cousins said, "the people of this city realized exactly the risk they were running. They saw each day the scars of the last explosion (of 1917). They accepted the risk unprotestingly, and as a man who comes from another part of Canada and who has had an opportunity to see the way in which Halifax citizens have stood up to the strain, I think Canadians elsewhere should know the situation."

In behalf of the citizens of the whole port community, we thank Mr. Cousins for his generous words and sympathetic understanding. He knows what he is talking about—no living person knows better or is in a better position to know.

How cheap, how tawdry, how puerile and stupid are the "causes" of the V-E Day riots when viewed against the background of the true situation. While the citizens of this great port community were being "derided and belied by fools," they were playing in this war the most vital part played by any community of Canadian citizens in a civilian capacity. But, as was said of a great man, so it may be said of a great people,

> Why should he heed the thing they say?
> They never asked if it were true,
> Why brush one scribbler's tale away
> For others to invent a new?

It is, of course, fatally easy for people living in some quiet, remote inland community to accept a lot of fantastic yarns and old wives' tales. But that is past and gone . . . and it is to be believed that hereafter, when someone with a petty or fancied grievance, speaks slightingly or abusively of this community and of its citizens, the people of the rest of Canada will repel the lies and nonsense vigorously and with indignation.

The citizens of this community are not perfect. They are just ordinary human beings—and being human, they have their faults and their shortcomings. They are not different from other Canadians; and they know that other Canadians, similarly situated, would carry on with all the steadfastness and courage that has been displayed here in this community, not in this week alone, but throughout the entire period of hostilities.

Passing through long hours of terrors and alarms, the citizens of this port community have been magnificent—men, women and children, old and young, the sick and the well, the aged and the infirm. There has been no panic, no hysteria. Here the people knew, as one writer has put it, "probably better than the residents of any other city in the Western Hemisphere" what the danger was and what measures had to be taken to cut down destruction and loss of life. To quote a Canadian Press news story in comment on the threat under which the citizens of this community "had been living for the last six years"—

"At least twice during that time the threat of explosion

was extra close. Once a burning freighter containing ammunition was sunk by shellfire in the harbour, and on another occasion a blazing ammunition ship was towed safely to sea, passing close to the heart of Halifax before it reached open water."

"It isn't, of course, anything to boast about, considering what the people of Britain and other lands have gone through in this war—but, at least, it is something to know the truth about. To represent the citizens of this community as an inhospitable, grasping, greedy, shameless horde of money-grabbers is disgraceful alike to the spreaders of such slanders and the people who accept and magnify them. Let it be trusted, and that most earnestly, that Canada has heard the last of this sort of thing."

In contrast to the rather critical tone adopted by certain Central Canadian newspapers in connection with the Halifax V-E Day riots, some of which showed a complete lack of understanding and appreciation of the vital part played by the port and city in two great wars, editorial comments on that Wednesday evening's near disaster, were kindly, generous and warmly sympathetic.

Halifax (said the *Ottawa Journal*), deserves well of this country—its contribution to victory in Europe is literally beyond computation. For its people, suffering this new blow, there will be widespread sympathy, and a desire to help them in every possible way.

For whatever damage was done, the government is responsible and no doubt the government will put its great resources immediately at the disposal of the harassed citizens of the Atlantic port.

Under the heading, "Honour is due," the Montreal *Gazette*, picturing the "anxieties and suffering experienced at that time in Halifax," suggested that this new misadventure brought forcefully to mind what the people of Halifax have endured in two world wars.

It points out that the situation of Halifax as a great ocean port had inevitably made it one of the chief concentration centres for Allied shipping, and at the same time a main storage point for dangerous munitions of war.

In the first war, the risk of such service has become "a matter of painful memory." Although in the latest conflict the continent has escaped being blitzed, Halifax could share with the war-broken cities across the Atlantic, "The experience of the sudden tragedy of death and ruin," it continued.

Halifax's services in two wars have not been performed without costs to its loyal people. For these costs it deserves the sympathy of all Canadians. More than this, the citizens of Halifax deserve to share in the honour and the praise which are rightfully extended to the citizens of Great Britain. For they have shared war's penalties, and for the same high purposes.

The Ottawa *Citizen,* expressing thankfulness that the casualties caused by the Naval Magazine explosions had been so few, and visualizing what must have been for the inhabitants "a most unpleasant night," expressed the hope that Halifax "which has come in for some rough usage at the hand of fate in recent years" may henceforth be spared.

The *Globe and Mail,* Toronto, noted that "the ancient city of Halifax has some reason to count itself a child of misfortune, considering the recent V-E Day goings-on, as well as the great tragedy which took place in 1917.

Under the heading "Guardian of the Gate" the *Herald Tribune* of New York printed the following editorial:

During two great wars Halifax has stood guard at the approaches to the North American continent. The navies and merchant marines of a world filled her magnificent harbour; much of the wealth of the west in men and materials, has flowed through the port to stem on distant battlefields, the threat of aggression and tyranny. The old fort crowning Citadel Hill has been a symbol for Canadians and Americans alike of common resolve and common action.

The enemy did not come to Halifax. But this city has paid dearly for its proud and dangerous rôle. One terrible winter morning in 1917, two vessels crashed in the narrow pass that leads into Bedford Basin.

This grim reminder that, in time of war, Halifax becomes a powder keg, has never been forgotten, and one can well imagine the terror that swept through the city on Wednesday night, when the huge Canadian naval arsenal in nearby Dartmouth went up in flames.

But Haligonians are a tough breed. The danger area was evacuated swiftly and without panic, and though the explosions continued all night it appears that the casualties have been amazingly low.

For this, Canada and the United States can join in congratulating Halifax and Dartmouth, while paying a tribute of respect to the guardians of their Atlantic gate.

In all the excitement and discussion that followed the explosion of the Bedford Basin magazine, one fact is unforgettable.

The response of men and women in the emergency organizations was magnifient.

They manned first-aid posts; they provided and operated transportation services; they supplied and distributed food and blankets; they policed the streets, even in the areas which were deemed most dangerous.

These volunteers turned out at the first call; they remained on duty until the last necessity for their help had passed; those who were compelled to leave their homes to seek safe places in which to stay owe and acknowledge their debt.

This public appreciation of a most valuable work, together with the satisfaction of having done a job well, is the only reward the volunteers receive. That is their payment for hours spent in training, that must, at times, have seemed unnecessary, and not one of them but would say that that is sufficient.

It always seems amazing—though it should not—to see great throngs of people facing danger without panic; steadfast when confronted with peril of unknown magnitude. The masses of men, women and children, especially in the northern end of this city, its suburbs, and in Dartmouth, had their courage tested and they responded.

The A.R.P. organizations typified the spirit of the community; it is thus singled out because it gave leadership and set the example. That will not be forgotten as long as the story of the explosion is told.

It is with pardonable pride that I quote herewith an excerpt from the Dartmouth *Patriot,* the weekly newspaper of the town on the eastern shore of Halifax Harbour, which suffered the major damage in this series of magazine explosions:

Halifax's Radio Station CHNS kept on the air throughout the hectic period and their periodic broadcasts on the progress of the north-end calamity were instrumental in quieting the fears of the entire populace. The staff there worked without rest for twenty-four hours, squelching rumours of impending blasts and bringing up-to-date information to their great listening public.

From our own observations in Dartmouth we are able to state definitely the "explosion" broadcasts sent out over CHNS probably contributed more to relieving the minds of the harassed public of Halifax and Dartmouth than any other means of communication, and their valiant staff are to be sincerely congratulated on the splendid way they performed their duties.

The staff of all the radio stations, newspapers, and communication systems stuck to their posts throughout the emergency and in fact, hundreds of unsung heroes did work beyond praise. Let us hope that from now on this great Eastern Canadian Port of Halifax will enjoy some well earned peace, and that everything having to do with war can be forgotten for a long time.

XIV

HALIFAX IN WARTIME

1939-1945

On every occasion since its founding in 1749, Halifax has become the North Atlantic focal point of military activity whenever the Empire was at War, and its citizens throughout the years have known the restrictions of war on many occasions, and have played a prominent part in the Armed Services and in Civil Defence of the "Warden of the Honour of the North," whenever called upon. The original settlers were organized into units to train in the use of arms, and Haligonians have been engaged in similar activity ever since.

During the last week in August, and the first week of

September, 1939, for the second time within a quarter-century, citizen-soldiers of Halifax were mobilized to defend the old seaport from attack by possible enemy action, and by the time news flashed over the radio that the Empire was again at war, motor trucks bearing troops were rumbling along shore roads to coastal forts, and within a remarkably short time, every military defence post along the coast was ready for instant action, if a German raider decided to attack.

Gun crews stood guard on the firing platforms at hidden coastal batteries; naval ships, stripped for action, steamed seaward; and overhead squadrons of planes wheeled and circled continuously beneath and high up over the clouds. Supporting troops were at their stations ready to be transported to any point needing them. Ancillary and departmental units were mobilized to the last detail.

Out of the Harbour mouth, smudges of smoke on the distant horizon heralded the arrival of ocean-going ships, seeking shelter from hidden perils of the sea imposed by war's outbreak. Plans prepared long before were put into practice, and as usual Nova Scotia stood ready to defend her coast line.

In addition to the Military Personnel, many thousands of citizens were quickly organized into a Civil Defence Corps, ready to do duty should long distance planes attack with bombs, or for any other emergency in which they could be of service. Like their fathers before them in the last war, our citizen soldiers, along with the professional or permanent force soldiers on these lonely outposts all along the coast of Nova Scotia, were ready to do their duty in order that the Province and the rest of the country could rest secure from surprise attack, as part of Canada's Atlantic Command, which stretched from Labrador down to the West Indies.

These active service volunteers, like their comrades on the Pacific Coast, performed a very necessary duty, and if they had their own choice would much sooner have been on the other side of the Atlantic. On August 6, 1940, the

importance of Canada's Coastal Defences was emphasized by
the Press releases, from Ottawa, which definitely set these
troops apart from other troops in Canada as follows:

RE-ORGANIZE VITAL ZONES

Appointment of Major-General William H. P. Elkins as
the officer in charge of Canada's new Eastern Military Command was announced today. In his new post General Elkins
will be responsible for the land defence of thousands of miles
of coastline.

Since 1938, he has been Master-General of the ordnance
at National Defence Headquarters, in charge of supplies for
the Canadian forces.

Now the long, indented shores of Nova Scotia, New
Brunswick, and Prince Edward Island, the similarly indented
shore of Newfoundland and the rocky coasts of the Gaspé
Peninsula, the north shore of the Gulf of St. Lawrence in
Eastern Quebec, and the coast of Labrador will be his to
guard against any invader who may cross the sea.

The forces which will eventually come under the fifty-
seven-year-old General include the coastal defence forces
now operating in the Maritime Provinces, the garrison in
Newfoundland, and all units of the Canadian Active Service
Force and the Non-Permanent Active Militia now stationed
in the area assigned to the command.

Creation of a military command of this type is something
new in Canadian defence history. It is designed to meet the
special defence problems which arise from the geographic
position and it is unlikely for the present at least, that any
similar organization will be established in any other place in
Canada.

The Maritime Provinces and adjacent territory are not
only the part of Canada lying closest to the Empire's enemies
in Europe, but they are a vital link in the chain of the
Empire's war organization. In that area are the ports of
departure for hundreds of shipments of supplies and troops
destined for the United Kingdom.

Large forces may eventually be stationed in the area.

The 3rd and 4th Divisions of the Canadian Active Service Force, now receiving training in various parts of Canada, will not be sent overseas unless and until the war takes a different turn than is now indicated. When they are ready for action, they will undoubtedly be stationed in whatever part of Canada is most likely to see fighting. That part now is the Maritime Provinces and the approaches to the St. Lawrence River.

Thus General Elkins may come to fill in Canada a similar rôle to that filled by Lieut.-General A. G. L. McNaughton in Great Britain.

General Elkins will be in command of forces which must be ready to move anywhere to meet an enemy who may strike from the sea or the air. General McNaughton commands an army corps, built around the 1st Canadian Division and engaged in defence of Britain.

General Elkins will command all the military forces operating in this area and will be responsible to National Defence Headquarters in Ottawa.

Naturally close contact will be maintained between General Elkins' headquarters and headquarters of the Royal Canadian Navy and the Royal Canadian Air Force for the Atlantic area but exact details of how the new organization will fit in with the sea and air forces and the existing military organization are in process of being worked out.

Major General L. F. Page, C.B., D.S.O., General Officer Commanding-in-Chief Atlantic Command, a successor to General Elkins, at Christmas, 1943, gave added confirmation to the importance of the Coastal Command troops' task, when he broadcast the following message:

I am extremely grateful to the Army radio programme "On Parade" and Radio Station CHNS for giving me this opportunity of speaking to all ranks of Atlantic Command at this season of the year.

I have become very proud of the Command during the short period I have commanded it, and I have had a good opportunity of seeing for myself the manifold tasks that fall to your lot and the varying conditions under which you have to live and work.

These conditions are not always easy but inevitably I have found that you have made the best of conditions and have faced them like soldiers. I doubt if there is a more difficult task to perform than that of constant vigilance in all weather with little or no excitement to break the monotony, but owing to the nature of our job, vigilance cannot be relaxed for a moment.

It is on this account that the Christmas and New Year's privileges that have been extended to troops in other parts of Canada cannot be given to you to the same extent.

Watch and ward must be maintained just as it has to be by our comrades in Italy and our sailors at sea. I know your officers will do everything in their power to make your Christmas as bright and as happy as circumstances permit.

And so to you all, I send my warmest wishes for the best Christmas possible, my thanks for your good work and the hope that 1944 will bring to you and yours the realization of what we all wish—Peace with Victory.

The foregoing shows that the authorities considered that these Coastal Command troops were on operational duties throughout the whole command, on the same basis as all their general service comrades in Newfoundland, Labrador and elsewhere in the world.

On the very night that Major-General Page broadcast his message, an alarm kept troops on the alert for twenty-four hours, along with all East-Coast troops from Newfoundland to Florida.

During the last war when German raiders were roaming the Atlantic, the Coastal Defence troops in Nova Scotia became the forgotten men, and as yet have not received recognition. It is good to know that this time they are to get a general service ribbon, even though it is on the same basis as those serving in training centres throughout Canada, which is quite different from serving on the Coast, particularly in winter on an outpost.

Many feel that all troops in the Atlantic Command should be treated alike and be given due recognition for their service by allowing them to wear the Maple Leaf on their ribbon. It is hard to understand why troops in Newfoundland under the same command should be marked differently from other troops of the same Atlantic Command, being subject to the same orders and conditions on duty, as General Service Men.

Perhaps it is not yet too late to rectify the injustice in the matter of recognition of service rendered, by a grateful government.

Enemy mines have been discovered and swept up by the Navy right at the very entrance to the Harbour, and if a munitions ship had hit one we would have had the closeness of the war brought home to us, in a similar manner to our experience in 1917.

Down where the big guns of the coastal defence artillery guarded Canada's Atlantic shores, and where the infantry patrolled the roads and coast line, constant vigilance was the rule. Men of the Royal Canadian Artillery mounted guard day and night to keep the seaways leading into important ports safe from the enemy.

At night, batteries of searchlights swung their beams seaward. The examination of passing ships was especially important.

Should the vigilant searchlight operators fail to spot an underseas boat, nets of steel cable were stretched across the mouth of these East Coast Ports, vital in Canada's war effort, to keep out any German submarine that might seek entry to attack ships laden with the supplies necessary to the Empire's war effort, or warships responsible for keeping open the Atlantic lanes, while refuelling and refitting. Nothing was left to chance, every necessary precaution was taken in the scheme of defence.

The anti-submarine nets covered every inch of navigable waters across the mouth of the port channel. They were kept afloat by stout steel drums and dropped to the sea-floor.

Two minesweepers of the First Great War vintage operated an ingenious "gate" to permit entry or departure of ships.

Even while the gate was open a U-boat could not get between the guarding minesweepers without showing her periscope. The channel was not deep enough at any point to permit entry of an entirely submerged marauder.

Had the call for action come, the Coast Defence artillery-men were ready to handle the big guns. Night and day there were crews ready for action when the alarm was sounded. Gunners were kept familiar with their work by daily "man-ning parades" in which they went through the motions of bringing the guns into position and firing them.

Artillerymen must have practical experience to work their batteries effectively. Every square yard within range of the guns was charted and regular target practice was heard both day and night. Sometimes, at practice, the target was theor-etically over the horizon, when an airplane high overhead acted as the eyes of the batteries and transmitted directions by radio to the plotting room.

The men at the position finder made the necessary cor-rections for wind, tide, temperature and speed of the target boat. They marked the position of the target on their charts and sent directions to the gunners.

Historic forts—built on sites first guarded by Imperial Troops whenever the security of the Empire was threatened —had been modernized to meet up-to-date wartime condi-tions. Where muzzle-loading relics of a colonial era once stood, modern, long-range coastal guns pointed ominously toward the open sea. These old forts along with the modern ones were ready at all times to give a good account of them-selves.

Scattered at hidden points below them on ocean-washed beaches, batteries of lighter artillery with protecting forces and searchlight units were there to repel landing parties should they attempt to run the gauntlet of fire from the forts.

Machine gun crews, thoroughly trained in the mechanics and routine of the rapid-firing weapons, were always ready for instant action should hostile planes swoop low over gun emplacements. Alert and decisive, sentinels patrolled ramparts night and day, keeping ever watchful eyes focused seaward. Sentinel duty on the ramparts overlooking the sea and at the many outposts on the Nova Scotian coast was a very cold and uncomfortable job at times, with very little glamour, but a very necessary task in the scheme of defence in this second world-wide war.

Although the coastal defence works had been modernized to the highest degree, remnants of a colourful past were still to be seen. Iron coal baskets of the eighteenth century vintage—used by Imperial garrisons in bygone days—were still in use in some of the fortifications. Discarded cannon cast aside during the passage of time were to be found acting as ornaments outside some of the older forts. Old casements and foundations of old mountings with their iron rails gave an interesting contrast.

While a few of the men at a time were enjoying a rest or a game of cards, their comrades were on constant watch for a possible raider or hostile plane, watching, watching and just itching to put into action the guns they knew so well. Theirs was as montonous a task as can be found, and only one who has spent a winter among these troops can realize it to its full extent.

There were many special units in addition to the gunners. The searchlight batteries were ever ready, just in case enemy airmen would attempt a raid, or reconnaissance, at night time. These specialists had powerful lights ready for instant use. In addition to scanning the surface of the sea, they had the whole sky to keep under continuous watch at night. Powered by electric motors, the lights could pencil a streak of light thirty thousand feet skyward. Each light was electrically controlled and could be operated by the man in charge of the apparatus for detecting the sound of approaching aircraft.

Guided by the noise of beating propellers, recorded on

the special listening apparatus, the operator had little difficulty in focusing the lights of his battery on the target.

Once caught in the mesh of searchlights any hostile enemy then would become prey to vicious fire from anti-aircraft batteries situated at strategic points along the shore-line.

Capable of firing many rounds a minute, these ack-ack guns were also operated and aimed by ingenious electrical devices. We know it now by the name of Radar.

Should a hostile aircraft be sighted, the guns would circle the plane in a ring of fire. In the event that he manœuvred himself out of the danger zone, the pilot would find other difficulties in the shape of Army co-operation squadrons of R.C.A.F. fighter planes of the latest design.

Piloted by crack airmen well-schooled in the art of aerial warfare, battle planes, capable of speeds exceeding three hundred miles an hour, carry stinging death in their wings.

Diving at a terrific pace and firing a great number of rounds of ammunition in sixty seconds, the defence planes were thundering engines of destruction.

Not only did the fighters patrol sky trails for enemy ships, but also escort fast-travelling reconnaissance bomber squadrons. These Reconnaissance planes, slower but still dangerous, were the "spotters" for the other flying units. Night and day they patrolled the sea areas for lurking submarines or enemy vessels. In constant touch with a central control bureau, the "Lookout" planes could advise land batteries within a few seconds of the approach of the enemy from the sea.

Operations of the entire area were directed from a closely guarded central control room. Here were to be found strangely dotted maps and charts bearing vital information.

Behind a battery of telephones were operators receiving and sending instructions. All units received their orders direct from the control bureau.

From these control rooms the Commander had a complete picture of the entire defence force of his particular area, and was in constant contact with all branches of the services which would spring into instant action, should occasion demand.

Nowhere in Canada was there such a complete defence scheme as could be found at the East Coast Canadian Ports of the Atlantic Command. The Army, Navy and Air Force being in constant communication, while each looked after its special function.

As long as the war lasted and any German planes and ships were afloat, vigilance could not be relaxed.

They were Active General Service Troops, who were expertly trained to do their job. Fate had assigned them to Coastal Defence, but each and everyone of them wearing those small red letters "G.S." on a little black circle on the lower left sleeve, had signed on for service anywhere in the world and would have given anything to receive orders to join their general service comrades overseas. In the meantime, vigilance was their watchword.

In addition to the troops of all branches, the Fortress Commander was in direct contact with the Civil Defence Force, who while the Armed Services would attend to military operations, would be responsible for the numerous tasks of Civilian Defence, and even evacuation of civilian population, if thought necessary in an emergency.

Citizens of Halifax gathering together for the purpose of being prepared to do their bit in case of an emergency is nothing new to this old city.

Just a short time after the city was founded, all persons from sixteen to sixty years of age were assembled to train in case of need, if any emergency should arise. Those who lived in the south suburbs assembled within the pickets opposite the end of Barrington Street by Horseman's Fort. Those of the north suburbs assembled between Grenadier Fort and Lutterals Fort near Jacob Street, and those of the town on the esplanade assembled by the present site of the Old Town Clock on the side of Citadel Hill.

In the old days, an emergency was a far different affair to what might happen today, and the organization was far less complicated.

During the war the Halifax Civil Emergency Committee, with its Air Raid Precaution Wardens, Firemen, Special Police and other specialists had a greater number of people on its strength than the whole population, both military and civil, consisted of in the early days.

The Civil Defence organization consisted of some six thousand odd citizens. Over forty-five hundred men and over fifteen hundred women made up of wardens, control staff, telephonists, industrial wardens, fire watchers, auxiliary police and firemen, doctors, nurses, first-aid workers, rescue squads, decontamination squads, demolition and clearance crews, telephone, gas, electric, public utilities, drivers, messengers, telephone, cable and radio communications groups and the Red Cross complete organization.

Their vast organization at their various posts throughout the city, in every blackout test, and in the case of a real emergency came under direction of the Control Centre Staff, headed by the Director of Civil Defence, Major Osborne Crowell, who supervised all phases of Civilian Defence, in close collaboration with the military by private telephone lines to the Fortress Commander and Anti-aircraft Gun Operations Room.

The whole organization which was supervised by an executive committee headed by the Mayor, at the end of June, 1943, launched one of the most comprehensive and educational Civilian Defence Weeks organized in Eastern Canada. The main object of the campaign was to impress upon the public the importance of Civil Defence in this vulnerable area with the hope that more citizens would join the A.R.P. organization and that the entire population would take the steps necessary to prepare for any emergency.

The success of the city's Civilian Defence Week was due to the individual efforts of civil defence volunteers. As proof, if any more is needed, of the necessity to maintain both military and civil defence, the following from the Halifax Press of December, 1943, is of particular interest:

Coastal defence batteries around Halifax went on the alert in the early hours of Christmas morning after a report was flashed from Washington that a "sneak air attack might be attempted by the enemy on Christmas Day."

The alert signal was simultaneously received by naval and air force units, as well as military units stationed in this area and personnel were ordered to stand on call. Pilots at coast stations in off patrols were ordered to stand by.

The defence units in the Halifax area, as well as along the Eastern seaboard, remained at the alert until Christmas night. Cancellation of the alert was announced by Eastern Defence Command in the United States at 9.05 p.m., E.D.T., three hours after it had disclosed that "protective measures" had been taken.

American army officials said they could not reveal the source of the report. While many Haligonians were returning from midnight church services, forces personnel along the coast were at their posts. Gun crews mounted the anti-aircraft units and shore batteries were held in readiness.

The flash came through to Halifax around 3.00 a.m., Christmas morning. Major O. R. Crowell, Director of Civilian Defence, received the report from army authorities at 3.10 a.m., and remained up during the morning ready to call out the six thousand A.R.P. wardens and first-aid auxiliary units if it became necessary.

Throughout Christmas Day, United States radio stations broadcast reports of the alert. Commentators from Washington said no information could be received as to the source of the alert signal. Authorities, they said, remained silent as to how imminent the danger, if any, was to American shores.

Authorities in Halifax likewise remained silent as to the nature of the reported danger of enemy attack.

In New York, stations carried a message from Mayor

LaGuardia: "Today is a holiday, but the enemy respects no holiday. Remember, in case of any emergency, act calm, avoid panic, obey orders."

Colonel C. S. Craig, D.S.O., M.C., Fortress Commander and Acting District Officer Commanding Military District No. 6, said the alert was received in Halifax early Christmas morning from United States authorities.

Personnel were ordered to stand by the guns, he said. Men on operational duty in this zone, he said, do not receive any Christmas or New Year's leave as in other areas in Canada. They remain at their posts continuously.

Major O. R. Crowell said the report of the alert on Christmas Day, 1943, would serve as a vivid reminder to the people of Halifax that "we are still in the danger zone."

The foregoing warning coming after four years of war made both the armed forces and civilian defence forces realize that it was their proud privilege to ensure that, even if their services were never actually required, they were at all times competent to discharge their responsibilities, and to maintain their defence organizations at the highest state of efficiency.

There were many things in Halifax and surrounding districts of which we had to speak with marked discretion in those days of war. That's natural enough, for this great port had a rôle in the Empire's war effort that was of such magnitude that it was difficult to fully realize. Now peace is restored, the story can be told in its entirety, and we get a true picture of the contribution of the Halifax district.

We may now visit in fancy together one of the most important links in our defence chain—a great base of the Royal Canadian Air Force. Not only did it serve as a means for the protection of our coast, and our city, but it served as a centre from which shipping on our sea lanes could be safeguarded and from which a definite and unceasing war was carried out against any venturesome enemy U-boats which came to our waters. That much is well known, and I am breaking no security regulations by reference to these special reasons for existence of the mammoth Eastern Coast Air Base.

First, let's look back through the years to get some facts about the start of aeronautics at this port. To do this we have to revert to the latter part of the First Great War. It was then that the United States established a seaplane base at Eastern Passage. It was then that a Lieutenant-Commander Richard E. Byrd was among those sent here in connection with establishment of the base, which was designed to serve the combined Allied war cause in that war.

Today, these many years later, the three original hangars, great buildings of that time, erected to serve the American airmen, are still doing service, but under a different flag. What was then the main building of the station is still standing and serves among other things as headquarters for the service police. The Lieutenant-Commander who was sent by the Americans to command this base in Canada was later to win world wide fame for his Arctic and Antarctic explorations, as Admiral Byrd.

But even before his polar exploits he had another link with Halifax, for he played a major rôle in carrying out the famous flights by the NC flying boats, which were detailed for the United States Navy's first trans-Atlantic flights. There are many in Halifax who will recall the evening set for the arrival of the NC aircraft, as they were called. Practically all in Halifax who could make their way gathered on the harbour shores of Point Pleasant Park, or at what was known as Greenbank, at what is now the southern extremity of the terminal development. It was a great sight that still dwells in mind as the tiny specks appeared in the distance and some of the great flying boats descended on the water and taxied in close where they could be more easily seen by the great concourse of people.

Days of peace did not see Eastern Passage continue as an important base for air operations: it had served its purpose for the moment. But aviation is something which is built on, looking ahead. Foresight is imperative, and with passage of time it was seen that necessity for existence of a base there was warranted. At first it was largely a case of using existing buildings. Then came expansion, but even then, only the property adjacent to the harbour waters were in service. At the start of 1937, came the government announcement of plans for the great military aviation base, to combine the seabase with a great land airport on the other side of the Eastern Passage Roadway.

By the spring of the following year the task of cutting out tree stumps was practically completed on the vast tract of land which had been bought up for the Airport. That summer great bulldozers swarmed over the land, steam-shovels sent their teeth digging into the hills. Fortunately this work had been taken in full stride, with realization of the world chaos that might lie ahead. And soon by the fateful fall of 1939, much had been accomplished in providing the great mile-long runways.

Since then, the work of building construction has gone on unceasingly, and expansion continues unabated. It's a big "plant" and with a personnel of proportions which are in keeping. The fact that a two-hundred-bed hospital, perhaps the largest such boasted by the R.C.A.F. in Canada is provided there, is a pretty good indication.

Interesting as administration buildings, with their countless offices proved, and the rooms and wall-size maps, with myriad markers showing various phases and facts of operations catch the fancy, they are only secondary to the visitor's eyes. It is the great hangars and the runways which hold first attention.

To study a complete air photograph of the R.C.A.F. Dartmouth Station, as it is officially known, is to really grasp its great extent. One group of buildings I am told is referred to as Hobbes' Hollow, named after the commanding officer of the station for some years, and who has played a very effective part in its development.

The entire personnel of the station, officers, airmen and airwomen, were on parade to witness the official departure from the station of the man who had been·its commanding officer since July 27, 1941.

Relinquishing command of the station to his successor, Group Captain Hobbes expressed the hope that the personnel of the station would render to Group Captain Carscallen the "same loyal support" they had given to him. Telling the men not to be impatient if they did not get overseas as soon as they desired, he declared they were doing a "splendid job" right where they were. Experience while he was in Britain, he said, had convinced him the Dartmouth station was "an important link in the chain. The defence against sub warfare in the North Atlantic would not be complete without that link."

This great Eastern Canadian Airport is a most interesting place. In addition to the hangars and technical buildings, one can find a Post Office building set up for speeding the mails to and from the vast personnel, the pigeon lofts close to the harbour waters, where the trained winged carriers are kept, the well-equipped machine shops, the small fleet of boats of the Marine Section, moored at the station's dock, or the powerful flying boats tethered to their big buoys in the comparatively quiet waters of Eastern Passage. It's a wonderful place to visit.

During the war, Nova Scotians were familiar with the precise plane formations which daily flew overhead at regular times, and vanished into the mists at sea, yet few knew where these squadrons went or what their particular duties were, or from whence they hailed.

To the Merchant and Naval vessels, they were well known and no matter on what part of the broad North Atlantic their course took them, they knew that one or more of the Royal Canadian Air Force Squadrons, fully armed, would suddenly appear and give them a thorough inspection, and report their progress from day to day.

Canada was divided into Air Commands. Canada's coastal areas formed part of the active service zones known as Eastern and Western Air Commands. All the rest of the Dominion was divided into four Air "Training" Commands, whereas the coastal zones are designated only as Air Commands. And that, in military or naval language, means a fighting command. Thus the men of the Eastern Air Command were fighting men; they were as distinct from the Empire training scheme, as the navy is from the army.

Headquarters for the Command was in Halifax and their bases were scattered all over the Atlantic area. Their activities were seldom publicized, but occasionally the press carried a story, released by the Minister for Air, which reminded us of the splendid service given by these lads. It was known that they patrolled Newfoundland waters. That they policed the St. Lawrence was revealed when they spotted and stopped an Italian freighter, until a Royal Canadian Navy Auxiliary vessel could catch up and seize the foreigner. And on that, as on countless other occasions, press reports contained little mention of the R.C.A.F. action.

Squadrons of the Eastern Air Command planes, with which we became so familiar, accompanied every convoy to sea, and before the ships departed, the planes searched the waters outside the harbour. In a huge, fan-shaped sector, radiating from the lead ship of the convoy, an air squadron radiated out on what was called sector search, and the squadron units each patrolled back and forth on a segment of the sector. Other special duties included a special search, often entailing thousands of miles of flying, to check on a fisherman's report that something suspicious was seen at sea, or in towing aerial targets high in the sky for anti-aircraft shore batteries to practise gunnery upon.

They operated under one of the most trying conditions known to airmen: Wireless Silence. No airman on convoy guard, for instance, was permitted to touch a wireless key. Use of wireless could give a submarine the bearings of a flotilla of ships. So rigid was the rule, that a plane forced down at sea even out of sight of the convoy, must not ask aid by wireless, the authorities being of the opinion that one aircraft and its crew were of less value to the United Nations cause, than a ship or a convoy of foodstuffs or armament.

On patrol they stopped ships at sea by light signal. Over the seven seas, the British had an involved, an intricate but foolproof system of codes that came into effect at varying hours of the day. Any ship in Canadian waters should know these codes. The airman must know them, so that their challenge in the current code may be answered correctly. They did not hesitate to stop any ship by diving at it, and then continually circled it in a wide arc within their view, until a surface craft arrived to search it. If no British or friendly ship was nearby, they broke wireless silence to summon a surface ship.

This action reveals one of the most important accomplishments of these airmen, navigation and chart-reading. At all times, without landmarks to use as aids, these airmen had to know their exact positions on the vast Atlantic, and the spot had to be designated exactly or the surface ship might race out to a spot hundreds of miles away.

This meant that the entire crews of these big bomber reconnaissance squadrons worked constantly during flight. The navigator sat at his desk, plotting his position. Every fifteen minutes he checked the wind drift, and "shot" the sun regularly. He checked barometrical readings. In other words, he had to be an expert, because he couldn't check his calculations by taking a peek at a nearby town or mountain range.

The Commanders of the crews of four in the big bombers are known as "captains" the only place in the Air Force where such a title is applied. That is because this Command was nautical in everything it did. It flew so many knots, and so on. Its captains had to have the equivalent knowledge of Naval Lieutenants. They never talked of maps, only of charts. Discussions centred regularly around such things as tides and drifts.

When a man, someone with years of flying experience, arrived at the Command, he was a fully qualified, highly trained member of one of the best Air Force organizations in the world. But here he started to learn new things, for instance:

He may have had to learn how to fly flying-boats, because the Command had several. This meant he must learn about tides and currents and how to reckon them and compute their speed. Then he had to learn about "Deicers," how to jettison gasoline in flight, the rules of the sea, how to read charts (not maps), the signals used by surface craft, the international code of the sea, navigation at sea, identification of ships, the handling of surface crafts, laying flare paths at sea, gale signals, and how to signal to ships, salvaging surface ships and aircraft.

And these are only some of the things he learnt. He had to pass tests on every one of them. Every type of naval vessel of the United Nations, as well as those of the enemy, must be recognized in a very few moments when one suddenly looms upon on the horizon, and so many hours were spent in study of silhouettes.

The young lads seen on the streets, our airmen, got practical war experience in coastal patrol work. Night and day, week in and week out, planes of Canada's airforce maintained a constant patrol of the vital sea lanes off this coast.

Reconnaissance planes, speedy low-winged fighters, fast and powerful bombers all formed part of the potent system of aerial defence thrown up to defend the Atlantic seaboard from enemy attack.

From hidden bases on the coast and inland, the present generation of Canadian fighting airmen were on the job.

Operating in close unity with the army and navy, the planes carried out important and many duties.

Merchant convoys clearing Atlantic ports for the high seas had their escorts of bombing planes which were there to aid the navy in keeping coastal waters clear of enemy undersea craft.

During the year of war, many of these young lads of

the Eastern Air Command had been credited with a submarine sunk and many more had been in action. It was only when the official reports were released some months later, that we realized their splendid contribution to the safety of our ships and supplies, and the official reports were always very conservative. For instance, in December, 1942, the Ministry for Air released the following, which summed up the attack by an R.C.A.F. plane on a submarine in the Gulf of Saint Lawrence, some three months previously: "Depth charges functioned correctly."

The crews of our aircraft, especially those who had been fortunate enough to engage a submarine, were the most enthusiastic young men imaginable. To hear them describe their exploits, one would get the impression that they had been out on a duck hunting expedition, instead of risking their lives in more ways than one, and we need have no fear of the coming generation being able to look after itself or that they will have any trouble living up to the traditions set for them by the men of 1914-1918.

Canada's airmen, all over the world in World War II, made a great name. In the list of accomplishments not the least by any means are the deeds of the lads of the Eastern Air Command, with their "Wings over Canada"—and the North Atlantic Patrol.

The Honourable J. L. Ilsley, Wartime Minister of Finance, in his opening words during a speech before the combined service clubs of Halifax, preceding Canada's Fifth Victory Loan, said, "It gives me great pleasure to speak in Halifax, a city that has a greater realization of war than any other Canadian city, a city where the actual operation of war is seen."

The citizens of Halifax have grown used to seeing anti-aircraft gunners at battle stations, Air Force bombers coming and going on their regular patrols, troopships and Merchant ship convoys sailing in regular procession, and Naval ships of all sizes down to minesweepers, sliding in and out of the harbour in fair weather and foul. After four years of war, when Mr. Ilsley made his speech even men of the services had said to themselves, "I wonder if it could happen here," but just the same, every day they went through their training, and "stood by" keeping a sharp lookout, ready for instant action at sea, on lonely coastal batteries, at wireless stations, lookouts, and in the air.

The airmen had their reward, and exciting moments, on several occasions when they had come across an unsuspecting U-boat on the surface, and had long become acquainted with the seriousness of their rôle in the defence of Canada's shores. From numerous encounters they knew it could and actually did happen here.

The Navy, for the most part, on their convoy duty had many experiences with U-boats that had made us mighty proud of them.

There was one branch of the Navy, which up to the middle of the year 1943, began to wonder, like other branches of the Service, if they would ever see any action, yet could not relax for one minute in their seemingly routine watches and drills. That branch was the mine-sweeping division which patrolled our harbour from the approaches and channels used by the many ships that had made use of this East Coast Port. Every day since war began, they, along with other branches of the Service, in fair weather and foul had been constantly on the alert, so as to be ready, if need be, to do their part. This type of Active Service was like the Army's rôle on the coast, the most trying in as far as keeping the men keen, especially after four years with no glory or praise such as was being showered upon their comrades overseas, but it was a type of service that was most necessary, if we were to be sure of our position in a war where anything could happen.

In September, 1943, a group of newspaper and radio men were taken out on a routine minesweeper patrol, in order that they might see first hand the type of service these men were performing. This trip was arranged by the Navy, as a preliminary introduction to these men, and at the conclusion of which, the Minister of Naval affairs made a most startling announcement of the fact that this very group whose work the newsmen had seen that day, had some three months before, in June, 1943, foiled the attempt by U-boats, to block up the very entrance to Halifax Harbour with mines.

It was officially announced by the Hon. Angus L. Mac-Donald, that enemy submarines mined the approaches to Halifax Harbour in early June in an arc intended to close the port to all shipping.

Minesweepers of the Royal Canadian Navy and the Royal Navy cleared a six-cable channel (twelve hundred yards wide) within one day to permit a convoy to sail, a feat which drew the congratulations of the Admiralty, he said. Mr. MacDonald paid a tribute to the units of the Royal Navy which were in Canadian waters and participated in the sweep.

Mr. MacDonald said the information that mines had been laid was kept secret for security reasons.

No lives were lost as a result of the enemy action, although a small freighter—two thousand tons—which was sunk in June is believed to have been mined. She was, however, a convoy straggler and was four miles inside an area which the Navy had declared dangerous.

The mines, he said, were doubtless laid by an ocean-going type of submarine fitted for minelaying.

Mines were first discovered and reported by ships of a convoy escort force. Plans which had been made long in advance were immediately translated into action.

The first task of the minesweeping fleet was to clear a channel for incoming and outgoing ships, and to maintain this swept route so the convoys might continue to move safely. The second was to make exploratory sweeps to determine the extent of the minefield and the third was to clear the whole-mine-infested area in "mopping-up" operations.

All of these duties, which were not only extremely dangerous but most laborious and exacting, were performed "like clockwork" the Minister said.

Mr. MacDonald had high praise for the officers and men of the minesweeping fleet, who since the beginning of war had not relaxed their vigilance in a tedious and monotonous job. They discharged their duty when faced by enemy action, he said, with a thoroughness and efficiency which could not have been excelled, without a single casualty, a greater degree of success than the most hopeful, knowing the hazards, could have expected.

Youthful and veteran naval men combined brains and brawn to sweep the convoy channels when Germany tried to seal Halifax Harbour—men from all walks of life and all parts of Canada.

The channel was cleared for shipping, the extent of the minefields next determined and the area "mopped up."

On the smokestacks of many of the sweepers today are white and blue bands—special marks of distinction for the job they did in cleaning out the entrance to the harbour of these hazards of war.

The white bands are for mines they destroyed themselves, the blue for "assists."

Proudest ship of the minesweeping fleet is a Canadian-built and Canadian-manned craft with the insignia of eighteen destroyed on her funnel.

Throughout the days and nights in clearing out the field there was stiff competition between the ships to lengthen out their rows of Mine Destruction Insignia.

Lieutenant John A. MacKinnon, R.C.N.R., of Charlotte-town, P.E.I., and Halifax, captain of one of the ships of the minesweeping fleet, and with more than ten years merchant service sea time behind him, in reference to this official announcement remarked:

The excitement was terrific and a welcome break after plugging away since the start of the war. It was nice to know we at last had results after months of work and training.

It was hard work all the way through. We worked long hours with little rest but as long as we kept getting mines nobody cared. The crews did a wonderful job.

We like to brag of the fact that our ship destroyed the first enemy mine ever to be blown up by a Canadian minesweeper. We were in on the blowing up of fifteen of them.

Skipper Sam Lillington, R.C.N.R., of Port Aux Basques, Newfoundland, another captain of one of the minesweepers and a former merchant seagoing man with more than sixteen years sea time behind him, felt it was a good job done but a nerve-wracking one. He supplied another sidelight to the dangerous undertaking when he said:

We had a close call when we were forced to cut across the bow of a merchantman which was heading straight for a mine in a heavy fog. We went as close as twenty-five feet to the mine to make the ship cut around us. We didn't dare get any closer. It was a close shave.

Lieutenant-Commander R. M. Barkhouse, R.C.N.R., of Halifax, port minesweeping officer, veteran of British minesweeping in the last war, the man immediately responsible for destruction of the mines summed up their work as follows:

The crews did a wonderful job. They worked untiringly for long hours day on end and there wasn't a complaint. The more they swept the more they wanted. Every man from seaman to C.O. was wonderful.

What he did not tell was that he himself went to sea during the first three nerve-wracking days to direct his fleet personally on knowledge gained as a sweeper captain earlier in this war.

Lieut.-Commander Barkhouse is well qualified for his job. A veteran deep-sea master, he captained a Royal Navy minesweeper in the Mediterranean in the First Great War. He lost his son, Sergeant Air Gunner Donald Barkhouse, in a raid over Europe. The flier was buried in Cologne.

Assistant to Lieut.-Commander Barkhouse was Skipper

Lieutenant M. A. Hyson, R.C.N.R., of Halifax, who remained on the job with his commanding officer until the harbour mouth was cleared.

The mines laid in June were of the "moored magnetic" type and were described by veteran minesweeping seamen as more powerful than they had ever seen before. They were moored to the ocean bed but were designed to explode magnetically.

The enemy made one fatal slip that gave his game away. He left one of the mines on the surface where it was spotted by a convoy escort.

The men who were continually seeking out these deadly explosives were not long seasoned and toughened sea dogs born to have no regard for the fear of the dangers of the ocean.

They were mostly young men, many still in their teens, who came down to the sea from the plains, the forests, the farmlands, the big cities and little towns all across Canada. They lived for the day when the cable of an enemy mine would snap in the cutters of their sweeper's kite otter and bob to the surface.

Their patrol was from the pre-dawn to almost dusk—seven days a week and fifty-two weeks in a year, unless they had the luck for a "refit" which would tie their ship up in port for several days.

One month after the announcement of the attempt to seal Halifax Harbour with mines had been foiled, Naval headquarters at Ottawa announced six Canadian naval officers and ratings had been granted awards by the King for "gallantry, skill and devotion to duty during hazardous mine recovery operations."

There was no doubt that the splendid work of the minesweepers of this Great East Coast Port, saved the lives of many seamen on this memorable occasion, and allowed the stream of our supplies to Europe to carry on uninterrupted. The mine laying U-boat did his work well, but so did the navy, who along with all other branches of the Services had a good look at the U-boat captain's "calling cards," left at our front door. From that day on they all realized it could happen here, and no relaxation was allowed in the routine, somewhat monotonous duty, the training of four years having proven that our boys could be depended upon when the call came.

It is a matter of satisfaction that the Canadian authorities gave suitable recognition during the war, by issuing a Canadian Voluntary General Service Medal for all active general service men and women who served on the Atlantic Command ready to do their duty on our coast or overseas, at whatever it may be, no matter how monotonous, and who had no choice as to what part of the world their duty placed them.

The faithful service of all our armed services made possible the splendid record of Halifax, a city as Mr. Ilsley said in his Victory Loan speech, "where the actual operations of war are seen," a city which is known far and wide for its part in World War No. II mostly as "An East Coast Port."

During the first two years of the Second Great War, my particular duties in the Active Army brought me in contact with thousands of officers and men, and also gave me every opportunity of observation of Halifax in wartime, both from the military and civilian effort.

We have covered the military activities, but to complete the picture credit must be given for instance to the wives of the men overseas who formed women's auxiliaries, for the purpose of keeping contact with our Halifax units, and the Reserve Battalions for keeping the names of our Active Units ever before us. The Red Cross, particularly their Blood Donors' Clinic, was very active, and Halifax, as usual in wartime, was one hundred per cent. behind the troops in every phase.

We must not forget that we had in Halifax a most efficient Civilian Air Raid Precaution Corps under full time direction of an officer who retired from the Active Army for medical reasons, but who along with thousands of our older men and women of all ages were doing their bit this way, practising every night to perfect the particular section to which they belonged, all getting familiar with gas masks, tin hats and practice black-outs, which were called without notice sometimes locally and sometimes Province-wide.

Hundreds of other men, particularly those who had been turned down for service overseas, and those who were key-men in different essential industries, were members of the Reserve Army, being civilians by day and soldiers by night and on Sundays and holidays. All sorts of men enlisting in the Reserve Army and the boss in the daytime, in numerous cases found one of his daytime employees acting as his superior officer at night. These men of the Reserve Army, along with thousands in the Active Forces, under all sorts of weather conditions, learned full well the meaning of the words of our National song—"O Canada, we stand on guard for thee."

Most Canadians are aware that recruiting figures for the Active Army showed the highest percentage in Canada from Nova Scotia and Prince Edward Island. Credit must also be given to the many women of Canada, in joining the Army, Navy and Air Force in increasing numbers every day, thereby releasing many men for Active Service.

Those who only know Halifax as a visitor of just a few days, had little idea of the tremendous changes that the war itself had made in the old garrison town. The population had grown from around seventy thousand to about one hundred and twenty thousand. Prefabricated houses as well as permanent structures took up practically all the vacant places, and thousands of war workers and Active Service troops from Upper Canada came to live amongst us, who, perhaps otherwise, would never have set foot in the Maritime Provinces. It must be said, however, that there was no more orderly city in the Dominion than wartime Halifax.

Every night radio programmes were broadcast featuring the Navy, Army and Air Forces of Canada, both locally and over the National Network, and many firms sponsored programmes of a patriotic nature. The newspapers were full of pictures of men and women who had joined for Active Service in the various branches and each week they featured a special summary of news and events which could be cut out to send overseas, the items having all been passed by the Censor, thereby relieving the home folk from worrying about what they could write. This was a splendid service, especially for Haligonians who had little time to spend in entertaining, writing letters or in showing visitors the beauties of the North West Arm and the lovely outlying districts of Halifax.

The majority of our wartime visitors did not, it would seem, get very far away from Barrington Street and the centre of the city, to see the many fine things of Halifax, or to learn about its storied past.

A description of Halifax in wartime as published in a Montreal paper by one of its star reporters, who was sent to get a first hand picture of Canada's great Eastern Canadian port in 1942, would confirm this view. He reported as follows:

Halifax is a city apart today. It is different from any other Canadian city yet it is unlike any European city. Nowhere as in Halifax does one realize that Canada is at war.

The streets are thronged with men of the fighting services, soldiers, sailors, airmen, Canadian and allied. On one corner will be seen a group of French sailors, while across the street are New Zealand airmen from the other side of the world.

At one moment the air is thick with English accents, Cockney, North Country, Devon and Oxford: the next American and Australian voices boast about their respective countries. Scotch sailors argue with Royal Marines, while French Canadian soldiers gesture to West Indian Negroes.

Air Raid Precaution posters warn the public "What to do —and how to do it—in the event of an Emergency." Searchlights sweep the sky from time to time and huge flying boats soar over the city day and night.

It gives the visitor an odd feeling to stand on a corner

looking up a patrol of the most modern airplanes, speeding through the skies, while at the same moment easy-going Negroes are driving ox-carts up Spring Garden Road.

And again, to stand in the Red Chamber of Province House reading a commemorative plate to the effect that His Majesty's Council met aboard the *Beaufort* Transport, July 14, 1749, present being His Excellency, the Governor Edward Cornwallis, while across the hall one hundred and ninety-two years later the Legislative Council of Nova Scotia is seeking new ways of expanding the Province's war effort.

Halifax, city of narrow streets and old-time architecture, dusty ship chandlers and modern marts, toy-like cars which shunt back and forth from double to single tracks, bearded sailors and smartly attired women, the majority of them amazingly attractive. Not New York at its best—no, nor Bagdad—could ever present a more polyglot appearance.

Barrington Street, the St. Catherine Street of Halifax, on a Saturday afternoon presents one struggling mass of humanity, pouring in and out of shops, spending the fruits of a prosperity Halifax has not known for years. The crush on the sidewalks is so great that pedestrians overflow into the street, making a passage that is already too narrow, even narrower.

An amazing feature of Haligonians is their amiability and familiarity. Taxicab drivers, waitresses, commission-aires, chamber maids, tram motormen, will begin a conversation without any inducement and will relate the story of their life, how they came by their present occupation, what they think of the war, and how it should be run, the price of food—an all important item of conversation in this city of sky-high meals—anything else the visitor may be interested in—or not as is more often the case.

Thus, Halifax was a city like no other. A wartime city. Dusty, narrow downtown streets bordered by old-fashioned buildings which in the suburbs turn into wide, paved boule-vards, bordered by lovely, comfortable homes. A city of hills, with the tang of the sea ever prevalent. A city of con-trasts, a hive of activity, a rapidly growing city, a cradle of tradition speedily being lost in the hum of Halifax at war.

While the needs of the Armed Forces made many changes such as the Old Market building becoming a military laundry, the Exhibition Buildings a training centre, and King's College becoming H.M.C.S. Kings, a few things still remained the same and are known to every soldier, sailor or airman who has been stationed there in the past. All during the war, Hector MacLeod, perhaps the best known police constable of the force, was still directing traffic on Barrington Street, and Brother Keeler, the coloured news-vender and some-time preacher was still at the old stand.

Haligonians and their wartime friends continued to spend most of their little leisure time in line-ups, waiting to get into restaurants, hostels, theatres, or hockey rinks, or trying to get aboard the too few trams, and with the now familiar rationing system in operation, housewives were to be seen with baskets on their arms carrying home their portions and many business men were reducing by riding to and from work on bicycles, instead of the family car as in days before the war, and the Old Town Clock on Citadel Hill, with its roots in the past and face to the future, ticked off the hours for Haligonians.

Halifax, which was founded for the express purpose of upholding British prestige, hit its stride as usual in time of war, in the manner of a true veteran. War was no new experience to its citizens, and no Canadian community can have greater pride or bears the scars of war comparable to Halifax in wartime.

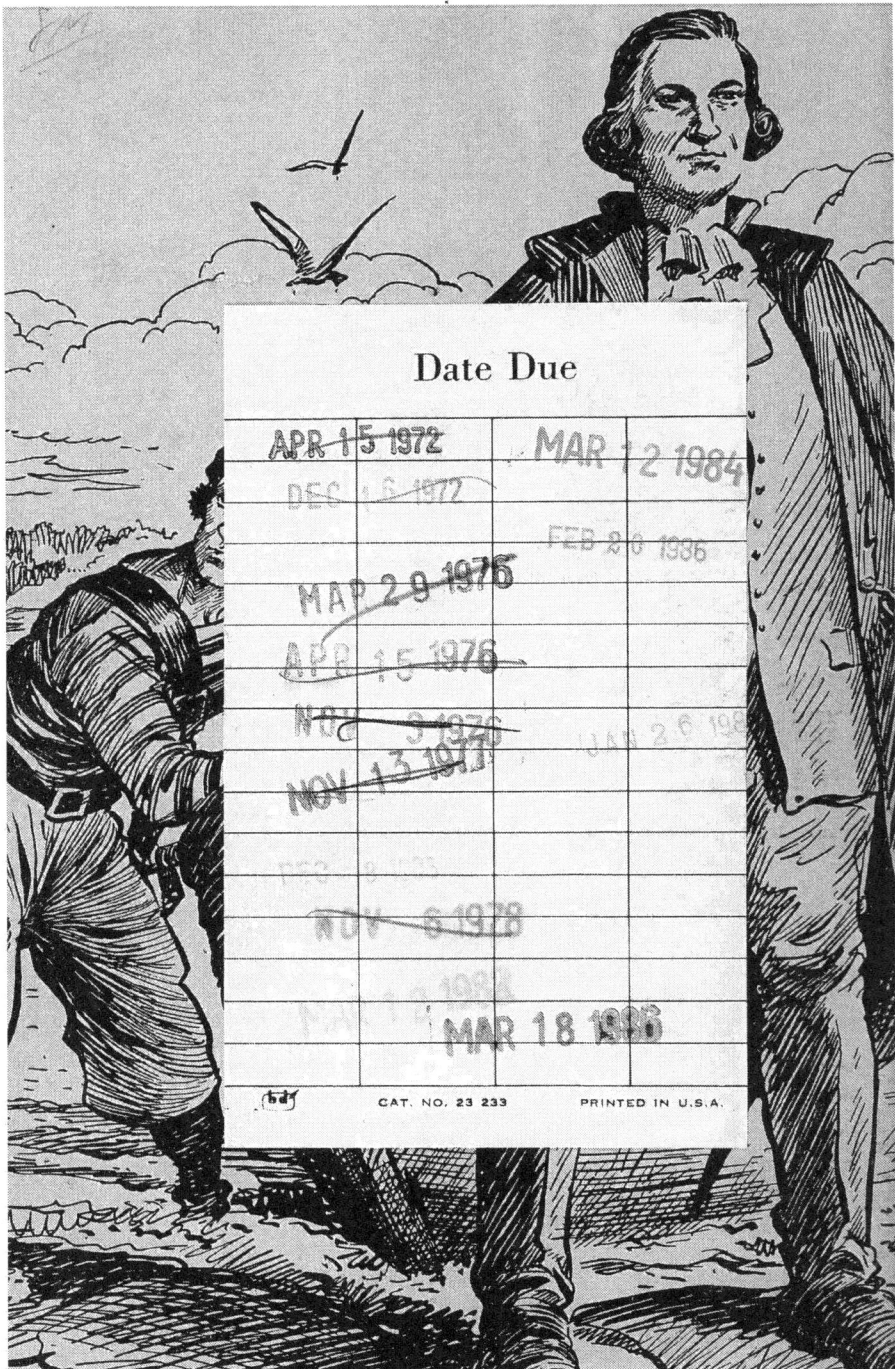

Date Due

APR 1 5 1972	MAR 1 2 1984
DEC 1 6 1972	
	FEB 2 0 1986
MAR 2 0 1976	
APR 1 5 1976	
NOV 3 1976	JAN 2 6 198
NOV 1 3 1977	
NOV 6 1978	
	MAR 18 1986

CAT. NO. 23 233   PRINTED IN U.S.A.

CPSIA information can be obtained
at www.ICGtesting.com
Printed in the USA
LVHW080802300822
727165LV00004B/83